Triumphant Living

Sermons from Five Decades
Celebrating the Liberal Gospel

Triumphant Living

Sermons from Five Decades Celebrating the Liberal Gospel

Rhys Williams

Eleanor Williams, Editor

PEARSON CUSTOM PUBLISHING

Boston, Massachusetts

Printed in the United States of America

10 9 8 7 6 5 4 3 2 1

BX
9843
.W595
T75
2003

ISBN 0-536-73395-3

BA 997211

DG

Please visit our web site at *www.pearsoncustom.com*

This book is printed on acid-free paper.

PEARSON CUSTOM PUBLISHING
75 Arlington Street, Suite 300, Boston, MA 02116
A Pearson Education Company

Dedication

To Our Grandchildren

Dylan Rhys Williams
Luke Sebastian Williams
Philip Rhys Kelly
Rhys Kiernan Williams
Grant Schuyler Williams

With love and hope that they will grow
to appreciate the gift of life and use it wisely.

Triumphant Living

Sermons from Five Decades
Celebrating the Liberal Gospel

Contents

❦

Acknowledgments

❧

The large outpouring of goodwill by many people of the First and Second Church, other friends, and institutional colleagues has been and continues to be a tremendous influence on my life. Many people have combined their efforts to bring *Triumphant Living* into existence. The sermons are presented to help us focus on the positive and to inspire a civilized future.

The loving support of my wife and soulmate, Eleanor, has been limitless. We have enjoyed a shared ministry in caring and reaching out to people in all conditions of life. As editor of this book, she has brought analytical insight and clarity of vision to its content and has been instrumental in choosing those sermons which, though given at a specific time, she felt had a timeless quality.

The catalyst for this book has been Graham Sterling. No other person has put more time and creativity into this project. His amazing ability to organize vast materials into computer format and to analyze publication procedures, plus his tenacious commitment, were invaluable in bringing this book into being. I express my deep appreciation to Graham and his wife Judy for their endless support of this project and their friendship over many years.

With affectionate gratitude I thank Forrest Church for valuable counsel and his positive foreword; John Burt for his sensitive biography; Robert Hettinga, whose technical genius helped me through the mysteries and challenges of the computer; Tom Dahill for his photograph of the Kepes window on the cover of this book and his drawing of the new church edifice; Robert Dancy for bringing to our attention and facilitating negotiations with Pearson Custom Publishing; and Howard Fuguet for his legal advice on behalf of our church.

Eleanor and I are thankful for the encouragement of our children, Rhys Hoyle Williams and Eleanor Pierce Kelly, whom we consider our finest achievements, and their spouses, Rebecca Williams and Philip Kelly. These sermons reflect the values and ideals we learned from our parents, Eleanor Lyles and William Rupp Barnhart and Lucita Squier and Albert Rhys Williams.

Editing and transcribing hundreds of sermons, from which this collection has been selected, have engaged many members and friends. In addition to Judy and Graham Sterling, who literally found and transcribed years of sermons, I thank: Lisa Beane, Sheldon Bennett, Laszlo Bonis, Barbara Centola, Carol Gilbert Hettinga, Jack Hardie, Walter Jonas, Elizabeth Kendrick, Pat Krol, Ellen Meyers, David Reno, George S. Richardson, Sibyl Senters, Lollie Sharpe, Ellen Slater, Glen Snowden, Josie

Sterling, and Nancy and Jack Sullivan. For guiding us through the publishing process, we are most grateful to Ellen Bedell, Director of Development at Pearson Custom Publishing.

In a time when peace is challenged, it is my hope that this book will help us all to embrace a larger focus of inclusion. May we look to the future with respect and love!

Rhys Williams
March 18, 2003

Foreword

∾

$\mathscr{B}$ETTER THAN ALMOST ANYONE I know, Rhys Williams exemplifies the optimism intrinsic to liberal religion. From his days as a ministerial *Wunderkind* to his active retirement after forty years in the pulpit of the historic First and Second Church in Boston, Rhys has put love to work for truth. The most remarkable thing about this collection of sermons, ranging over five decades, is how constant both the voice and message remain throughout. We are born free and held responsible for the lives we make and the life we serve. The world doesn't owe us a living; we owe a living to the world. Success in life comes from every investment we make that enhances the life placed within our charge. Triumphant living is nothing more and nothing less than living in such a way that our lives will prove worth dying for.

For this reason, although individualism and freedom—Rhys's watchwords—echo throughout every sermon in this book, he remains the most dedicated institutionalist I know. The list of charitable and cultural institutions in Boston that Rhys has served is almost endless. His service extends from Hale House to the Boston Opera Company, from Emerson College to the Urban Ministry. He is as generous with his time and energy as he is unprepossessing in extending himself for others. Rhys learned long ago a lesson that comes hard to many in the ministry: *It's not about him.* A devoted minister places him or herself at the disposal of others. For Rhys, triumphant living has nothing to do with personal glory. Its bounty can be enjoyed and measured in direct proportion to one's gift of life and self to others.

In an age laced with irony and cynicism, it is refreshing to read pages from a life work that is so affirming, so brimming with hope. Rhys doesn't agonize; he brainstorms. His ministry, so well reflected in his preaching, is solution-based, not problem-based. Comfortable in but never boasting of the Enlightenment tradition, Rhys is a modernist in outlook. Yet he invests modernism with a moral dimension that too often gets muted by the march of progress. I suppose you could say that he is an old-fashioned modernist. He nurtures in his life and preaching the most redemptive elements of rationalism by infusing thought with spirit. For this reason, no matter what subject he tackles, his sermons are always uplifting. They blow like a fresh breeze, refreshing our appreciation for life's abundant possibilities.

Increasingly complex and fraught with danger, the modern age tempts many thoughtful people to succumb to sophisticated resignation. Knowing that the problems besetting our world are so very great, we may resign ourselves to the inexorability of their grip. Rhys resists this temptation. His cup is not simply half full—it overflows. Not unmindful of life's tragedy, inequality, and sorrow, Rhys nonetheless empties himself to be filled (and to fill us) with a deeper appreciation for the oft-forgotten blessings of being, and being *here*, and being here *together*.

The philosopher William James distinguished between the once-born, for whom life is a gift, and the twice-born, for whom it is a burden that must be redeemed for its worth to be secured. For almost two centuries the liberal religious tradition, which countered the Calvinist preoccupation with sin with faith in basic human goodness, was the epitome of a once-born outlook—positive, hopeful and hearty. That tradition has been darkened by the umbra of modernism. In an age when even the once-born are often tortured souls, Rhys holds firm to the old Unitarian gospel. Even those of us who cannot walk with him all the way down the wide and straight path welcome his company, for it brightens our journey.

Dozens of Unitarian Universalist ministers began their life work under Rhys's tutelage. The intern program at First and Second Church is unique. Rhys gave to many seminarians the opportunity to begin their parish work at First and Second Church. I owe my own ministry to Rhys Williams. Taking me under his wing during my years as a master's and doctoral student, he guided me from the academy to the parish. His direction was so deft that I remained completely unaware of it. He didn't pressure or cajole me. He simply took my hand without my knowing it and led me. I don't owe him my faith, but I do owe him much of my faithfulness. He didn't give me my gospel, but without hearing his good news I might never have sought it.

For all of Rhys's seminarians and for devoted parishioners throughout the decades, this book is a treasure. To a new generation of Unitarian Universalist preachers and congregants, it offers testimony to the enduring witness of liberal religion in a pure and uplifting form. Rhys's light shines gently yet clearly. A perfect antidote for an age in which knowledge conspires with hopelessness, his companionable wisdom will brighten your journey and help redeem your days.

Forrest Church
All Souls Unitarian Church
New York City

Biography of Rhys and Eleanor Williams

By John Burt
Professor of English, Brandeis University
and Member of First and Second Church

RHYS AND ELEANOR WILLIAMS have nurtured, encouraged, taught, ministered to, shaped and led the First and Second Church in Boston through their forty-year ministry and beyond. Their unique partnership brought to the ministry of the oldest church in Boston the insight, human warmth, wisdom, generosity, energy, and love that led it into the twenty-first century as one of the leading churches in Boston and as one of the flagship congregations of the Unitarian Universalist movement. Emerson described History as the lengthened shadow of a man; from 1960 to 1970 the history of the First Church, and since 1970 the First and Second Church in Boston, has been marked by the lengthened halo of Rhys and Eleanor. This collection represents a sampling of the human depth, the intellectual power, the moral passion, and above all, the warm optimism that Rhys brought to the pulpit of a great church. But it represents only a small fraction of what Rhys and Eleanor brought to the life of that church, both in fostering its work and life every day, and in shaping an institution that looks back on a long history and forward to a strong future.

Both Rhys and Eleanor were the children of clergy, and both came from families with histories of commitment to liberal religion and social justice. Churches have human lives, and in finding their calling at First and Second Church, Rhys and Eleanor have guided a Church that continues to shape and be shaped by the human beings who give themselves to it.

Rhys was born in San Francisco, California, February 27, 1929. His grandfather, David Thomas Williams, was born in Wales, where he worked in the coal mines at age 11. Coming to the United States, David Thomas attended the Bangor, Maine Seminary and was ordained to the Congregational Ministry. He and his wife Esther Rhys had four sons, all of whom became Congregational ministers. Two of the four later became Unitarian ministers. Rhys's uncle, David Rhys Williams, who served the First Congregational Society (Unitarian) of Rochester, New York from 1928 to 1958, was an active pacifist, an early supporter of birth control, a campaigner for racial equality, and a labor arbitrator in wage disputes between International Structural Steel and the Iron Workers Union.

Rhys's father, Albert Rhys Williams, began serving a Congregational Church in East Boston. He worked to support the mill workers in Lowell and Lawrence during the labor struggles there. Taking a sabbatical in 1913, he became a foreign correspondent and stayed to cover the First World War. He did not return to the ministry. He arrived in Russia before the October Revolution and followed the course of the Russian Revolution closely, befriending John Reed and Louise Bryant—and knowing Lenin, on whom he wrote a book. Although inclined as a social-ist, he was never a joiner of any political organization. His expe-riences during and after the Russian Revolution are eloquently recorded in his books.

In 1919 Albert was living in the bohemian world of Greenwich Village. There he met Rhys's mother, Lucita Squier. Her ancestors had been members of the First Church in Boston in 1632. She spent summers in Mexico where her fam-ily owned a silver mine near Saltillo and a small railroad. Her family lost everything during the Mexican Revolution of 1911. At that time she was studying in Paris but returned to the United States. She trained as a stenographer but then went to Hollywood, where she first advised the producers about cos-tumes, especially for historical dramas. Then began a long career as a writer of scenarios for Hollywood luminaries including Mary Pickford, Colleen Moore, and many other stars and directors.

In the wake of the 1921 famine in Russia, Lucita Squier joined Quaker Relief and entered the Soviet Union. She and Albert Rhys Williams were married in Moscow in 1922. She became fluent in Russian, and the couple worked in villages in the Volga region. Not wanting their son to be born in the Soviet Union, they returned to San Francisco in time for Rhys's birth in 1929. They moved to a small house in British Columbia. The isolation of life in British Columbia made Rhys determined to live the city life when he grew up.

The Williamses alternated between living in Canada and in California. They lived for some time in the literary and artistic community in Carmel, where young Rhys collected abalone shells on the beach with the poet Robinson Jeffers. When Lincoln Steffens was bedridden, Rhys remembers having many conversations with him. Friends of the family included the actor/singer Paul Robeson and the poet Langston Hughes. In the third grade Rhys was sent to boarding school in Ojai Valley, which he did not like. Later he lived on a ranch in Ojai Valley with a friend of his mother's.

Rhys's father went to Europe as a correspondent during the Spanish Civil War and considered moving the family to Europe in 1938 but was dissuaded by the increasing likelihood of war. Instead, the family moved briefly to Chappaqua, New York in the early 1940s. They returned again to the West Coast. Rhys received a scholarship to attend Vermont Academy but was unhappy living a continent away from his parents.

He had planned to attend Stanford University, but his Uncle David persuaded him to attend St. Lawrence University, where there was a program which provided scholarships for young men and women who might be interested in the ministry and a special curriculum that enabled them to do much of the early work of seminary training while still undergraduates. During the summers of his graduate years, Rhys was a sight-seeing bus driver and agent at Glacier National Park in Montana. In addition to his B.A. and M. Div. from

St. Lawrence, he received an LL.D. from Emerson College in 1962 and a D.D. from St. Lawrence in 1966.

In the fall of 1953 Rhys accepted the call to Charleston, South Carolina. The Unitarian Church in Charleston is the oldest Unitarian Church in the South. It has a distinguished history. Under the ministry of Samuel Gilman, known also for writing "Fair Harvard," it was the most important of the antebellum Unitarian churches in the South, although after the Civil War many of its leading families became Episcopalians.

In 1955 he traveled to Europe with the Sherwood Eddy seminar group of ministers and professors to discuss international affairs and to interview prominent European leaders such as Clement Attlee, Willy Brandt, and Josip Tito. In London's Toynbee Hall, the settlement house that inspired Jane Addams to found Hull House, he met Eleanor Hoyle Barnhart.

Eleanor was born March 19, 1932 in Frederick, Maryland, where her father was a professor of religion and philosophy at Hood College. William Rupp Barnhart was an ordained Congregational minister, as was Eleanor's grandfather, and served often as guest speaker in churches in the Baltimore and Washington areas. In 1944 he became Executive Director of the Washington Federation of Churches, but after a year he chose to return to his position at Hood College, as he preferred teaching to administration. He was an advocate for social justice and social equality. Eleanor's mother taught Latin and history at Frederick High School, from which Eleanor herself graduated, winning the Maryland State Scholarship to Goucher College.

At Goucher Eleanor majored in political science and international relations. Through her religion and philosophy courses, she became interested in Unitarianism, to which the progressive theological convictions of her father had already inclined her. The summer before her senior year at Goucher, she was one of six interns from the United States at the United Nations, where she worked in the human rights division and met Eleanor Roosevelt, who entertained the interns in her home. At the United Nations, Eleanor was able to observe closely the negotiations that brought an end to the Korean War. After graduating from college, Eleanor received a Fulbright Fellowship to the Netherlands where she studied the politics of the recently decolonized world and early efforts of European economic cooperation such as the Coal and Steel Community.

At the completion of her academic year, Eleanor joined her parents and sister Joanne, already with the Sherwood Eddy seminar group. Eleanor's curiosity about Unitarianism immediately drew her to Rhys. Their courtship continued that autumn after Rhys returned to Charleston and Eleanor became a teacher of history and English in Baltimore County.

In September 1956 they were married. They enjoyed very much the beauty of Charleston and the warmth and enthusiasm of their congregation. But by late 1958, Rhys felt he had done as much as he could to influence the mores of the community. The church was growing and had many loyal and active members. Rhys felt this was a good time to seek another church.

Rhys received calls to be the Candidate for Ministry from two churches almost simultaneously in the summer of 1959.

First Church was the smaller of the two in membership, but it had a distinct flavor, played a unique role in Boston and in the Unitarian Association, and had a deep tradition of intellectual openness that Rhys and Eleanor found very attractive. The other church was going to have to build a new building in order to make way for a freeway, and having completed a parsonage in Charleston, Rhys felt (little did he know what was in store for him) that he did not want to engage in another building project.

In Boston, Rhys enjoyed a thirty-three year collaboration with First Church's Music Director, Leo Collins, and a thirty-year association with the Church Administrator, Susan Twist. From the beginning of his ministry he reached out to new groups. With Gerry Krick's efforts, First Church became a presence in many area colleges, such as Boston University, Emerson College, Fisher College and Bay State College. Discussion groups were held on campus and social evenings were organized at First Church.

In the middle 1960s Rhys began training field education students and ministerial interns, starting a tradition which brought First and Second Church fame as the training ground for excellent ministers. Dozens of field education students and ministerial interns benefited from Rhys's generous tutelage, and some of these are among the most distinguished young clergy in the denomination. Increasingly, First and Second Church became known as a place for superb training. The interns taught First and Second Church as much as they learned and were a continuous source of new ideas, new perspectives, and new voices, bringing with them also tremendous reserves of esprit de corps and loyalty.

Under Rhys, the Church developed a distinguished history of founding institutions to serve the public good. The John Winthrop School for young children began in 1966, originally using one room in the parish house and a second room in the basement of the old First Church building. Beginning in 1965, a committed group of church members formed the Edward Everett Hale Corporation and began investigating possible sites for an assisted living facility for elders. An existing home for older women at 273 Clarendon Street was about to close. In 1971 this building and two adjacent houses became Hale House, named after Edward Everett Hale, the great Unitarian minister and orator of the nineteenth century. When the Frances Mary Barnard Home closed in Milton, Hale House gained its resources and became Hale-Barnard Corporation. In addition to providing a residence for fifty-six men and women, it maintains an outreach program for people in other areas and a bill-payer program to help elders. In the 1990s First and Second Church played a significant role in creating the Peter Faneuil Corporation which bought the old Peter Faneuil School on Beacon Hill and rehabilitated it into mainly single-room occupancy housing. Also on Beacon Hill, the Corporation built new housing for persons with AIDS.

On March 29, 1968 First Church was destroyed by fire. Only the spire of the old church building and the facade on Marlborough Street remained. A fortuitous closing of the fire doors saved the parish house from sharing the fate of the church building. Fortunately, church records dating back to 1630 had been moved from the church to the parish house.

Churches from other denominations were generous to First Church during this difficult time. The First Lutheran Church of Boston shared its sanctuary that first Sunday and the Church of the Covenant welcomed the John Winthrop School. Emmanuel Church (Episcopal) gave First Church the use of the Leslie Lindsey Chapel gratis for four years, and our services were held at 9:30 every Sunday morning until the new church was built.

The early stages of the rebuilding process went rather smoothly. Committees were organized to explore the possibility of merger with other churches or joint use of facilities. In 1970 the Second Church (then located in Brookline) merged with the First Church. Committees were formed to select an architect and to oversee the building of a new church. The treasurer of our Trustees, State Senator Oliver F. Ames, persuaded the insurers that the new building did not have to be an exact copy of the old one.

About half of the $2.8 million needed to rebuild the church had been raised when, on December 1, 1969, the Church received a series of non-negotiable demands from an organization called the Fellowship for Renewal. This organization was formed specifically in response to First Church's attempt to rebuild. Their demand was that the Church turn over the money it had raised, so that they could use it to rehabilitate a building on Massachusetts Avenue for housing. The Church's stand was that the money donors had given for one purpose could not be arbitrarily diverted to another purpose.

Although the Fellowship for Renewal phrased its demands in the language of Black Liberation, its membership was entirely white. Many of its members were Unitarian Universalists. They frequently demonstrated at services, once causing the service to be dismissed. They obtained the church's mailing list and harassed the membership through the mail. The Fellowship for Renewal's campaign went on for some six months. When they persuaded representatives from a predominantly African-American civil rights group to meet with them and with a delegation from First Church, the representatives from the civil rights group saw that the Fellowship for Renewal's agenda was not worth pursuing, and the Fellowship for Renewal ceased to exist shortly thereafter. Throughout this, First Church had the friendship and support of the clergy and parishioners of Emmanuel Church, who warmly assured Rhys that, "This too, will pass."

The new building of First and Second Church, under the joint ministry of Rhys Williams and John Hammon of Second Church, was dedicated on Palm Sunday, 1972. It is a handsome and striking building, designed by the architect Paul Rudolph, incorporating a modern sanctuary and narthex and the steeple of the old First Church, expressing in its very contrasts the union of old and new of which First and Second Church is proud. 1981 marked the completion of the faceted stained glass window by Gyorgy Kepes that graces the Edward Everett Hale Chapel and which is reproduced on the cover of this book.

In addition to his dedicated ministry at First and Second Church and his involvement in the John Winthrop School project, the Hale-Barnard project, and the Peter Faneuil and AIDS Housing projects, Rhys has distinguished himself with the advice and leadership he has provided to many of the leading charitable and educational institutions of Boston. He serves on the board of the Franklin Institute, which has trained young people, among them many immigrants, in technical areas since it was founded by a bequest of Benjamin Franklin. Rhys served for over forty years on the Board of Emerson College, cementing a relationship that has been of profound benefit to both institutions, enabling Emerson to use rooms at First and Second Church as classrooms during the week and establishing a live broadcast of church services over Emerson's WERS radio every Sunday. He has been president of the Benevolent Fraternity, now the Unitarian Universalist Urban Ministry, which has served the needs of urban Boston since the nineteenth century. He continues as president of the Unitarian Service Pension Society and the Society of Ministerial Relief, the latter of which supports retired ministers and their widows in North America and in Transylvania. He is active in the Ministers' Club of Boston and is on the New Horizon Board for Higher Education of Russians in the United States. He is a past president of the Unitarian Universalist Ministers' Association, the professional association for Unitarian Universalist clergy. Both Rhys and Eleanor are on the President's Council, an advisory group to the president of the Unitarian Universalist Association. Rhys has served for over twenty years as Chaplain of The Society of the Cincinnati, which is headquartered in Washington, D.C.

Eleanor also has a distinguished record of service and leadership in Boston. A founding incorporator of the John Winthrop School, she served on its Board of Trustees for thirty-four years. For ten years she was president of the Fragment Society, one of the oldest charitable foundations in Boston, founded during the War of 1812. She has been a past president of the Dedham Temporary Home for Women and Children (now generally called the Chickering Fund). She is a vice president of the Lend-a-Hand Society (founded by Edward Everett Hale) and for many years was on the Board of Managers of the home for the elderly now known as Goddard House.

Eleanor has been actively involved in the life of the Church. For many years in the spring and sometimes fall, Eleanor, Leo Collins, and I would lead walks to historic Unitarian and Universalist sites. Members and friends looked forward to the annual Christmas party given by Rhys and Eleanor in the parsonage on Beacon Hill and to other dinners and meetings graciously hosted by them in their home.

The sermons in this book are selected from the work of five decades of ministry. These sermons exemplify both the intellectual depth and the tender human common sense of a great minister. Over the years, Rhys's theology became broader, as he sought to engage people with very different views in a common search for meaning. At the heart of each sermon is Rhys's ability to speak to all parishioners as people with moral concerns and spiritual hungers, people who are looking for ways to become better, more decent, more kind, more thoughtful human beings. During his many years of ministering to a turbulent world, Rhys brought to his work a warm and far-reaching spirit of optimism —seeking, through gentle and realistic encouragement, ways in which all of us can become, with the moral and psychological equipment we already have, closer to the kinds of people that in our best moments we hope to be.

After a forty-year ministry at our church, Rhys retired at the end of January 2000 and became Minister Emeritus. We look forward to many years of his friendship and wise counsel.

First and Second Church in Boston as it appears today. Completed in 1972, following the great fire of 1968, the stone tower and façade on Berkeley Street are the only remains of the 5th building of First Church which stood from 1868 to 1968. Drawing by Tom Dahill.

Unitarian Church, Charleston, South Carolina. Built in 1772 as a Congregational Church, it became a Unitarian Church in 1817. Interior remodeled in 1852 after Henry VII Chapel, Westminster Abbey, London. Rhys was minister here from 1953 to 1960.

Wedding of Eleanor and Rhys, Frederick, Maryland, 1956.

Rhys Williams, 1966.

(Photo courtesy of Bacbracb Photographers)

Christmas card sent by the Williamses, 1968. Rhys Hoyle (age seven) and Eleanor Pierce (Norie) (age four) standing in ruins of church. Under the photo was written, "Christmas proclaims hope and new beginnings."

Interior of the new sanctuary of First and Second Church, dedicated December 10, 1972.

Flower Communion Sunday, May 1995. Margaret Scadden giving flowers to Vanessa Southern, an intern (now minister of the Unitarian Church, Summit, New Jersey) and Rhys.

June 1999. Leo Collins, Music Director, Emeritus; Jack Sullivan, Vice Chair, Standing Committee; Rhys Williams; Gordon Sterling, Chair, Standing Committee; Marlin Lavanhar, an intern (now minister of All Souls Unitarian Church, Tulsa, Oklahoma).

Eleanor and Rhys in Jericho, 1985. They were part of a group from the Semitic Museum, Harvard University, traveling in Israel.

Eleanor and Rhys in front of 7 Chestnut Street, Boston. Photo by Nigel Harvey, taken for celebration of Rhys' forty-year ministry at First and Second Church, January 2000.

*Norie Kelly and Rhys H.
Williams in foreground.
Rebecca Williams holding
Rhys K. Williams,
Dylan Williams, Philip
Rhys Kelly, Luke Williams.
Thanksgiving 2001.*

*Dylan, Rhys, Luke, and
Grant Williams, March
2003.*

*Norie, Phil, and Philip
Rhys Kelly, January 2002.*

Sermons from Five Decades

MEETING
NEW
CHALLENGES

A Religion for
a Changing World

*L*AST WEEK A CARD came to my desk from a high school I attended in Vermont. It asked for information concerning the present address of my parents. This academy had sent a letter to them in Cedar, British Columbia, Canada, but it had been returned. Cedar, B.C., a few years ago, consisted of houses thinly spread over a five-mile radius, a school of three rooms with twelve grades and a general store. Since we have moved away from this community, startling changes have occurred. The school no longer exists. Parents believe their children receive a better education from a consolidated system.

Mr. Rayer, who ran the general store, has retired. When Mr. Rayer ran the store, all customers were his friends. He pumped gas into their cars. He listened to their problems. He had a substation post office in the store, and you daily picked up your mail

5

from him. If you moved away, he sent you a Christmas card with the local Cedar news, and, of course, forwarded any mail that might have come. But Mr. Rayer has retired and times have changed. Supermarkets have replaced the general store. The mail is now delivered by a rural carrier from the main post office in the city, nine miles away. Housing developments have sprung up.

Here in Charleston this past month, Rodenberg's old supermarket became modern. They moved all their butchers from the visible scene and replaced them with packaged meats on open refrigerated shelves. Perhaps it is more efficient, but it is sad that there is no longer a human face connected with the food we buy.

American Motors, which once built Hudson and Nash automobiles, as well as its present product, is talking about a merger with Studebaker Packard Corporation. This will mean that four automobile manufacturers will be turning out products that look basically the same. Thirty years ago there were over 100 automobile firms. Their cars were distinctive, from the giant Pierce Arrow and air-cooled Franklin to the tiny Moon. Americans were producing cars of distinction and grace. Perhaps four consolidated companies from over 100 would be fine, if only individual styling and a choice of taste could be maintained. But they are not. "Bigger and bigger" becomes the motto. Eating the family out of house and home with its gargantuan appetite for gasoline, bulging out of one's garage like a sixty-year-old man getting into a tuxedo he wore at eighteen, these elephantine products of consolidation and mass production are robbing us of financial solvency. This is the way we are heading. Is it really what we want? We see consolidation taking place

around us and in every direction . . . but too often this consolidation is towards the lowest common denominator.

Edward A. Weeks, Jr., Editor of the *Atlantic Monthly*, reported
at the Unitarian May meetings that in the 1920s, they had one
million discriminating readers. After supposedly better educational techniques, thousands of new schools, and many millions
of increase in our population, they have today the very same
number of discriminating readers.

Is consolidation leading Americans to forget their individuality and their dreams and visions? Is it robbing us of our individual initiative, our individual development? In many cases I am
afraid it is doing so, for we take this enthusiasm for consolidation
in our business life and move it into the area of our spiritual
development. As a few top directors in automobile production or
T.V. presentations set the taste and pattern for American buying
and viewing, many feel that they should turn over their spiritual
life, their religious development, to a few top hierarchical men in
churches. Let them mass-produce our religious laws and insights.
Let them tell us what is spiritual and religious and what is not.

I talked with a scientist recently who said, "My religious
leader and church don't understand some of the laws of the
Universe that I do . . . but I am an expert on astronomy; they are
not. They accept on faith what I tell them. Consequently when
they tell me ideas and doctrines that don't make sense to me, and
there are many, I accept these ministrations on faith. I'm an
expert scientist. They are experts in religion."

Through consolidation and mass production you may be
able to bring an automobile to every garage and a T.V. to every

home, but I am firmly convinced that you cannot bring a meaningful religious faith, a religion for a changing time, by similar methods. Our minds and our religious yearnings cannot be mass-produced. This era of mass production and consolidation has brought about a higher standard of physical living. But the examples we see of world hate, revolution, of growing crime and juvenile delinquency, of our emotions being controlled by artificial tranquilizers, indicate all too clearly that our religious life, our yearning for more noble living, and our hope for a world of peace cannot be found in mass-produced spectator religions.

With great advances in technology and knowledge occurring at unimaginable speed, it is time Americans sought to discover and embrace a religion that is willing to keep up with these changing times. The first premise of a religion for changing times is that religion is an individual matter that must stress and practice the dignity, the wonder of human personality. Religion must be individual, rather than the end product of mass production and consolidation. We, rather than a hierarchical church, must be finally responsible for our spiritual development. For as Jesus said, "Every one that asketh receiveth; and he that seeketh findeth." Jesus was not referring to an organization but to individuals. Shakespeare later reinforced this idea when he said in Hamlet (lll, 3), "My words fly up, my thoughts remain below: Words without thought never to heaven go." Churches can mass-produce pious sounding words, but only you as an individual can take them into your heart, dwell upon them in your mind, and lift them out into life with positive intent.

Since religious organizations and their rituals often fail to inspire individuals to seek peaceful and respectful living throughout the world, it is time that religion be taken out of those church agencies that mass-produce religious formulas and be placed back in the hands of the people. To counteract the great spiritual lag, each one of us must assume his own religious responsibility. Our churches must inspire each of us to seek the highest that is known. Our churches must encourage each of us to share our insights with others. Our churches must be an open testing ground for our spiritual experimentation and growth. There is wisdom given in Romans 12:2 where it says, "Be not conformed to this world, but be ye transformed by the renewing of your mind."

A religion for a growing, changing world must emphasize the importance of every living person. The sooner we discover the hidden talent, the unused goodness within our own human breast, the sooner we will be able to encourage these same characteristics in others.

A religion for a changing world must call out from us our highest and noblest sentiments. It must make us aware of our own preciousness and that in others. It must point to living examples of goodness in other people, such as Albert Schweitzer, and call us to develop these same noble qualities in our own life. It must make us aware that behind the greed, the impatience, the selfishness, lies a spark of reverence, of potential for love.

Take this reverence for our own individuality and the individuality of the other person into every area of life that we touch. Then we will have embraced the first step in a religion that shall meet our needs in a changing world. A religion to meet such a challenge must not only encourage individuals to develop their potentials of goodness and nobility, their highest individuality, but it also must promote the quest for a vision, rather than the preservation of a doctrine.

It was William Ellery Channing who wrote: "The great end in religious instruction, whether in the Sunday school or family, is not to stamp our minds irresistibly on the young, but to stir up their own; not to make them see with our eyes, but to look inquiringly and steadily with their own; not to give them a definite amount of knowledge, but to inspire a fervent love of truth; not to burden the memory, but to quicken and strengthen the power of thought; not to bind them by ineradicable prejudices to our particular sect or peculiar notions, but to prepare them for impartial, conscientious judging of whatever subjects may be offered to their decision; not to impose religion upon but to awaken the conscious, the moral discernment, so that they may discern and approve for themselves what is everlastingly right and good."

The importance of the individual and acceptance of responsibility, the desire for newer and nobler visions, and the quest for greater truth and knowledge comprise the religious emphasis needed to meet the challenge of this changing world.

If more people would assume their responsibilities as individuals and would embrace a religion that would encourage them to do this, they could find a growing concept of God that they could genuinely worship. They could lead a life that would bring joy to themselves and to others.

It is not consolidation or mass production that will raise our spiritual qualities and insights but individual development, searching, and responsibility. May our church never impede us on this continual quest. May it always point us in the direction of these words from Philippians 4:8: "Finally brethren, whatsoever things are true, whatsoever things are honest; whatsoever things are just, whatsoever things are sure; whatsoever things are lovely; whatsoever things are of good report, if there be any virtue, and if there be any praise, think on these things."

Religion for the Sixties

JANUARY 8, 1961

$\mathcal{A}$S WE ENTER THE SECOND YEAR of this decade, fraught with its threats of violence in the world, yet permeated at the moment with comfort and conformity at home, we should become more acutely aware of some of the big spiritual questions. In 1961 can religion be a vital force in improving personal and social conditions? Can we throw off the signs that foretell a life of obliteration rather than one of developmental affirmation? Are our real hopes those that inspire us to increase the noble content of our humanity and that of our world? Are these questions of the spirit matters that really concern us? Are we really interested in them, or do they get a passing thought, if any at all?

If we were to look over the various publications talking about this decade, we would be startled to see how religion has become respectable but not truly respected. What has superseded religion? What occupies our avenues of communication, our areas of genuine concern? Mammon, bodily comfort, selfish expediency? We should learn from the epitaph of Rome, for no state ever excluded the ideal from its national and social life so strictly as did Rome, with the exception of Nazi Germany. It taught prosaic commercialism to all its provinces. It died a slow, lingering death after achieving one of the greatest seeming successes in history. Its citizens served mammon in place of God with more than usual dedication. The power they worshipped carried them along for the moment. Eventually, their own decadence enabled barbaric forces to shower the bricks of their civilization down upon them. This was a tragedy, for Rome's empire with its social structure still looms as one of the greatest reared through human ingenuity. The lesson of Rome's fall should be a stark reminder to the most prosperous nation in our twentieth century.

Where are the deep questions of religion being talked about today? Almost nowhere. Take a recent issue of *Newsweek* emphasizing this decade of the sixties. There is much space devoted to politics, to defense, to the mobility of our population, to the demand for a share in material prosperity by the awakening continents of Africa and Asia, to future products and luxuries, to sputniks, space probes, and the stock market. At the end is a small section devoted to religion.

A more sophisticated publication, the *Saturday Review*, previews the decade we have entered. It talks about science, leisure time, education, the European Federation, health, defense, and underdeveloped areas as the big issues we face in these next ten years. Certainly all these topics are important, and I don't mean to depreciate them but are they enough in themselves? "Wait a moment," you say, "it may be true that our main channels of communication stress these aspects for the decade, but don't sixty million church members in America indicate that we are religiously concerned? Isn't there a greater proportion of our population in churches today?" Many of us are worried by the failure of so-called church members to bring their professed beliefs into the mainstream of their lives. There seems to be no dynamic transfer from the pew to the home or the business. We see no profound religious journals dominating the newsstands. We find no overall dedicated cry from church members to reduce the world's corruptions.

Dr. Robert McCracken of New York's Riverside Church spoke of this recently in a sermon, declaring, "The current upsurge of piety in the nation should arouse our concern. In particular, the discrepancy between the size of churches and their impact on the national and international life would suggest that, for the majority, religion presents an escape from reality. From problems of delinquency at home to the international scientific arms race dominated by a strategy of obliteration . . . the great public issues are not grappled with. The churches are mainly devotional societies, detached for the most part from the life-and-death struggle going on in the contemporary world. The result is that the general tendency of society in its organized forms—government, trade unions, professional associations—is to pursue its affairs without reference to the religious view of man."

We have a great lag between the idea of the Church and our individual lives. Why? One reason is due to the Church's failure to face our spiritual needs. Another is due to our complacency. The tragedy of the lag is shown all too clearly when we see people turning to scientists rather than to clergy for solutions to the great human yearnings.

Religious leaders did not always come in last. At one time they were prophetic and skilled at leading people towards spiritual solutions. They used all the knowledge that was available in order to live life abundantly and with the flame of hope. The writings of the ancient Hebrew prophets and Jesus with his Sermon on the Mount and Beatitudes are the culmination of centuries of human struggle brought together for all to see.

The Gospel writers drew from the best available knowledge of their era in order to make their writings more graphic and convincing. The Gospel writer Matthew, in describing the story of the Magi following the star until it rested over the place where Jesus lay, went outside Jewish sources for his material. Magi were not Jewish wise men but Zoroastrian priests from Persia. Similarly, in the Mithraic religion, then dominant in Rome, there is an account that in the year A.D. 66, before Matthew wrote his Gospel, three wise men brought gifts of frankincense and myrrh to Nero, the Anti-Christ, and worshipped him as Lord and Savior. If the Anti-Christ was paid such homage, could Jesus receive less?

It is certainly a fact that some of our ancient religious writers used the ideas of many traditions and sources to weave their stories and to put across their religious concepts concerning Jesus.

16

Luke's parable of the talents is a vivid portrayal of why it is necessary for us to put all our knowledge and abilities to use. What is not used will be lost. Jesus symbolically indicated that unless we use that which is available to us—in a democracy the genuine practice of freedom and human rights—eventually we will lose it for ourselves.

Darwin said the same thing, only in different words. He scientifically demonstrated to the world that unless we can adapt to changing circumstances and use our various abilities, we will become biologically useless and eventually extinct. The Church in Russia is a dying institution because it has always buried its opportunities and talents by not relating to the changing needs of society.

Dr. McCracken is warning Americans, and particularly American churchgoers, about the tremendous lag between a religion of life and deed and one of vocal but unpracticed creed. The Church in the sixties should be a full, talented institution, not satisfied merely to exist on the visions of a dark and superstitious age but willing and able to hold its head high along with other areas of human endeavor where experimentation and the wide range of all knowledge are applied to create a better life for humanity.

What then should be the emphasis of religion for the sixties if it is to reduce this tremendous lag? First, religion must show that there is a purpose leading us towards constructive and altruistic good will in this world, beset today by war and fear, and that we are a part of this purpose. To reinforce this view we must not only point out Jesus and his works but also must speak of others' sacrifices and good will. We must see civilization as a progression from the caveman to the United Nations. We must tell people about Darwin, who showed us that species change to adapt to a different environment.

We must carry these observations into the philosophic realm. For instance—why did not all life remain at the level of a starfish, which has survived for centuries? What is humanity's unique contribution? Is it not love, sacrifice, tolerance and understanding, when the animal passions demand of us greed, selfishness and survival at any expense? Is it not coming to terms with the planet—humbly and appreciatively coming to terms with what we are and how we came to be? Is it not developing a higher sense of values and purpose?

Dr. Pitrim Sorokin is Professor of Sociology at Harvard. Although he was condemned to death by Stalin, one of his books is titled *Altruistic Love*. He says that social organizations built mainly through conquest, coercion, and hate—for example, the Empires of Alexander, Caesar, Genghis Khan, Tamerlane, Napoleon and Hitler—have had, as a rule, a relatively short life. He points out further that selfish business interests, without concern for the overall good of the community, such as certain drug and cosmetic manufacturers, have a business life of four years. On the other hand, the longest existing organizations are the great ethical-religious traditions such as Taoism, Confucianism, Hinduism, Buddhism, Judaism, and Christianity. Sorokin tells us that the secret of their longevity probably lies in their dedication to the cultivation of love in the human universe.

The Church must focus the human mind on such facts, pointing out a growing morality and harmony in the universe and in the evolution of human beings. Today, if religion is to be dynamic and convincing, it must call on the talents of non-religious leaders such as scientists to affirm such observations. We must call on those such as Arthur Compton, who has stated that "The chance that a world such as ours should occur without intelligent design becomes more remote as we learn its wonders," and Dr. Kirtley Mather, Professor Emeritus of Geology at Harvard, who has declared, "We live in a universe not of chance or caprice, but law and order."

Not only scientists such as Sorokin and Compton but religious people who think for themselves in terms of twentieth-century knowledge need to be heard today. It was Halford Luccock, the former Dean of Yale Divinity School, who said a few years ago that there was a long road between the primitive Galilee man and the Man of Galilee: "There is evidence here that there is an upthrust in the universe, an emergent purpose, an evolving plan. The Galilee man is the type of creature from which we have evolved; the Man of Galilee is the type of man towards which we move." Religion in the sixties must be ready and willing to incorporate the latest revealed truth and the newest scientific knowledge and to demonstrate that these may be in harmony with the thoughts of shepherds and the wisemen many years ago that behind this universe is a purpose that is leading us towards harmony and unity and beauty. This wonderful purpose we call God.

Another direction of religion in the sixties should be in reducing ignorance, in making people aware of problems that

need solving, and in inspiring them to act intelligently and spiritually to see that realistic solutions are reached. The old saying,
"five percent of the people think, five percent think they think,
and ninety percent would rather do anything else but think" has
been stated more profoundly by Samuel Johnson in these words,
"Mankind has a great aversion to intellectual labor; but even
supposing knowledge to be easily attainable, more people would
be content to be ignorant than would take even a little trouble
to acquire."

Fortunately, this attitude is changing. With shots to the
moon and man in space, with the realization of the evil and fragmentation caused by prejudice and hate, with the weapons of
total destruction, we are beginning to acknowledge that we must
understand more than ever before. We are beginning to see that
going to the moon is not going far enough. The great distance
lies in us—between what we are today and what we must become
by tomorrow.

If our ability to manipulate things is getting dynamic new
attention, so religion in the sixties must give both strength and
encouragement to developing the human spirit. Alexis Carrel
writes in *Man the Unknown:* "Humanity's attention must turn
from the machines and the world of inanimate matter to the
body and soul of man . . . to the organic and mental processes
which have created the machines and the universe of Newton
and Einstein." Religion in the sixties, instead of being an escape
from reality, must be a means to it. We must acknowledge that
the happy and contented individuals are not those who have
escaped the usual misfortunes of living. If, like Anne Frank,

we can be mistreated and still be happy, we have gained a valuable insight. Peace of mind does not depend upon what life has done to us, but rather it depends upon the degree of internal enlightenment with which we react to the pressures of living. If we are willing to grow intellectually and spiritually, we will soon realize that we can live actively with purpose in a most troublesome world. We will have the knowledge that we are an important cog in reducing the ills and in affirming the good. Thus, religion must help give to us the faith and confidence to face realistically and intelligently the paramount problems today—war and peace.

The old doctrine of original sin must be evaluated in the light of modern developments in psychology. If others tell you that you cannot do something, such as jumping over a ditch, and you likewise convince yourself that you are not capable of this act, you probably will not try it and consequently will not accomplish it.

Emperor Asoka in the third century B.C., horrified by the "abomination" wrought by his victorious wars and under the influence of Buddhism, radically changed his belligerent policy to one of peace and friendship. Through a policy of "love begets love," he was able to secure peace for some seventy-two years. As Professor Sorokin has pointed out in his writings: "Considering that such a long period of peace occurred only three times in the whole history of Greece, Rome and thirteen European countries, Asoka's achievement strongly suggests that the policy of real friendship can secure a lasting peace more successfully than the policy of hate and aggression."

Through the years there have been examples of peace shining through war. It must be realized that humanity is more richly endowed with the capacity for love and cooperation than for hate and destruction. In the year A.D. 1139 at the Lateran Council, the use of the crossbow was forbidden under the penalty of excommunication. Poison gas was banned for use in World War II. In view of the destructive power of modern-day weapons, the Church should be encouraging the banning of war to solve human and national difficulties and should be active in the work of alleviating the conditions which breed wars.

Religion must emphasize that we are capable of creating an atmosphere of peace and cooperation among all peoples on national and international levels and in our homes. There are talents in the scientific, business, and social world that can enrich the human spirit. The Church must bring to fruition a synthesis of these concepts along with the ideals of its own historical, ethical heritage. You and I must strive towards this truth. This is our task, our hope, and our opportunity!

How We May
Make Moral Decisions

JANUARY 30, 1966

*I*N OLDER PROTESTANT THEOLOGY, the doctrine of atonement was stated in legal terms. Calvary was conceived as a transaction between God and Jesus in which God accepted Jesus' sufferings as the penalty of original sin. Throughout the Bible we are aware of codes and laws that speak of the way we should behave. They run from the Ten Commandments to the Sermon on the Mount.

For centuries we developed a code that we did not always follow but that we acknowledged pointed to the eternal life. There was always hypocrisy. Ibsen in his play *Ghosts* sought to point out the gap between the morality we declared publicly and the sin we lived privately. Writing in the 1880s, he shocked his world by exposing the double standard.

Today the sins that were private are now exposed publicly. A poll in Toronto, Ontario recently came up with these attitudes: "Seventy-five percent of the people said they would, if they could avoid being detected, cheat on income tax, keep any extra change a cashier or teller might give them, drink until they were drunk, if that was the mood of the party they were attending, keep an extra bag of groceries a supermarket clerk might hand them by mistake, hoodwink employers by manipulations that amount to outright fraud, and attempt to get ahead in their jobs at the expense of subordinates."

The sinews that have held civilization together for centuries are rotting. We are not finding new bindings for peoples. We are losing a sense of a higher purpose. We no longer sense we are part of something ongoing and eternal. We have accepted the criticism of Ibsen. We have eliminated many of society's hypocrisies, but we have chosen the lesser choices. We have even captured the pessimism of Ibsen that we are on a never-ending treadmill. The troubles that befall us come from fate. They are beyond our power to control. They are beyond our capacities to understand. Thus we can be one of the statistics in the Toronto poll by ignoring our responsibilities and trying to forget the hard work that needs to be done. We say everything is relative, that life is purposeless, and we will be happiest if we can forget our world and strive to be happy. James Stephens has captured this thought in these lines:

> "Good and bad and right and wrong
> Wave the silly words away.
> This is wisdom to be strong.

This is virtue to be gay.
Let us sing and dance, until
We shall know the final art;
How to banish good and ill
With the laughter of the heart."

We cannot be unmindful of our times. Events grab hold of us: the specter of war, the diminished respect for law and order, the refutation of ideals that have held civilization together, the lack of constructive and positive substitutes. They all cry out at us. We cannot ignore them. We cannot forget them. If the codes of the Bible and the ancient doctrines of the church no longer grip us and transform us, how then shall we make our moral decisions?

A writer in one of the leading scholarly magazines has called for the substitution of beauty for the codes of duty and righteousness. This would be the new morality to replace that to which we barely give lip service anymore. The old idea of duty to a code is dead. It is gone forever, we are told. An empty place has been left to be filled. The aforementioned writer proposes beauty.

We can be sympathetic towards this suggestion only if we make clear what it may imply in our lives. Is there not a beauty that is moral? It is the beauty that Kant recognized when he said: "Two things fill the mind with admiration and awe: the starry heavens above and the moral law within." It is the beauty that Wordsworth recognized when he called duty "the stern daughter of the voice of God."

The morality that religion should be talking about today is too high and sacred a thing to be limited by a finite code from the past. Moral beauty is being free from statutes imposed from without. It is to substitute spiritual principles governing life from within. This is what Jesus was talking about with the child-like spirit. He called for that openness, spontaneous wonder, and the wakening joy of the child.

If most people no longer are blind adherents to the codes of the past, how may we make moral decisions? How do we keep the childlike wonder? How can we come to know what is right and what is wrong in this fast-paced and changing world?

First, we need to recognize that human beings have the capacity for conscientious behavior. We are capable of moving beyond instinct and making decisions based on judgments. As Michael Servetus did, we can give up our life for ideals. No one compelled Servetus to stand up for the religious principles in which he believed. It was his inner decision. Theodore Parker broke with his peers when they were cruel to a turtle by a pond. The external code for Servetus was to accept the prevailing Trinitarian belief in Christianity. The external code of Parker's friends was to tease and taunt helpless animals. In the case of both Parker and Servetus, there was an inner voice. In religious circles it has been called the voice of God in the human soul.

Conscience as a moral notion did not exist with the classical Greeks. The thundering wrathful God of the Old Testament imposed external authority. Judgments depended on a fearful external authority. It is only later that we find the Hebrew prophets calling for personal judgments. Conscience comes into the vocabulary through the writings of the Roman Stoics. This is continued with Jesus. The eighteenth-century moralist, Joseph Butler, described it in these words: "We have a capacity of reflecting upon actions and characters and making them an object to our thought, and on doing this we naturally and unavoidably approve some actions, under the peculiar view of their being virtuous and of good desert, and disapprove others as vicious and of ill desert." That we have this moral approving and disapproving faculty is certain from our experiencing it in ourselves and recognizing it in others.

If we recognize the capacity of conscience in others and ourselves, how do we translate it in connection with moral decisions? How do we move to embrace the idea of conscience as the "still small voice within"? We should understand conscience in three parts: First, we know it as a way of feeling. This, however, does not account for conscience being a source of moral knowledge. Therefore, second, conscience contains the element of reason. This reason is directed upon a moral situation. This reason enables us to judge the rightness and wrongness of an action; for example, "Our conscience told us lying is wrong." Third, it contains the element of "ought," as in "You ought to do this now." No one aspect is conscience. Rather, conscience contains strands of all three elements. To say we have a conscience means that we do in fact make moral judgments on our own, that we have a disposition to feel certain emotions in connection with the performance of certain actions, and that we have an active tendency to do actions judged right and avoid actions judged wrong. How then do we obtain this conscience? Is it something innate? Or is it the product of education?

We are not born with a conscience. We have an innate capacity, however, for moral reflection that can be developed by training and education—even from our first day of life. Our powers of speaking and reasoning are trained and developed through education, through exposure to childlike wonder and openness. That is one reason why our Church has never had a creed. The creed adequate for today stifles growth and vision tomorrow. Consequently, we have encouraged the affirmation of the highest religious ideals that we know now. But we always keep the mind open, ready for new light and possibilities.

It seems clear that we make the best moral decisions and judgments if we have educated consciences. We may find a certain wisdom in the codes and laws of the past. The experiences of the ancients cannot be discounted. The reasons we choose the do's and don'ts may vary from age to age, but the eternal truths of the ancients' findings deserve our attention. In many instances the taboos of the Old and New Testament have validity today. They suggest which attitudes and transgressions lead to tragedy and despair and which bring us to fulfillment and meaning. Churches have existed for centuries to remind us of what codes were and to tell people how they might be applied to problems they faced. If the church held the code too tightly and stifled growth and change, then people suffered. But if the religious organization used the codes of the scripture as a foundation and guideline, and from them urged individual refinements and developments, then the person and the community flourished in the deeper spiritual sense.

An educated conscience will not only gather the best from the written and oral traditions of religion, but it will be enlightened by the community, by family and associates, by local, national, and international events, and by many areas of endeavor that have expanded and continue to expand our vision.

This means that there is no ground for maintaining that conscience is an infallible guide to right conduct. The phrase "my conscience" is a compendious way of referring to one's moral beliefs about right and wrong. That they are liable to error leads us to the next step in the question—how may we make moral decisions today?

If our conscience is fallible, is it ever right to go against our conscience? Can conscientious action ever be wrong? The answer is yes, for we have stated that conscience is not infallible. It is colored by our environment and by lacks in this environment. Also, there are situations where conscience fails to give a clear-cut answer. During times of national crisis and war, men are inducted into the armed services. We are experiencing such a period in our history today. The law of our land, the general mores and conscience of our community, tells us that this is the right action. However, there are certain men who are sincere conscientious objectors. They sincerely believe fighting in a war is morally wrong.

Today we have sincere differences of opinion over the resumption of the bombing of North Vietnam. There are voices from the South in the Senate and Congress that call for resumption. From other sections of the country there is a majority opinion in the Senate and among the people not to resume the bombing. I am sure both groups speak from sincerity. Both are expressing their conscience based on the restrictions of their particular environment. We may say in such cases, "I think that what you're doing is wrong, but I appreciate that you really believe that it's right, so I cannot entirely blame you." Even if one is mistaken, that individual is acting from a morally impeccable motive.

How can we move beyond relativism to make judgments that have a moral foundation? The nineteenth-century utilitarians suggested that when rules conflict, we should decide upon the rightness of particular actions by estimating their probable consequences. That is one response.

Second, there is the philosophic answer that when our fundamental principles come into conflict, we must examine the whole situation until we find a conviction forming within us such that to follow one set of rules rather than another becomes morally important to us. A question arises in my mind. We have nothing beyond the principle to justify this moral decision.

The existentialists present another solution. Faced with conflicts, they claim we bring ourselves to the edge of an abyss. We become oppressed by how completely arbitrary all our fundamental moral choices are. We must choose for we must act, but we appear to have no grounds for our choice. I question whether we have to accept their premise that we are forced to make choices that are groundless or entirely arbitrary.

The idealists offer a better solution. Here it is suggested that we consider what is achieved by each of the conflicting rules within the fabric of social life. We then follow what we judge to be most important. Our judgments should be weighed on what builds up a family, a community and a nation. Judgment is seen in the light of service. It is witnessed by establishing beauty where there often has been ugliness. The importance stems from the awareness of a power and beauty beyond ourselves to create, but towards which our lives may grow. This is where the religious element can enter our lives. It can offer the continuing vision of beauty, seen in order and in the harmony and love between persons. The religious element is beauty in principles that are changeless and eternal. It can speak of that beauty lived into being by each of our lives, when the rightness of our moral decisions brings inward strength to us and creative power to our society.

As Spring Came

MARCH 31, 1968

*(The service was held at the First Lutheran Church in Boston
two days after the burning of the fifth building of the First
Church in Boston which had been completed in 1868.)*

*I*T IS A STRANGE FEELING to have to give a sermon
of this type. I see in our congregation this afternoon Dr. Max
Kapp, who was dean of the Divinity School of St. Lawrence
during my training. He prepared me for many services, but not
for this one, except by example. He, too, experienced the burning down of a building; in his case, his theological school.

We as the First Church in Boston, gathered in 1630, enter
the spring of 1968 with our sanctuary gone. So many centuries
ago as spring came, a man rode on a donkey into Jerusalem. He
felt that his message of a new order and a new way was about to
be accepted by the masses. Jerusalem's people would be one—
even the Samaritans. Her slums would disappear and beauty
would reign where ugliness had held its grip. Violence as a means
of solving differences would be retired, and a new communica-

33

tion of understanding would permit horizons of love to appear between peoples and nations and generations. And yet, almost overnight, the outstretched hands were withdrawn. Was Jesus to be a failure? Was all that he stood for to die, and nevermore to be? We know he was crucified. But the ideals to which his life had been committed would ever serve other people as a way towards which the individual and his society must travel. What was essential for the spirit gained a new emphasis, a new beginning, and a new resurrection following his death.

As spring approached in 1968, the First Church in Boston seemed to be taking on new depths, new dimensions, and new fulfillments towards the ideals of Jesus. Never since the beginning of my ministry in our Church in 1960 have we had more varied and active groups than at present. Never has our outreach beyond ourselves been broader than today. We have felt that something of us had become fulfilled when we opened Hale Chapel to groups outside our own congregational needs. We felt that we were encouraging responsible people to remain in the city when we were the catalyst for the development of the John Winthrop Nursery School, which now has a waiting list and which needed space for a kindergarten. And this spring the Social Concerns Committee has created channels for our people to act constructively in other areas of our city where needs are often greater than our own and where the resources to meet them are less known. For a long time there have been many things we have been doing for others through the John Clarke Fund and the South Friendly Society and many other agencies. Here, however, in a new way, with a new approach, and a new avenue for our people, we were helping others to learn better how they may help themselves.

We have enjoyed increasing interest in our Sunday morning programs, from the worship service to the Laymen's League Breakfasts, the Beacon Book table, the display of different concerns and opportunities, the sermon discussions, and those uplifting paintings of Alice Holcomb's. We seem to be increasingly giving witness to the spirit of those men and women honored on our historic church walls: Simon Bradstreet—"responsibility and trust," Anne Hutchinson—"a persuasive advocate of the right of independent judgment," John Winthrop—"who spent his strength and his substance in the cause of New England," Henry Vane—"a foe to every tyranny, and a life-long champion of the Rights of Man." I felt that we were on the verge of new breakthroughs, new commitments, new enthusiasms and growth. Perhaps in a sense we were beginning to feel the exhilaration of Jesus at the time of his triumphal entry. And then suddenly in one night, our home, our historic center of worship built by loving hands and maintained to glorify God and the ideals of men and women, was gone.

Friday morning, at 2:15 a.m., the phone rang. Was it a tragedy that had befallen a family or an individual? Was it someone with a serious problem? Such thoughts race through your mind at such an hour. The call was from a neighbor. The worst fire she had ever seen was raging near Berkeley and Marlborough Streets. "Was it our church?" She didn't know. I dressed quickly. The phone rang again, and this time it was my mother, who had seen a fire in the same area. Even then, I couldn't believe that our church was aglow with flames.

Entering a taxi, I asked to go to Berkeley and Marlborough Streets. "I've just been down in that area," he replied, "but I won't go back in that area. It's terrifying. The church is going up in flames. The whole city may burn." "What church?" was my quick question. "The First Church," was the answer, "the Unitarian Church." "I'm one of its ministers," I said. As he dropped me at the corner of Arlington and Marlborough Streets, the man was almost in tears. He refused the fare and said in a very low voice, "I'm sorry."

As I walked up Marlborough Street, the flames were shooting above our tower. The cinders were flying in a wide arc. It was obvious that the building was going. There was no hope of saving it. It is then that your thoughts go to the responsibilities ahead. As you see the church burning and buildings nearby catching fire, your concern is for the loss of life that could be occurring. Should you notify the Chairmen of the Standing Committee and the Trustees? But they are both doctors; they need their sleep, for people's lives rest in their hands. And there is nothing now to do but watch and to mourn—to think of the irreplaceable memorials that are gone.

And then in the daze of the flying embers, you see Park House. Here are the records of the Church that existed for centuries. Can they be saved? You finally find someone in authority to give you permission to enter.

You see that the office is locked and filled with smoke, and then you notice the portrait of Dr. Park and you take it off the wall to remove it from the building. You are thankful he did not live to see this moment. The beauty of his spirit lovingly nur-tured our church for almost sixty years. But then you are assured that they are going to save this building, because a member of the Social Concerns Committee had returned, after leaving Park House at 11 o'clock that night, to confirm that the fire door between Park House and Hale Chapel had been closed. And it was because of this thoughtful act that our records going back to 1630 and the base of our programs and operations were saved.

Watchfully through the night, you see the fire die. You still look at Park House, hoping the flames will not ignite the roof and wincing slightly as you see water hit the windows and break one or two. It is, in a sense, like an hour at the cross. Everything that so many for so long had striven to accomplish and to achieve, and which was symbolized in this sanctuary, seems to be destroyed, and the words of Job stab your thoughts: "My days are past, my purposes are broken off—even the thoughts of my heart. And where is my hope?"

Then, through the numbness of the dawn hours, you think of the members of this Church who have come to you in tears, but with affirmation that, "We will go on! We will rise to greater triumphs." And the coffee you drink, that is brought by a mem-ber of the Church, has another type of warmth. People who have always passed you silently on the Back Bay streets begin to come up to you one by one or in couples. They tell you that though they seldom go to church, though they are not Unitarians or Universalists, they always have felt that the First Church is their church. To them it was more than just another church in the Back

Bay. It was like the parish church that crossed the lines of history and even nations to represent the pioneering spirit. They want to do anything they can to help—to see this congregation rise again like a Phoenix from this rubble. They offer to type, to push brooms and to do just about anything we might ask them.

After you leave the scene, you find your home clustered with friends and parishioners, with offers of help coming from every quarter. The first donation for a new start comes from a *Globe* reporter. You begin to realize that the days and idealisms of the First Church are not just of the past. Perhaps with this new sense of purpose rising amidst us, this tragedy, sorrowful as it is, will not defeat us.

As notes and telegrams have come in, expressing such sentiments as Lawrence Perrera's, "I am hopeful that you and your vestry will determine to re-build on this important site, and I want to offer on behalf of the Back Bay Neighborhood Association any encouragement and assistance I can in enabling you to do this." Or the words in a telegram from the Executive Director and Chairman of the Dorchester Area Planning Action Council, where just recently we have sought to be of assistance, "Due to your great loss our hearts go out to you and your congregation. All is not lost because with God's help, we, the staff and Board of Directors of the Dorchester APAC will extend our hands in whatever way we can to help you to re-build your church." As all of these and so many more from Florida, South Carolina, Illinois, California, offer their hearts and their support, it makes me quite realize that we have become more alive as a congregation now than perhaps we have been in recent years.

We will have to work hard. We will have to go the second mile with each other. We will have to learn to communicate in ways that we never thought possible. We will have to hold each other together by our mutual and loyal participation. But this challenge is an opportunity. For more than brick and mortar, we are people. We are a living church. We are the ones that decide whether a church is more than a past, more than rote present, but a challenging and leading spiritual force in the mainstream of a growing, creative part of humanity. This is the spirit that will bind us together in these homeless days. The First Lutheran Church, which has so kindly let us use its sanctuary this afternoon, turns often, I am sure, to these words of Martin Luther, "For the sermon of God comes in order to change and revive the whole earth." This is a spirit that we as a living church must carry forward—continuing our works, sharing in our worship, and looking to new avenues of service. These will not be easy times.

First. We will have to call on our faith to a much fuller degree than we probably have been doing.

Second. We will have to remember the wisdom in Hebrews, "Wherefore we also are compassed about with such a cloud of witnesses, let us set aside every weight and the sin which doth so easily beset us and let us run with patience the race that is set before us."

Third. We will have to keep in mind real needs in our community as we go about the details of our building re-development. These lines from Rhoda Denison give us the warning signal that we can become so wrapped up now in ourselves and our own needs that we will forget the needs of others whom we must continually serve during this period: "It was a city of lilacs, a city of fragrant sanctity, a city of churches and synagogues. It thanked God for making it liberal, for making it tolerant of its brethren, the untouchables, the different. It opened its purse, and money poured on the halt and the blind. There seemed to be no limit to its generosity, its outreach, its concern for the needy, for those in want, unless, of course, the want was a decent place to live, a clean place of fields and skies, of fresh air and freedom. Then the lilac city, the city of sanctity, closed its purse, closed its doors, closed its heart, and hurried away. To forget by loud talk, by forming committees, by endless and eternal business, and once again, Love was nailed to the Cross." In facing tomorrow with imagination and vision, let us not lose sight of the spiritual outreach that we must not only continue but also expand.

Fourth. We will have to keep in mind that the essentials of religion are rooted more in people than in buildings. Therefore, the building that is constructed should have aesthetic effects that are proper and fitting for the religion and the idealism that we espouse. Religion is inherent in people's hopes and desires and ideals. Largely, it shapes the nature of our moral community and spiritual life. Beauty in our symbolic church has profound responsibilities in sustaining our spirits towards higher goals.

Fifth. We must remember that the essentials are still with us. Your ministry is intact. There was no loss of life in the fire. You as a congregation have visibly rallied in your determination to live on, to grow and to expand in every way. Next Sunday, Palm

Sunday, we will recognize new members. It is a time when people who have often thought about membership with us can come forth to a new experience where they will know that they are not only needed but where they will enjoy an exhilarating and creative period ahead as members of our congregation. And on Palm Sunday, the Covenant of our Church dating from 1630 will be read. This document has survived five buildings and the Revolution. What is it but a suggestion of the permanence of the deep, essential truths on which a living church rests?

Can we survive this crisis? The answer is assuredly, "Yes!" When people are happy together, they build something eternal. No fire destroys this. As Daniel Burnham has phrased it, "Make no little plans; they have no magic to stir man's blood, and probably themselves will not be realized. Make big plans; aim high in hope and work, remembering that a noble, logical diagram once recorded, will never die, but, long after we are all gone, will be a living thing asserting itself with ever growing insistence."

May the stones that we build with our lives be sacred, because we touched them with our creativity and vision. May they touch people and transform lives. May they uplift and carry us and others through the deep valley that we now experience to new high peaks. We are not forsaken. We have been handed a mantle of trust and responsibility in a major American city. How symbolic of these times when people so often wish to tear down. But let us, through our hard work, dedication, commitment and love, build a new church that will inspire and develop people to greater fulfillment. What we do will stand as a symbol of patience, insight, outreach and concern. We will speak with significance and challenge to this day. We will become a symbol of a people who had imagination and vision for those who come after us.

According to the ancient mystical legend, the Phoenix, sacred to the Egyptian Sun-god, Ra, every five hundred years built a funeral pyre of wood, which it ignited, and with its fanning wings, rose to new heights of strength and power.

Now, is this not the opportunity for us and for those who will join with us in this exciting adventure ahead? Where the stones have fallen, we will build with new brick. Where the beams lie charred, we will re-create with new timbers. Where the word is unspoken, we will build with new speech a church for us all, a work for us all, a chance for us all to participate with the ideal and with the divine. As spring came this year, the First Church in Boston and its members and friends see amidst the darkness a light leading to new vistas of beauty and service and love.

Let us pray. O God, as we go forth to do our part and to expand our horizon, may our hearts in sympathy go out to those persons who suffered with us in this fire. For those who lost their homes and their treasures, give us the strength in the midst of our sorrows to be a stay and a help to them. Amen.

Benediction

As long as you know you are pure inside,
as long as you can look up into a cloudless sky,
you will know that you will still find happiness.

Anne Frank

May the Lord bless you and keep you. May the Lord make His face to shine upon you and be gracious unto you. May the Lord lift up the light of His countenance upon you and give you peace, this afternoon and forever more. Amen.

Freedom in the Age of the Temper Tantrum

APRIL 5, 1970

Text: James 2:12 So speak and act as those who are judged under the law of liberty.

THE LATE A. POWELL DAVIES was perhaps the most eloquent spokesman for liberal religion in the early 1950s. His sense of commitment, his emphasis on being for something, his courageous strength as a spokesman for freedom made the Washington, D.C. area vibrant with Unitarian growth. Like spokes protruding from the hub of a wheel, Unitarian churches sprang forth from the city center to the circumference of our nation's capital. It should be clear that the number of churches and church members is not the ultimate criterion of good, but they are nevertheless symbolic of creative effort.

Whether Dr. Davies talked about Jesus, or God, or a current issue, the central theme of freedom flowed through all his thoughts and actions. His stress on freedom had a particular cast to it that liberated and elevated people. To Dr. Davies, freedom

45

was bound up with the totality of life. His particular strength lay in clarifying the issue of freedom as it was raised by the complexity of living in the '50s. Freedom was not just doing what pleased a person, or as we might say today, "doing your own thing" apart from other people. Instead, Davies saw freedom as a commitment to a larger and constructive possibility. It consisted of abstaining from injury to others, whether it was to an individual or a group, while positively ascertaining certain actions that would liberate people from curbing restraints.

We should recall that the early '50s were not an easy time in the story of our greatness. There had been the Berlin Airlift. The Cold War was hot. But perhaps the voice that was most challenging and affected American life most strongly was that of the late Senator Joseph McCarthy. He was a master at the art of innuendo. There were mass resignations from the State Department. Persons who had thought of diplomatic careers shifted gears and went into other fields. When he cast his eye upon some person or some department in government, there was fear and trembling. He proclaimed that he was freeing America from subversive influences. But others interpreted his very method as one that was destroying the freedom that he was seeking to save. While declaring that he was saving America for freedom, he was, through his approach, undermining creative possibilities for many Americans and destroying their lives. While many ministers, university and political leaders, and government workers remained silent, Davies stood up as David before Goliath. He saw that the techniques of smear and innuendo and temper tantrums were destructive and adolescent. There was not an opportunity for creative action if there was fear, if there was irrational interference, if there were non-negotiable demands.

We weathered the age of McCarthyism in America. It may seem remote and removed from today, and yet there are new and larger forces using the same tactics. They intimidate, demand, confront, and strike fear in the hearts of citizens. They are not unlike Senator McCarthy, who proclaimed that he was saving freedom, while using tactics that diminished freedom. Can there be liberty today when there seems to be license to do your own thing without considering with empathy the consequences it may have on individual and group life?

Following World War II, America became the world's greatest power. If the Christian missionaries, in a type of arrogance, could tell the natives of Asia and Africa what they should do religiously, we as a nation took on a form of arrogance in believing our way and our philosophy should dominate the world. Like the Christian missionary, who was saving man through Christ, or Senator McCarthy, who was preserving freedom by denying it to those who didn't accept his methods, so we as a nation said that the democratic way was the best way for all people to live, regardless of their development. To be fair, in spite of our arrogance, we may remember that the United States has done more for more people than any other nation in history. There is often idealism behind our actions, as well as self-interest.

We had a generation growing up during the '60s who saw our nation expanding its reach all over the world. They saw us interfering in the internal life and decisions of nations. They witnessed the fact that if we didn't like the way things were going, we were capable of setting up puppet governments and causing revolutions. They were taught the tactic that if you didn't like what some group or someone was doing, you had a right to interfere and even destroy.

We should remember this as we view the crises our nation faces in the '70s. In the name of freedom, of self-determination, universities and colleges have become centers of violence. Yet does anyone gain freedom from this? In the name of freedom and self-determination, religious denominations have become divided, with irrationality and emotion triumphing over reason and dialogue. There seems to be a new urgency to leap without seeking to understand, to denounce and divide without creating and uniting. In the name of greater freedom, we are having less freedom. I have called this time the age of the temper tantrum.

Adolescents, as a group, tend to rebel against their elders. An adolescent has to do battle against something or someone if he is to achieve his own identity and sense of worth. Usually the adolescent strikes against people who mean the most to him, who have done the most for him, and who care the most about him. That is perhaps why the protest and the demands today are not made against companies erecting huge buildings, or the Mafia, which takes billions of dollars out of our economy through graft and corruption. The demands and the insistence are against organizations that have cared the most about other people: the church, the college, or the welfare program. These organizations are symbolic of caring institutions. True, many of them have not done enough. True, many of them are lethargic.

48

True, many of them are self-satisfied. But still they are doing something for others. To those persons and groups who would denounce them, the question should be asked, what have you done beyond rhetoric and violence? Because there has been some degree of good in them, they become vulnerable to attack. It is the great universities like Columbia, Harvard, MIT and the University of California, or even a church, such as the First and Second Church in Boston, seeking to rise like a phoenix from the ashes, that become the targets for these groups. It is the caring institutions, that seem to be doing something and which represent power and commitment to people, that receive the focus and the attention in these times. This call for opening up and liberating institutions has validity. But if we are to obtain a larger freedom and good, we cannot do it by destroying the freedom and the liberties of others.

At our First and Second Church in Boston, we are in the midst of such a test. In early December, members of the Fellowship for Renewal (FFR), a totally white group, informed us that they would enter our Sanctuary during services on December 7 to make a statement. Our church, which was gathered by Governor John Winthrop in 1630, and our nation, which came into being in the next century, were founded on the principle of congregational polity and freedom of worship without coercion. We negotiated for many hours with the Fellowship for Renewal and they finally agreed to make their statement following rather than during the service. Unfortunately, however, they brought the news media, which took pictures during the service against the expressed wishes, not only of our Church but

49

also of Emmanuel Episcopal Church, where we are meeting for worship. At a later date, we allowed the FFR to talk to a congregational meeting. We informed them that our million dollars of insurance claims, which they insisted we give to low-cost housing, was not available because of the deed of trust under which our Trustees bought the insurance. We had a committee negotiate with them to no avail. When we did not turn over $1 million to build low-cost housing in another part of the city, this FFR Group went to radicals seeking their support in disrupting our services. Several groups would have no part of this. In desperation, and after several of the more rational members of the FFR seemed to understand our situation, a few members of this group went to some extreme individuals. These people were happy to join with the promise of $1 million in hand. First they picketed a service. The following Sunday the Fellowship for Renewal withdrew themselves, and a militant group disrupted our service to the point that our service had to be dismissed. Since then they have entered twice to disrupt the service and once to denounce us at a coffee hour.

We are facing a deliberate attempt by certain individuals to destroy our Church, which is now a merger of two Unitarian Churches. The First and Second Churches merged in February of this year. Our harassment continues with an open letter to us saying we have until May 6 to deliver $1 million if we wish to alleviate the disruption of services. Symbolically, if the oldest church institution in Boston were destroyed, Pandora's box would be opened and other institutions seeking to serve the community would be subject to the threat of harassment and destruction. In fact, our church, through its subsidiary corporation the Edward Everett Hale House, Inc., set up several years ago, is providing seed money for a $15 million, 800-apartment rehabilitation and new construction project in the South End. The interest of certain parties seems to be more in obtaining power than in providing housing.

Dr. Bruno Bettelheim has been analyzing the politics of confrontation for these times. He sees in these methods the psychology of adolescence no matter what the age of the protester. While consciously demanding freedom and participation, a commitment to Mao and leaders like him suggests an unconscious need for controls from the outside, since without them, confronters cannot bring order to their own inner chaos. People seeking to find their own identity today are not being helped by indifference or an easy-going approach that passes for permissiveness. Whether it be the child who holds his breath and turns blue in the face so that he can get his own way or the adult who in the name of freedom uses totalitarian methods to undermine the freedom of others, we are not helping anyone to find themselves if we do not stand by our values. We must not forsake those ways that have survival value.

If the temper tantrum psychology has changed from the McCarthy innuendo and smear to the demanding insistence of our era, this does not mean that the problems of society should be whitewashed. The problems will never be surmounted unless we hold fast to those concepts that expand people's freedom and give them in the end the most hope. These concepts are familiar to us all. They include reason, tolerance, the search for justice and good will, the seeking of truth, the sense of an infinite beyond the finite, the democratic process in human relations, and a responsible individual freedom of belief. If we hold fast to these values that have been very much a part of our Unitarian Universalist religious heritage, then we will be able to act creatively.

With our freedom to act creatively, let us move beyond the tensions of the moment. I believe each person and organization has to do some soul searching. We can no longer afford to do our own thing apart from other people. We must become totally involved as human beings in the spectrum of life. Dr. Davies' whole thrust was abstaining from injuring others while positively asserting that action which liberates people. The Church is a group that can help in this great time of human want. We need the message of transcendence. But we must have more than this today. Without a caring society, we sow the seeds of greater poverty, mass famine, disease, and enslavement.

Poverty in an age of unparalleled prosperity and seemingly unlimited promise tells us something is wrong. Pollution of our environment, decay of our cities, continuation of wars, and threat of war, and everywhere a vague but widespread discontent with the general quality of life confronts us. If we stand strong in the areas that we cherish and see that freedom is not diminished by the demagogues of violence; if we reveal some of the achievements of the past and confirm our commitment to build on these, we will be more likely to achieve those goals that are vitally needed today.

Hope and DNA

*I*N THE 1950s the Rev. Billy Graham described heaven in specific and concrete terms. It was located thousands of miles from earth. It was a land of milk and honey. Pear and apple trees lined the streets. There was plenty for everybody. It seemed to be a paradise.

Throughout history people have often been deluded by the idea that paradise is a place where there are no challenges, no pain, stress or difficulties. Effortless living and overabundance would bring ultimate happiness. That is why people have yearned for the Garden of Eden. Yet truth should tell us something else. There was never a Garden of Eden and there never will be one in the future. A life without challenges, without developing talents and discovering new truths, would be utterly wasteful and boring.

There is the story of a person who died and found himself in what appeared to be a very pleasant place. He assumed this must be heaven. He was addressed by a man who said he was his servant. The servant would provide anything of a material nature that he wished. The man who had died thought for a moment and decided he would like to go fishing. All during his lifetime on earth, he had enjoyed the sport but had never been very successful. The servant provided him with a boat and the finest fishing tackle he had ever seen and took him to a river. He cast his line. Immediately a fish was at the other end biting the hook. Time and time again he did this, filling the boat with fine edible fish. This went on for several days. The man began to feel uneasy. It wasn't so much fun, pulling in fish after fish. There were no challenges, no problems, and he was becoming bored. Finally he went to the servant and with some humility said, "I know I wanted to go fishing, and everything has gone so very well. I am catching more fish than I can use, but I find myself getting bored. Perhaps I might do something else." The servant asked what else he had liked to do on earth. He replied, "On earth I liked to play golf, but I always shot over 100. Perhaps I can improve my game now that I am here." So the servant said, "This is no problem." He took him to a golf course; the beauty and magnitude surpassed any from his past experiences. He was presented with the finest golf clubs. Immediately he went out on the course and with his first stroke of a club had a hole in one. This happened every time he hit the ball. After several days of perfect golf, the same uneasiness and boredom set in. Finally he returned to the servant and said, "First I went fishing and was bored because I did so well. Now I am playing perfect golf and the same feelings possess me. I had no idea I would feel so depressed in heaven." The servant turned to the man and replied, "What makes you think you are in heaven?"

Human beings need to have challenges. We need to see potentialities and possibilities. Although we do not always triumph, we need to work towards the possibilities of new accomplishments.

As we approach the twenty-first century, the possibilities for a better society on earth seem to be diminishing. We are in ecological trouble. Our fossil fuels are running out. Population is growing. Extremes in weather are causing disasters. We are in economic trouble. Debts are rising. Inflation is growing. Doing things in the same way will not solve the gigantic problems ahead. We must approach the future with new insights. There are truths that presently exist that we do not now know about, and there are truths we have inclinations towards but have yet to harness. We must discover them and learn to harness them to help surmount our difficulties, solve our problems, and give us hope for the great possibilities that do lie ahead.

In the year 270 B.C. when everyone saw the sun rise in the east and set in the west, Aristarchus of Samos made some observations that led him to believe that the earth circled the sun. His views were rejected because everyone could look at the sky and obviously see that it was the sun that went around the earth. Centuries later Copernicus read Aristarchus's conclusion and found more evidence affirming it. But he did not dare publish his book until he was on his deathbed. Then came Kepler. He did not worry about public or popular opinion. He knew the truth. In the closing of the preface to his book, he wrote, "Here I cast the dye and write a book to be read whether by contemporaries or by posterity. I care not. I can wait for readers thousands of years seeing that God waited for millions of years for someone to contemplate his work."

New possibilities opened up with the discovery of the truth that the earth went around the sun. It has lead to our probes in space and the possibility of orbiting space vehicles gathering solar energy and transmitting it down to earth. We are now at a time when we must accelerate the pace of discovering existing truths that will help solve some of the gigantic problems facing us.

I believe the greatest scientific discovery of this century has been the recent research on deoxyribonucleic acid or DNA. It has given scientists the ability to do biological engineering. Someone has said DNA is to biology what nuclear fission is to physics. Nothing since the early days of atomic weapons has caused so much dismay as the real or imagined threats associated with the development of genetic engineering and recombinant DNA research. DNA carries our genetic heritage. DNA allows a species such as human beings to reproduce its own kind. But if there is some intervention into DNA of a molecule, then the genetic heritage is altered. Scientists in DNA research use the e-coli bacteria that are found in our digestive tract. Science knows more about these bacteria than any other living organism. Dr. Stanley Cohen of Stanford University, using e-coli bacteria, spliced the DNA of a South African toad to it. From that time forward this e-coli bacteria and its offspring produced the DNA genes of a South African toad.

If the DNA message is altered, the effects of doing so are far reaching. Very simply, the new technology enables the scientists to take DNA from one organism and splice it into DNA from another to create something absolutely new—new living molecules, new genes, and, therefore, new life.

The set of techniques developed in 1974 make it possible to cut the long threadlike molecules of DNA into pieces with the aid of certain enzymes. Then they are recombined with the DNA of another carrier. The combined DNA of two or more sources is introduced into an appropriate host cell to propagate and possibly to function. There has been a bitter debate ever since concerning the wisdom of DNA research and development.

In that same year—1974—scientists, realizing the potential benefits as well as potential hazards of DNA research, sought to bring together those persons who were researching DNA and come up with some guidelines to prevent any potential biological hazard. One hundred and fifty scientists representing sixteen countries gathered at the Asilomar Conference in California. In February 1975 they produced a resolution, which said that certain types of experimentation with DNA should be abstained from. They also produced a sliding scale of danger. In the most dangerous experiments allowed, they agreed to use bacteria that could not survive outside the lab. These guidelines were affirmed by the National Institutes of Health in June 1976.

In the Western world no group of writers has ever shown such restraint. The suggestion that an author should not write the truth as he or she sees it, regardless of what offense or damage it may cause, would be met with cries of dismay and warnings that any such action would inflict irreparable damage on the human spirit and stifle the creative mind.

Scientists did not abandon DNA research, but they put themselves on notice that they would use a "go slow" approach in this new area of amazing potential good and possible harm.

Dr. Clifford Grobstein, in the July 1977 issue of *Scientific American*, describes the four-year-old controversy over potential biological hazards presented by gene splicing. He speaks about the best-case and worst-case scenarios. The gap between them symbolizes the high degree of uncertainty that surrounds this major step forward in molecular genetics.

In the worst-case scenarios, the fear is not so much of any clear and present danger as it is of imagined future hazards. The classic response to such fears is rigid containment: the Great Wall of China, the Maginot Line between France and Germany before World War II. Some scientists feel the basic hazard about DNA is the introduction into bacteria of genes that would make the bacteria more dangerous. In the simplest case, such a gene might give one strain of bacteria a resistance to all known antibiotics. The worst-case scenarios envisage worldwide epidemics caused by newly created bacteria, the triggering of a catastrophic ecological imbalance, or the power of some mad scientist to dominate and control human beings.

For years we have had means of controlling people through education and propaganda. We also have had the means to develop a superior species and an inferior one through the stock breeding of human beings similar to what we do with animals in developing better cattle and poultry.

H. G. Wells wrote about a future time when beautiful and intelligent people called the Eloi would dominate the world. They were served by comparatively unintelligent, docile but physically strong people.

Some scientists believe the danger comes not so much from the professional in the laboratory but from some of the untrained support services such as those who clean the laboratories. They realize that many scientists are already engaged in potentially hazardous research with radioactive materials and pathological bacteria. Those who work with them are trained to take precautions. Accidents are rare. But they feel with DNA, special precautions should be taken.

The guidelines approved in 1976 by the National Institutes of Health do not apply to work being done in private laboratories. Mayor Valucci of Cambridge, Massachusetts, was able to put some restrictions on DNA research in that city. Senator Kennedy has sponsored a bill in Congress to place federal controls on DNA research.

Scientists are in disagreement concerning the dangers. Dr. Norton Zender of Rockefeller University said there is no way that any inspector can find out what is being done in a laboratory. Some scientists believe that the general public will become more disillusioned with the work of scientists if the potentials of DNA breakthroughs do not live up to the promise.

On the other hand, there is the best-case scenario. DNA may provide major new social benefits through more effective and cheaper pharmaceutical products such as insulin, better understanding of the causes of cancer, more abundant food products, even new approaches to the energy problem. There are more than 2,000 diseases that are caused by gene mutation. DNA research might enable us to eliminate them. Crops depend on fertilizer made from oil products. Food crops such as grains and vegetables could be redeveloped through DNA gene splicing so that they could draw most of their needed fertilizer from the air. This could open up vast new uncultivated territories that are not viable for commercial agriculture today. The most substantial benefit might be rapid advances in the detailed understanding of gene action. This in turn might add substantially to our knowledge of immunology—resistance to pneumonia, cancer and other medically important subjects.

There has been no disaster from DNA research to date. There are those scientists who feel that their colleagues who are extremely cautious or who are against DNA research are looking for a black cat in a dark room, which may not be there. They feel their colleagues are crying wolf without having seen or heard one.

Dr. James D. Watson feels that the guidelines from the Asilomar Conference are too restrictive. He writes, "I did not then nor do I now believe that all recombinant DNA research is necessarily totally safe. The future automatically entails risks and uncertainty and no one person experiments in directions where he anticipates harm to himself or others. Instead, we try to adjust our actions to the magnitude of risk. When no measurement is possible because we have never faced a particular situation before, we must not assume the worst. If we did we would do nothing at all."

Dr. Watson feels that the conference was hasty in setting up unjustified bureaucratic roadblocks that set back the course of legitimate science. He believes that there are types of experimentation under the original moratorium that pose no real threat to the general public. Dr. Barnard Davis of the Harvard Medical School believes the guidelines are excessively severe. He also believes that society and science are sufficiently mature to use DNA research in positive ways.

I do not look at DNA as a scientist. But from a religious and social view on society, DNA offers the potential for existing truths to help solve our great social problems. Throughout the Bible there is evidence showing that the great seers and prophets have found positive potential in human beings. The Psalmist called men and women "little lower than the angels."

We are now at a threshold where the truths that we have found and harnessed for our benefit are not sufficient for the tasks facing us in the next hundred years. We will need new breakthroughs to find what are now unknown truths and to apply them to the work at hand.

Four years ago a breakthrough to a new understanding of an already existing truth occurred. This was the ability to splice the genes of one species to another. The end product, for example, might be a new DNA molecule consisting of sections derived from both bacteria and human cells. These hybrid molecules can be put back into bacteria, thereby creating new forms of bacteria capable of synthesizing human proteins.

There is an amazing potential that can come from this process. I do not believe we can hold science back any more than we stopped the development of the H-bomb after the atomic bomb had been developed or any more than we are stopping the development of the neutron bomb. Today, rather than place more controls, it seems to me it would be more productive to encourage DNA research. Herein lies hope and the possibilities of new breakthroughs to existing truths that may be harnessed for the betterment of humanity.

If research in DNA lives up to its potential promise, some of the dire predictions will not be realized. DNA offers hope for potential possibilities to not only sustain our life on earth but to enrich it and to broaden it. It offers hope to places such as the third world which as of now knows it will never have a chance at many of the benefits enjoyed in the Western world. DNA hopefully will allow humanity to have more time to develop its talents so that we all will be more creative, loving and caring human beings. The world we know is changing. Let us face the future with assurance!

Survival and Space

SEPTEMBER 23, 1979

THERE IS A NEED TO IMAGINE the future and then attempt to achieve it. This became an imperative need following the atom bombs that fell on Hiroshima and Nagasaki in August 1945. Up to that point in history, there was little doubt that the human race probably would survive for many more thousands of years. This is no longer a surety.

After the first atomic bomb fell on Hiroshima, the Council of Six, advisors to Emperor Hirohito, believed that it was a one-time phenomenon. It would take years to develop another atom bomb, they counseled. But on August 8, 1945, one thousand miles from the coast of Japan, a B-29 bomber took off into the night sky carrying a bomb weighing 10,000 pounds and shaped like a watermelon. Six hours later, the B-29 reached the coast of Japan. The primary target was Kokura, Japan. This was Japan's largest military arsenal. When the plane came close to the target, smoke from previous bombings obscured the crew's view. One hundred miles away was Nagasaki, and because of dwindling gasoline supplies, the plane headed for that city. Forty thousand people worked there in armament plants. Although there was a seventy percent cloud cover, the men in the bomber were able to see their target. The bomb was released at 30,000 feet. It exploded as planned at 1,500 feet. The B-29, in trying to get away, was rocked by five shock waves but managed to stay intact. The closest landing field was Okinawa, 350 miles away. The gas gauges were on empty. Two engines stopped, but the plane landed safely.

Two hundred thousand people lost their lives at Nagasaki. Due to radiation exposure, thousands have suffered. It is known that the Japanese had planned an all-out last defense of their country. It is estimated that there would have been casualties of at least one million Allies and more than one million Japanese. Ten hours after the bombing of Nagasaki, Japan unconditionally surrendered. From that time on, the world was never to feel that its continued existence was unquestionable.

From 1945, life on earth would be considered finite—not merely from an aging planet but in the near term from a nuclear war. Now in 1979, we know also that there are finite natural resources that cannot maintain indefinitely the lifestyle that has become common in Western society. Some of these resources, especially fossil fuels, will be exhausted in a few hundred years.

Are we at the end of our evolutionary development? Or do we possess the potential ability to find and reach in the universe "a land," as the poet Thomas Wolfe phrases it, "more kind than home"? Are we the link to the future of higher evolution? I, for one, believe we are.

If human beings represent a growing and hopefully a forward thrust in the evolution of this vast universe, what evidence do we have? Astronomers have the now certain knowledge that the same chemical elements exist everywhere in the universe. The physical laws that apply here on our earth also govern planets millions of light years away. Recently, radio astronomers discovered that the universe is teeming with carbon-based molecules. They are the building blocks of life. "It looks as if God was an organic chemist," says Dr. Cyril Ponamperuma, who is in the field of chemical evolution at the University of Maryland. He goes on to point out that no matter where you direct your telescopes, you find two molecules, hydrogen cyanide and formaldehyde. These two provide the basis for everything else. They imitate the primitive conditions under which life arose on earth billions of years ago.

Dr. Gaylord Simpson, a retired Harvard University paleontologist, in his book, *This View of Life*, likens evolution on earth to a lottery. "Most ticket holders have been losers," he says, but "human beings happen to be the descendants of a long line of organisms that drew winning tickets in every successive adaptive change."

Because all solar systems in the universe are governed by the same physical laws, many scientists believe that there are parallel, but not identical, developments of life elsewhere. In short, biologists see life forms on other planets following evolutionary paths that coincide to some extent with our evolution. But they

65

doubt that there will be exact duplicates of our earthly development. They believe that there are life-bearing planets that resemble earth closely, even having blue skies, but they will not be perfect replicas. There may be intelligent human beings that look humanoid, but the difference will be fundamental and profound. Dr. Simpson and other biologists persuasively have argued that evolution is "nonrepeatable and irreversible."

There is a haunting but positive lesson in discovering that we are alone in this universe as unique, unrepeatable beings. The knowledge that intelligent life, as we know it, is found only on one fragile planet should be very sobering for us.

We have been given the biology of the winner. When at our best, we are humane and kind; when we are at our worst, we tinker with lethal arsenals of death and destruction. Our survival, as we face the finite resources of earth and the munitions of ultimate destruction, requires from us in the years ahead both higher technology and greater humanity. It will require the application of our human characteristics that we share with other known species. We uniquely have the capacity to rise to mental challenges, to be curious about the unknown, to leave tunnel vision and look out towards the farthest horizon. Neither climate nor plague has stopped this adventure. Even when disaster has struck, human beings have picked up the pieces and indomitably gone forward.

Our new horizon is space. If the finite limits of this earth spell eventual destruction for human beings, our future hope lies in space. It seems to me we have the potential capacity to survive as a species beyond the life support system of this earthly planet.

Human beings in the past have imagined. They have envisioned, and then they have achieved their goals. This is what we must do again.

Certain human beings in the past have, as Shakespeare said, "seized the tide in the affairs of men, which, taken in the flood, leads on to fortune." They used their vision and imagination and followed through to expand their horizons. One productive period occurred towards the middle of the fifteenth century in Europe. Raw materials were becoming scarce. Most people believed the sun circled around the earth and that our earth was flat. The Americas were unknown in Europe. If you sailed west, some believed, you would fall off the rim of the world. But there were others who dared to question old beliefs. They were filled with speculations about the nature of this world and universe. Although not much solid evidence was available, clever minds pasted together the fragments and achieved quite remarkable deductions.

Prince Henry, the Navigator of Portugal, occupies a unique place in history. He never captained any of his ships. He never sailed on any voyage of exploration. Actually, he stayed at home, reading books, listening to new rumors and ideas. From this mixture, he constructed a view of the world that was extraordinarily accurate. He died about thirty years before Portuguese explorers proved his theories.

Christopher Columbus had very little solid data to work with, but he had clever intuitions and a powerful capacity to piece together odd bits of information. This led him to the conclusions that resulted in the discovery of America.

Nations at that time had to decide whether they wanted to participate in the exploration of the world and to what degree of commitment. Portugal and Spain, who made early decisions, gained empires of amazing wealth. Others such as Germany and Italy, whose imaginations did not reach outward, suffered grave disadvantages and never caught up. This imbalance was among the causes of World War I and II.

The most important dimensions of these explorations and discoveries were not primarily the exploits of daring captains or the economic advantages for the nations that they represented. The most lasting and profound effect was on the spirit of the times. It was an enlarging of the human consciousness. It made people realize that the old definitions no longer applied. The world consisted of a great deal more than Europe. To have missed the exploration was regrettable, but to have missed this spiritual awakening would have been disastrous. The vitality of ideas and imagination can be seen throughout history. Ideas are always more powerful than empires.

Certainly the world was changed by ideas transformed in the cascade of brilliant industrial inventions produced in England in the late eighteenth and early nineteenth century. We live today on the consequences of the Industrial Revolution. Our nation's capacity to financially organize and manage large industrial corporations is felt throughout the world. It is only when felt needs spur the imagination that certain accomplishments become possible. We are at that point again today. If we as a species are to survive and to evolve through future centuries, we need to know how to use space and to live in space.

Human beings living upon satellites in space was imagined long before its reality. One hundred and ten years before *Skylab* made its fiery return to earth, a satellite of fire resistant brick was launched into orbit from a township in Maine. The launching of this miniature moon occurred only on the pages of the *Atlantic Monthly*, but the author, Edward Everett Hale, worked out the details entertainingly and quite plausibly. (Dr. Hale was minister of the South Congregational Church in Boston, Unitarian. It merged in 1925 with the First Church in Boston.) The story was entitled "The Brick Moon." It was published in three installments and was straight science fiction. This satellite was to be an aid in navigation. It would orbit the earth at the Greenwich meridian, go over both poles, and thus give mariners as exact a measurement of longitude as the North Star does for latitude. It was decided that the satellite would have to have an altitude of at least 4,000 miles. The optimum design would be a 2,000-foot diameter hollow sphere. It could be sent into orbit by utilizing the energy of two giant flywheels rotating at such terrific speeds that they would literally fling this sphere into space. As a trip through the atmosphere would be fast enough for the frictional heat to melt any metal, the satellite should be made of fire-resistant brick. Thirteen hollow spheres strongly joined together were to fill the interior. As the work neared completion, thirty-seven of the workmen took up temporary quarters in the spheres inside the brick moon. The night before the scheduled launching, the brick moon vanishes. During the night the ground settled far enough to cause the brick moon to slide gently onto the moving flywheels. It is shot into space along with its thirty-seven inhabitants.

Like all good science fiction, the brick moon is a clever combination of the probable, the improbable, and the impossible. The survival of the inhabitants is explained with considerable ingenuity. They lived through the initial acceleration because the accident happened at night when they were in their hammocks. They avoided cremation because the brick moon shot into the atmosphere so quickly that the heat failed to penetrate the interior. They could breathe because the air within the sphere stayed inside. And it so happened that a couple of the interior spheres were full of ice and snow, so there was plenty of water. By luck they had with them a quantity of seeds, hens and vegetables and were all set to live out a peaceful and tranquil existence in their new world. Edward Everett Hale had an entertaining story in 1869. What he imagined has become a reality.

Each era of history progresses to a point when human beings are required, if they are to progress, to wrestle with the great problems of that period. For the ancient Greeks, it was the organization of society. For the Romans, it was the organization of empire. For the medievalists, it was the spelling out of their relationship to God. For the men of the fifteenth and sixteenth centuries, the mastery of the oceans. For us, it is how we can live in harmony on this finite globe while we establish ways of continuing life in space beyond this earthly existence.

You see people destroy themselves because the will to survive has been lost. You watch nations go down because of fatal wrong choices. This occurs when inner convictions are lost or when there is a sense of general frustration or a lack of purpose.

At the Smithsonian in Washington, D.C., there is a film that shows space taking the place of the oceans as the new frontier. It predicts that explorers in the future may leave their homes not just for a few months or years but also for their lifetime and the lifetime of their children and ensuing generations. They will, in the words of Thomas Wolfe, "lose the earth you know for greater knowing, lose the life you have for greater life."

Right now we must spell out our humanity in more humane ways between one another. Right now we should not doubt that human existence would be sustained and evolve beyond the finite resources and life on our planet earth.

There is the story of the man who died and went up to the gates of Heaven. St. Peter was in an expansive and bragging mood. He remarked, "Up here a minute is like a million years, and in fact, a penny is like a million dollars." And so the man said to St. Peter, "Will you lend me a penny?" St. Peter replied, "Of course I will. Just wait a minute." We do not have the luxury of this type of minute in 1979.

Let us get on with our task! I believe we are unique in the universe. We must expand our technical knowledge and spiritual vision. We must be the link for the greater fulfillment and purpose of the universe. Let us expand our horizons. Let us think of survival and space, of survival in space!

MANAGING
YOUR
LIFE

Finding Happiness

*I*N DECIDING ON A SERMON TITLE this week, I was more cautious than this summer when I gave a title to the Ellsworth, Maine, Unitarian Church, "Broad and Irresistible." It was sent to several newspapers for two-column, block advertisements. One paper, the *Bar Harbor Times*, edited the ad to read as follows: Ellsworth Unitarian Society—11 a.m. "The Broad and Irresistible, Rev. Rhys Williams." With that experience behind me, I was wary of using a title for today such as "The Happy Person." I do, however, want to talk about the subject of happiness this morning because so often happiness, joy, laughter seem to be lacking in modern society.

In the second paragraph of the Declaration of Independence, we read these words: "We hold these truths to be self-evident, that all men are created equal, that they are endowed by their Creator with certain inalienable rights, that among these are Life, Liberty, and the pursuit of Happiness." You will note that the Declaration of Independence says that we have a right to pursue happiness. We are not guaranteed happiness.

When I use the term "happiness" this morning, I am not talking about witless frivolity. I am speaking of an authentic, deeply felt, passionate enjoyment of life, which is often brought about by self-fulfillment and involvement with causes and institutions that uplift and expand the horizons of persons.

In sharing these thoughts with you, I believe that some of us may be handicapped in finding happiness due to a religious heritage that equates happiness with a sense of guilt. Bertrand Russell speaks in an essay on our irrational fear of happiness and the blight of this fear for millions of people. He writes, "It would be shallow to regard this aversion of happiness as applying only to the happiness of others. There is, deep in most human nature, a feeling that one's own happiness is dangerous." Impulses have very deep roots. The Greeks dreaded Nemesis and felt that hubris or excessive pride would surely be punished. Most of us are afraid to boast of good health or good fortune, out of a superstitious fear that to do so would bring bad luck.

What Bertrand Russell is saying applies to most persons who have had orthodox religion in their backgrounds. It would not have occurred to John Calvin, the founder of Presbyterianism, or John Wesley, the founder of Methodism, to say to any congregation that a person is entitled to find and enjoy happiness on this earth. The sermon I recently preached on John Winthrop showed he was a happy person and that he displayed love to his family, but to enjoy life too fully, to find happiness too abundantly, would be foreign to the life the Puritans envisioned.

Three thousand five hundred years of Judaism and two thousand years of Christianity have left millions of people with an undefined fear of a disapproving Deity. In this latter part of the twentieth century, the Deity has lost some of its terror. But even if we deny Its presence, we often feel a need for apology if we really enjoy many aspects of life.

My grandfather and father were Congregational ministers. Even though our family became Unitarian, my father always held to the idea that for any enjoyment or happiness that came to you, you must pay for it by experiencing some suffering or denying yourself some pleasure.

C. P. Snow has observed, "We are in a new Elizabethan age of discovery." The space capsule replaces the sailing ship. The solar system replaces the seven seas of our small planet. It is time for discoveries not only in outer space but also in knowledge of ourselves and in our sources of happiness.

We are in this Unitarian Universalist Church by choice. We are not gathered together out of fear of punishment after death. In spite of our liberation, however, many of us have surviving traces of guilt of which we may be unaware. The stifling aspects of Puritanism in us die hard—perhaps more so than the virtues of Puritanism. As a whole then, even if we are free from the vestiges of orthodox religion with its sense of guilt and fear of happiness, some of the perils of modern Unitarian Universalism are still with us.

What is one of our weaknesses as a denomination today? You may be familiar with the following story. One night a person had a dream. He saw a vast hall down which row upon row of men and women were advancing. At the end of the hall were two doors. Over one door was the inscription "This way to heaven." Over the other door was the sign "This way to a lecture on heaven." The sleeping person must have been a Unitarian Universalist, for most in his dream were entering the door leading to the lecture. Perhaps this should be a sign to us to stop discussing happiness and try it ourselves.

Another danger that applies to some of us is an obsession to serve others. We remember the words of the poet: "For we must share if we would keep the blessings from above; ceasing to give, we cease to have, this is the law of love." But here we must be on guard. The impulse to serve others can become a longing outstripping a reasonable possibility for fulfillment. To yearn to render a service far beyond our capacity or opportunity will create stress. If serving others becomes too great an obsession, we are doomed to disillusionment and frustration.

We often equate happiness with acquiring things or power. These when they become ends in themselves are often happiness killers. If we seek happiness at the expense of others, we will not be happy.

There are increasing numbers of people who are unhappy because there are always others who have something that they do not have. There is a desire for equal opportunity—equal achievement—equal results, often without the prerequisite responsibility and self-development that is really required.

Too often, instead of enjoying what we have today, we wish for something different for the future. There is a cartoon of a fireman. There are two pictures of him. In the first, the fireman is counting the months and the days until he will be able to retire from his job and move to a country farm. The second picture shows him a year after he has retired. He is back at the engine house. He is talking about the good old days. Too often we believe that if we only had a change of scenery, a new job, new friends, then happiness would be ours. But happiness really depends, I believe, on our inward state.

There is a myth that is told about Zeus, the king of the gods of Olympus. He became very tired of hearing prayers of constant complaints. It seemed as if everyone would gladly exchange the burden he carried for some other burden. So Zeus made it known that on a certain day, everyone could assemble on the plains of Olympus, throw down his burden and exchange it for another. Each person who came was glad to be rid of his burden and picked up another. Each thought himself happy as he picked up the burden discarded by his neighbor. But after a time, most persons came back to the plains. They begged Zeus to have their old familiar burdens returned. They found that the new burdens hurt in a way that they had not imagined. They knew how to deal with the ones they had discarded.

To gain happiness we must have time and space to develop a philosophy of life. Everyone needs air, food, leisure time to think, someone with whom to talk, and fortitude to exercise the muscles of the mind and the body. Thoreau writes in *Walden*, "I went to the woods because I wished to live deliberately, to front only the essential facts of life, and see if I could not learn what it had to teach. . . ."

One of the ministers in our denomination has made a survey over the past fifteen years asking people to tell their fantasies of perfect happiness. His questionnaire contained several preferences such as: inheriting a million dollars, traveling around the world, standing alone on a windswept beach. The majority chose as important "standing alone on a windswept beach." This shows that while human beings are social and crave to be with other people, the deepest human need is first to accept oneself. We need time to see ourselves in relationship to the whole world around us.

Oscar Lewis's *Children of Sanchez* points out how limited are the opportunities for happiness in the life of any person who is in a straightjacket of poverty or prevented by twelve and fifteen hour work days from a chance to know many of the delights of both the spirit and the flesh. To find happiness, spaces of time are needed where we can reflect on the past, view the present objectively, and develop a sense of purpose as we face the future.

A second ingredient necessary for happiness is to have something worthwhile to do. People who are satisfied in their work or hobbies are most often happy individuals. It may be your good fortune, as it is mine, to find a great deal of satisfaction and meaning in our chosen vocations. But for millions of people, this is not so. Currently the recession has forced people into unemployment and welfare. Many are placed in jobs below their training and interest. Automation in modern industry has created thousands of jobs that are dull, repetitive and destructive of human initiative. There is psychological fulfillment in performing a job and knowing that the work is useful and necessary. We all know the damage done to the personality of many unemployed, of pensioners and invalids when deprived of useful work.

People today have more leisure time. If our vocation does not give us self-fulfillment, let us hope that our leisure time may be spent in avocations where we find rewards of achievement and fulfillment. If we do, then we are likely to find happiness.

Another ingredient for happiness is to have something to love. All people have an affectionate side. The more we pour our affection and love out on people that are worthy of love, the more we are like the fountain of water that is connected with an exhaustless sea. We have deeply ingrained in our biological nature a need to love. This can be dangerous as well as good. We may be so filled with the need to love that if we cannot find worthy objectives, we find imperfect substitutes. Sometimes, we cannot find another person. Love of a pet, a worthy cause or some absorbing interest will enable us to find fulfillment.

The final ingredient for happiness that I shall mention this morning is to have a sense of hope. We all see unhappy people who spend their lives living in the past. They feel they have nothing left to live for. They may have already obtained many possible pleasures. They now fail to associate with others, to make new friends or find joy in the achievements of someone else. They have no hope for themselves or for others.

To find happiness we need to improve our personal life, making it more balanced, more rational, and more loving. This is needed not only on a personal level but also for society as a whole. Individual salvation and social salvation are tied together. Individual and social growth go together. One does not automatically bring the other into being. But if one finds hope for oneself as a person, one needs to explore and extend oneself so that a similar hope may be infused in the community around us.

In summary: We need a philosophy of life, something meaningful to do, something to love and something to hope for. These are not dramatic new truths. They are known probably to all of us. Our problem is that too often we forget these simple things of life. In all our striving for happiness, we too often forget to enjoy what we do have. Why not give happiness a chance?

Embracing Maturity

OCTOBER 22, 1978

*F*RAGMENTATION EXISTS today in our society in many forms. While diversification and decentralization may have positive attributes, they carry dangerous elements as well. The immature selfish group, the lobby that has only self-interest and no great vision for the nation as a whole threatens to destroy society rather than revitalize it. Whether it is the Sun Belt versus the Snow Belt, state versus state, lobby versus lobby, there is a growing fragmentation towards smaller loyalties in regional, economic, biological, political, and ethnic areas.

This trend has been stressed in a series of articles recently appearing in the *Boston Globe* entitled, "The Now Generation Is Thinking 'Me First'." In brief, the series points out that the individual is eclipsing the family; the nest egg is being blown on monthly charges; self-denial is being replaced by self-gratification.

In the words of an NBC special on California, "They want it all now."

The evidence is seen in the flood of self-help and self-improvement books, in therapy groups of all types, in gadgets galore for a new you, in exotic clothes and even fragrances for the "aware male." The stress is on being good to yourself. Seldom do we hear about one's responsibility to another person and to society at large.

The new emphasis has marks of immaturity. One of the major causes of immature behavior is arrested psychological development, usually originating from childhood. A child has a traumatic experience and instead of working it out, represses it. This may consciously be forgotten but often festers in the unconscious. Later in life we see an adult act in some childish way. The child who got his way by having tantrums and screaming at his parents often as an adult uses the same tactics in dealing with his employees or fellow workers and family. Another sign of immaturity is the practical joker or one who puts other people down by making them feel uncomfortable.

My purpose this morning is not to spend time on the psychological foundations of immaturity, except to mention the importance of child rearing in developing healthy, mature adults. Rather, my purpose is to develop criteria for maturity and to suggest what we might do to embrace it.

What are the criteria for a mature person? First we must realize that we are not self-contained units. We are linked to the environment around us both by nature and by culture. Immature persons have few linkages to either. They may live only in the past or live in the present without relationship either to a past or to a future. If a person is reactionary, only the past seems to have vital importance. If a person is neurotic or psychotic, there is a relationship with an environment that does not really exist. The person's responses, therefore, will be reactions to dangers that are projections of that person's own fears, to slights that are the projections of his or her own self-doubting. If we choose the mature life, we find that it is one that fulfills its possibilities through creative linkages with reality.

A second criterion of maturity is social growth. It is exemplified by an individual who does not just build up a limited, exclusive relationship with family, friends, colleagues and acquaintances, but continually expands into inclusion of people who were once strangers. When we think of people who are culturally, politically and ethnically different from us, we often only think of the dissimilarities. The mature person, on the other hand, knows that human beings are all members of a single species. All of us share what is known as human nature. The differences arise from cultural, environmental, family and peer influences. But ultimately there is a biological unity among all persons.

Mature persons find that their linkages with life grow stronger and broader. They are socially concerned. They are not creating barriers and walling out new experiences or people. Their growing understanding will keep pace with their power to execute actions.

A third criterion for maturity is never to stop learning. As human beings we are basically born ignorant. Other than an instinctual reaction such as the ability to suck, we come into the world ignorant and helpless. Specific knowledge gained by a person over many years does not by itself make that person mature. One person may be a specialist in cooking, another in treating someone with a disease, and a third in piloting a plane. Two people may take a hike in a national park. One may know the names of all the plants and trees and the nature of these species. On this account alone, we do not call one person mature and the other one not. The life work of the person who knows the plants would have required him or her to learn about them. It is not knowledge of this or that fact that marks the mature person but his or her attitude towards knowledge. If a person bluffs knowledge he or she does not possess, that person is immature. If a person, through adult strength and status, exerts influence that calls for a certain kind of knowledge but makes little or no effort to obtain that knowledge, that person, too, is immature. If we take for granted that our present store of knowledge is sufficient for the rest of our lives, we are immature. In many professions today it is said that the present knowledge a person possesses will be obsolete in six years.

A fourth criterion of maturity is a sense of responsibility. We are born helpless; we are irresponsible. There is little we can do for ourselves and nothing for others. The mature person takes responsibility commensurate with his or her power. To do this he or she has to accept a human role. No one has asked to be born. But to be an enlightened human being means progressively to accept the fact that the human experience is a shared experience; the human predicament, a shared predicament. Last year the newspapers carried the story of a criminal who was suing his parents because he said they were responsible for bringing him into the world. That is immaturity. If we are constantly looking to blame others for our failures and shortcomings or if we think we are always the exception, then we are not ready to accept responsibility.

Another dimension of responsibility involves the development of the sense of function. The person who wants the prestige of a certain type of work or lifestyle but resents or neglects the routines that go along with it is immature. Function requires the development of habits to support that function. When we see a person self-excusing or self-dramatizing, we are aware that the individual has not assumed sufficient responsibility to go along with the acquired position in life. The White Queen in *Through the Looking Glass* is an example of a distracted, not fully functioning being. She is bedazzled, always on the run; her words, like the mind behind them, go in all directions at once and arrive nowhere.

A fifth criterion for maturity is communication. We are born alone, but we will build word linkage between our human world and ourselves. Speech plays a major role in our lives. It is our primary influence on other people. Speech at its best becomes the means of moving from the narrow to the universal.

A sixth criterion of adulthood and maturity is the specific and creative sexual relationship. We are born creatures of diffuse sexuality. We reach sexual maturity when we accept our own sexual nature without common guilt, incorporate that nature in a rational life plan, and make the sexual experience the basis of a sustained, mutually fulfilling and creative relationship with another person.

A seventh criterion is empathy. This is the opposite of ego-centricity. It is making new wholes out of familiar parts. Empathy has been defined as "the imaginative projection of one's own consciousness into a person outside oneself." Empathy is imaginatively entering into another's life as if it were our very own.

These criteria for maturity rest on moving beyond isolated particulars and moving toward wholeness. Certainly we need pluralism. There are many roads to the mountaintop and various ways to reach it. But wholeness is seeing some common denominator, something that ties and binds and brings it all together in a governing, orderly philosophy.

Keeping in mind these criteria, how can we become mature individuals?

First we can hold out for higher expectations in our own lives. If we feel that going from childhood to adulthood is an anti-climax, then there will be no maturing. William Sheldon, in his book *Psychology and the Promethean Will*, has this to say: "The days of youth teem with fragments of living knowledge with daring philosophies, morning dreams, plans. But the human mind at forty is commonly vulgar, smug, deadened and wastes its hours. Everywhere, adult brains seem to resemble blighted trees that have died in the upper branches but yet cling to a struggling green wisp of life about the lower trunk." Is this what adulthood is? Most of us would answer, "No."

The good news is that the mature person can grow in happiness and competence by linking positively to life. This is done through accepting reality, social relatedness, and continual assimilation of knowledge, responsibility, clarifying our ways of communication, sexual understanding, and empathy.

A person in a family makes a mistake. The reaction might be angry outrage or cruel jests. The mature person will recognize that people do make mistakes, and though not condoning the act, the mature individual does not blow the error out of proportion. An adolescent may bring home ideas that vary from the family view. There can be shocked disapproval, or there can be a careful drawing out of why the adolescent thinks that way. This is done by listening with honest interest and expressing honest doubts when it seems necessary. Both these examples may seem insignificant on the subject of maturity. Yet it is out of the little things that the atmosphere for mature or immature attitudes is created. Edna St. Vincent Millay says it in this way: "It is not love's going hurts my days, but that it went in such little ways."

Every life situation offers opportunities for mature and immature reaction. A sign of maturity is knowing what is important and what is not, when to raise issues and when to let them drop.

Every organization presents opportunities for mature and immature responses. It is easy and immature to sulk or to quit an organization if things do not go to your liking. Mature persons stay with it and continue to share their best with others. We as individuals need to associate ourselves with organizations that promote maturity. There are many group situations that call upon our time. Some bring out the childishness and selfishness in us. Others encourage us to remove those individual and social situations that hold people back from fulfilling their potential.

To embrace maturity is to come up with a working plan for the continual growth of our minds so that we can increase the depth and breadth of our lives. This means coming to understand our environment and ourselves. Carl Binger, in his writings, sums up what it means to be mature. He writes: "As people move toward emotional health, and as adolescent children solve conflicts with their parents, they acquire a degree of self-knowledge which enables them to learn from the past and not only to suffer from it. They grow to accept and respect their own uniqueness and that of others; they develop the capacity to tolerate frustration and disappointments; and they find pleasure and satisfaction in living and working in their associations with other people." Embracing maturity is a lifelong commitment for each of us.

A Meaningful Life amidst Changing Times

SEPTEMBER 21, 1980

The 350th Anniversary Service of the First Church in Boston

TODAY WE FACE SUCH DRAMATIC changes in attitudes and values that a flood seems to be sweeping over us. Often we may feel as if a dam has broken or a hurricane is converging upon us. At times each of us may feel powerlessly swept along on torrential currents. So we may feel tempted now, as past generations have been tempted, to let go. We may feel like a rudderless ship in a storm. At times our faith may seem to have deserted us.

I am reminded of a retired minister who decided to fulfill one of his great dreams—to climb Pike's Peak in Colorado. He had almost reached the summit when he slipped and fell 30 feet. There he grasped at a branch and found himself dangling over a 3,000-foot precipice. He held on with all his strength, struggling to gain a firm footing. But it was to no avail. Soon he became

91

exhausted. He thought of his religious faith as he was almost giving up hope. Turning his face skyward, he called out, "Is there anyone up there?" A voice boomed back, "Yes." The minister asked, "Who is it?" The reply came back, "I am God." "Will you help me?" "Of course." "What must I do?" "First, let go of the branch." There was a very long pause, and then the minister called out again, "Is there anyone else up there?"

As today marks the commemoration service of this Church's first 350 years, we give thanks to all those men and women who had strong faith and dared to venture forth and create a new city in a virtually unknown land. They, too, lived in changing times, but they did not give up. They had the faith and courage to lead meaningful lives by committing themselves to building a better society.

We cannot deal with the next 350 years by beginning the 1980s with a pessimistic attitude and a resigned sense of helplessness. The impersonalization of society today is evident to all of us, as is the apparent meaninglessness of life to many people.

Loren Eiseley warns of the numbing of human hope in his book, *The Night Country*. He writes: "I had come into the smoking compartment of a train at midnight out of the tumult of a New York weekend. As I settled into a corner, I noticed a man with a paper sack a few seats beyond. He was meager of flesh and his cheeks had already taken on the molding of the skull beneath them. His threadbare clothing suggested that his remaining possessions were contained in the sack poised on his knees. His eyes were closed, his head flung back. He drowsed either from exhaustion or liquor, or both. In that city at midnight there were many like him.

"By degrees the train filled and took its way into the dark. After a time the door opened and the conductor shouldered his way in, demanding tickets. I had one sleepy eye fastened on the dead faced derelict. 'Tickets!' bawled the conductor.

"Slowly the man opened his eyes, a dead man's eyes. Slowly a sticklike arm reached down and fumbled in his pocket, producing a roll of bills. 'Give me,' he said, and his voice held the croak of a raven in a churchyard, 'Give me a ticket to wherever it is.' The dead eyes closed. The conductor's hastily produced list of stations had no effect. Obviously disliking this role, he selected the price to Philadelphia, thrust the remaining bills into the man's indifferent hand and departed. I looked around. People had returned to their papers, or were they only feigning? In a single poignant expression, this shabby creature on a midnight train had personalized the terror of an open-ended universe where persons have no idea where they are going."

Each of us today, as the spiritual descendants of the founders of this Church, has the obligation to be a positive force in this era of accelerating change. To be positive we should recognize the major new trends affecting us so that we may deal with them intelligently and effectively. What are some of these changes we face?

First, we should understand that the United States is shifting from a mass industrial society to an informational one. Informational occupations are involved in creating, processing and distributing information. This ranges from banks to education and governement. The effect will be more profound than the shift in the nineteenth century from an agricultural to an industrial society. Banks, educational institutions, and governments all create process and distribute information. The labor force in 1950 found sixty-five percent in the industrial sector. Today it is thirty percent. Informational occupations made up seventeen percent of the labor force in 1950; now they exceed fifty-five percent. In industrial societies the strategic resource is capital. In the post-industrial informational society, the strategic resource is knowledge and data. This is not only renewable but self-generating. This helps explain the entrepreneurial activity that is exploding around us.

But as we move from an industrial society to an informational one, we notice a powerful anomaly developing. When knowledge and wisdom are needed more than ever, many schools are giving us an increasingly inferior graduate. SAT scores are on a sharp decline. For the first time in our history, many of those graduating from high school are less skilled than their parents. Yet on the positive side, more young people today are getting an equal chance for an education and a wider choice of job opportunities.

The restructuring of society means that the traditional groupings of goods and services will not work any longer. We will need new concepts if we are to understand where we are and where we are going. It is up to our religious faith to give us high standards to help us on the way. It is our faith that can unify the parts into a meaningful whole.

The second change in our society is the growing momentum for decentralization. Power seems to have shifted from the Presidency to Congress. Now we see a new trend from Congress to the states and localities with such referendum questions as

Proposition 13 in California and Proposition 2½ on the ballot in Massachusetts.

The centralizing events of this century were industrialization, the Depression, and World War II, but in the late '60s, diversity began to be in vogue. Black, Polish and Latino became beautiful. Ethnic restaurants became more popular. Today, bilingual classes are demanded as the melting pot myth explodes. The national urban policy to save our cities has not succeeded, but some of our cities will be saved because of local initiative. Due to the growing diversity in the United States, a top to bottom monolithic policy will not be effective in the '80s. Democracy is on the rise, with the voters of Maine deciding by ballot this week whether they will close their Yankee atomic electric plant or keep it open.

The mass phenomenon of the industrial society is on the decline. Our great automobile companies are not competing well with the Japanese because we are still bound by old techniques while the Japanese allow greater autonomy and independence among their workers. The general magazines with mass circulations such as *Life* and the *Saturday Evening Post* have given way to special interest publications that are proliferating. The year that *Life* and the *Post* folded, 300 special interest magazines were established. Today there are more than 4,000 of these publications. Network television has started on the decline, while special interest television stations, with cable TV and new channels as a real possibility, are on the verge of an explosion.

The huge department stores are yielding to small shops such as boutiques and the many specialty shops one can find in such centers as Quincy Market. Chain supermarkets are closing their doors and individually run late hour stores are opening. National political parties are on the decline, with the rise of independent voters and even an independent presidential candidate for 1980.

We are not conferring leadership as we did in the past. Current leaders have a much more limited mandate than they used to possess. In the old Taoist model of leadership, there was a saying, "Find a parade and get in front of it." The parades are now smaller and less frequent.

The third major change we face in the '80s is the ushering in of a truly global economy, due partly to instantaneously shared information. The United States and Western Europe and the other developed countries are on the way to losing the great proportion of industries such as steel, automobile, railroad equipment, machinery, apparel, shoes, textiles, and appliances. It is estimated that by the end of this century, twenty-five percent of the world's manufactured goods will be from the Third World.

Yesterday is over. New adventures are ahead. A job revolution is occurring. A recent headline said, "Forty million people will be needed to run computers by 1990." Reading further, the question is posed, "But who will train them?"

We must begin to think and learn in terms of such new adventures as computers, bio industry, alternate sources of energy, and mining of the rich resources of the seabeds. We must stretch our imaginations in literature, art, and music and in organized religion.

The new work environment is changing from top-down, to bottom-up. We see a change of personal values across the past two decades. Production rate is on a dismal downtrend, while at the same time there is a growing demand for more satisfaction in life. We see workers refuse to produce. Some even sabotage the product of their work. More pay and a four-day workweek are not the panacea some people had hoped for.

The Japanese take thirteen hours to build a car. We take thirty hours. It is not because the Japanese are robots. It is the opposite. They are given enormous freedom to plan and execute their own work. They are allowed to solve problems on their own without interference from managers. The workers make many crucial decisions. Is this what the American worker can expect in the future?

Three hundred and fifty years ago a cohesive group of Puritans gathered this Church. But Americans of 1980 reflect not merely the culture of Western Europe but the mores and values of the seven continents. Too often today, differences are stressed, rather than the common denominators. We must begin to find new, acceptable ways to communicate with one another. In developing a meaningful life, we must discover a larger loyalty, not because it is imposed from above, but because it flows outward from within ourselves.

In a time of such accelerating changes, our values and ideals are of more importance than ever. Cyra MacFadden, author of the best-selling novel *The Seria*, comments on a recent experience at California State College. She had assigned a short story by Ray Bradbury. One student responded: "I picked up his vibes, but just couldn't get behind him." When MacFadden threatened to flunk someone for not completing several assignments, he said, "I'm not into value judgments, so don't lay your power trip on me."

If society is not to become a jungle, it is imperative to choose those values and goals that enhance life rather than negate it. Our Church is one institution that asks you to commit yourself to positive and altruistic choices that, in turn, will be the ingredients of a meaningful life. Let us join in the succession of those seers and heroes found in the history of this Church, who sacrificed for their altruistic hopes and dreams. Let us pick up their mantle as we venture into the future with its risks and unknowns.

Unlike a watch in which all parts must function perfectly, our lives may be better likened to a wheel. No one is successful in every dimension of life. Not all our dreams and hopes will be fulfilled. Several spokes of the wheel may be broken, but the wheel spins on, serving a purpose. Constant care of the spokes, however, must be taken, for if too many are damaged, the wheel will not be effective.

Although we all make mistakes, particularly in a society in crisis with tremendous changes in values, lifestyles and employment, we must not despair but must continually work at integrating the parts, constantly keeping our values and goals before us.

The Puritans also lived in times of great change. Though they failed in their attempt to create a godly community, they have been a positive force in the development of this land. We know that we, too, will never live in Utopia. Human nature will not be perfect in our lifetime. But what we do with our lives will affect the quality of our lives and the quality of life for others. We must help one another develop and maintain a meaningful life amidst these changing times.

A Triumphant Life

APRIL 26, 1981

*F*ORTY YEARS AGO Professor Walter Cannon of the UCLA Medical School wrote a paper on the subject of voodoo medicine. Cannon wanted to know how a witch doctor could say to a person, "You will die forty-five days from now, two hours after the new moon comes up" and forty-five days later that person could be claimed by death. This happened numerous times. Cannon wondered how this could possibly occur. He found that no trickery was involved. The voodoo doctor did not kill the individual. What happened was that the will to die had replaced the will to live at precisely the point that the individual accepted as reality the prediction of death. The moral of this story is obvious. People can be programmed to die. But the corollary is equally true. If people can be programmed to die, they can be programmed to live.

We need in these times to be programmed to live triumphantly. It is especially important now, for we live in an age of anxiety. Many of the old certainties seem to have disappeared. Our generation, in Henry Hesse's words, "is caught between ages, two modes of life and the consequence is that it loses all power to understand itself. It has no standards, no security." There are those who react to this fact by clinging all the more frantically to the outworn creeds of earlier days. They are like the woman who recited the prayer, "Good Lord, we pray that this evolution business is not true, but if it is true, give us grace to hush it up."

Dr. Rollo May, in his book *Man's Search for Himself,* discusses the anxiety that is prevalent because of the nature of our modern world. He writes, "Just as anxiety destroys our self awareness, so awareness of ourselves can destroy anxiety." That is to say that the stronger the consciousness of ourselves, the more we can take a stand against and overcome anxiety. Anxiety, like a fever, is a sign that an inner struggle is in progress. As fever is a symptom that the body is mobilizing its physical powers and giving battle to an infection, so anxiety is evidence that a psychological or spiritual battle is in progress. "Our task," concludes Dr. May, "is to strengthen our consciousness of ourselves, to find centers of strength within ourselves which will enable us to stand, despite the confusions around us."

One person associated with the career of George Washington was a Captain John Callender. He was an officer of the Massachusetts Militia who was guilty of cowardice at the Battle of Bunker Hill. One of the first duties Washington faced when he assumed command of the forces in Cambridge was to order the court-martial of Captain Callender. "It is with inexpressible concern," wrote Washington in his official orders, "that the General upon his first arrival in the army should find an officer sentenced by the General Court-Martial to be cashiered for cowardice—a crime of all others, the most infamous in a soldier, the most injurious to an army, and the last to be forgiven." So Captain Callender was deprived of his commission and expelled in disgrace. This could have destroyed this man's self-image. He could have become a very negative person. But this did not happen. After having been expelled as an officer, Callender re-enlisted in the army as a private, and at the Battle of Long Island, he exhibited such conspicuous courage that George Washington publicly revoked the sentence and restored him to his Captaincy. From a disgraced position, he transformed himself into a triumphant, courageous person. Such a conversion of life is, as Paul put it, being transformed by the "renewing of one's mind."

Personality can be changed, but some disagree with this statement. "By the age of thirty," said one psychologist, "the character is set like plaster and will never soften again." I could counter with the example of the immense change that came over Tolstoy when he was fifty. Yet, personality in many ways does get set, and we should keep this in mind.

A personality can get set in certain positive ways. What are some of these positive aspects? Personality becomes dependable. It develops a style so that one can count upon it. One knows in advance what some of one's friends will do. One can rely on their established character. One knows their predictable qualities. We can count on them. Their personalities are set in positive ways.

However, when personality has set in negative and defective ways, the person is presented with the most crucial problem. How can one be changed into a positive, more triumphant person?

The first thing we should keep in mind is to look not so much for a cure, but for prevention. There is something dramatic about a coward at Bunker Hill displaying such courage at Long Island that he recovers his commission. But from the standpoint of Callender, that was a terrible experience. Why go through such a difficult period if it is not necessary. The story of the Prodigal Son, feeding the swine in a far-away country, then coming to himself and returning home, has stirred the imagination of people for centuries. But from the standpoint of the Prodigal Son, it was a terrible experience. Why put yourself through such misery if it can be prevented?

Personality can be changed, but it requires willpower and conscious determination. It requires effort. For personality basically does get set and once set, it is not easy to change. To live triumphantly requires care right from the beginning of our conscious development. The importance of our actions on young people and of religious education in the home and in the church school should be clear.

But after I have said this with all possible emphasis, there remains the fact that no one has ever solved all the problems in one's life by prevention. Some will do this better than others, but no one has ever solved all the problems by just starting right. Everyone here, I am sure, understands John Callender and his deep need to change. And everyone here knows that within our own lives there are some dimensions of immaturity, some dimensions that can be changed for the better, some ways to make our personalities more triumphant.

"Adult infantilism," says one of America's distinguished psychologists, Dr. Joseph Collins, "is our chief deficiency as a people. Our most conspicuous shortcoming." How many of us can say with Paul, "When I was a child, I spoke as a child, I thought as a child, I felt as a child, and when I became a man I put away childish things"? Many have succeeded in putting away many superficial aspects of childhood. But all of us retain, even subconsciously, some traits and behavioral patterns of the child. It was Henry Ford who described a certain individual this way: "He met misfortune like a man. He blamed it on his wife." An executive has this motto on his desk: "A man can fail many times, but he isn't a failure until he begins to blame somebody else." We recognize many other areas of immaturity, such as craving praise and gratitude for most everything we do, the desire to want everything "my" way, the selfishness of "I" instead of the larger, embracing "we" as the prime motivator in our lives, and the expectation that life owes us a good living. I am sure you are all aware of many more aspects of immaturity.

It should be clear that there is a need for everyone to be transformed from having aspects of immaturity into having aspects of a more triumphant personality. Even though we are set in some of our ways, the negative ones can be worked on and in many cases changed.

We see in life sudden change occurring all around us. In your garden a plant gradually grows, but suddenly one day it flowers. We can predict in advance that a magnolia tree will produce magnolia blossoms. But we cannot predict the moment that every flower will burst forth. So it is with the human personality. In the hour of crisis, will it bring forth the flower of triumphant living or will it droop and die and never fulfill its potential?

Many years ago in London, there was a young man from India, anxious to be a social worker. He dressed well. He was socially charming. He took lessons to play the violin and to dance. We know him in history as Mahatma Gandhi. How unpredictable that a young socialite would become a powerful ascetic. Later in life he lived on goat's milk while holding in his frail hands the spiritual and political destiny of India. This was unpredictable, but it happened.

John Callender all the rest of his life was probably more courageous because he had been a coward at Bunker Hill. The very place where his personality was weak, that area grew the strongest. Courage took the place of cowardice. In our physical bodies, if a broken bone heals properly, it becomes stronger at the point of the break than the rest of the bone.

Let us take this a step further to say that not only in crisis and in sudden change may we move from negative to positive personality but also when a new person comes into our experience. A new person coming into our life may make a vast difference in what we become tomorrow. This may have been the case with John Callender. Convicted as a coward, he stood face to face with George Washington and something happened to him. It was not that Washington was easy on him. He heard himself called "infamous," and "most injurious to the army." But Callender refused to stay that way. Washington perhaps was the catalyst for Callender's conscience and will. Each one of us here has been touched and affected by such a person—a mother, a father, a friend, so that we have risen above negative responses to positive ones.

If a person can be a positive influence on each of us, so can an idea. Ideas germinate best in an atmosphere and community where they are nurtured and reinforced. A great emphasis of our Unitarian Universalist faith is individual freedom—but this must be practiced within the context of relating responsibly to our fellow human beings. Lillian Smith suggests, "All morality is based on this central truth; that people in their different ways must meet each other's needs, and in the doing, will find a larger, freer life for themselves." Thus the self-discovery, the self-awareness, the self-affirmation that we seek are served by acting responsibly within our freedom. In a denominational study entitled "A Free Church in a Changing World," a stress is made on individualism; it says, "For us the individual is central," but later it says, "Only in community can the individual attain the highest development."

So we come together for help in reinforcing these ideas and values that lead us to become triumphant personalities. First we are an intellectual community. We are here to share ideas and grow from the wisdom of each other. Emerson said once, "When two people think exactly alike, one isn't thinking." We come together with some common shared values but also with some diversity of thought. This provides a stimulus that enables each of us to grow, to develop, and to confirm ideas that have positive effects upon us.

We also come together as a social community, responsive to each other's feelings as well as thoughts. We share joys and sorrows, fears and hopes, and find in this mutual caring for one another emotional self-awareness and strength for living positively. There is a story of a man who visited a psychiatrist. He made himself comfortable on the couch. The psychiatrist turned on the tape recorder and said, "Talk about anything you wish while I go out and have some coffee." At the next session, the patient brought with him his own tape recorder and said: "I am going to let my tape recorder talk to your tape recorder and we'll both go out for coffee!" What he wanted and needed and what we all need are personal relationships.

We also come together as a purposeful community, responsive to a world of need beyond our own walls. Through this sharing and caring, we discover a corporate identity—a positive self-awareness we could never know individually. Just as the completely self-centered existence of a human being is destructive, so it is for any group of people. The Church, in reaching out beyond its own self-interest, finds greater significance and self-identity.

In this era of anxiety and change, it is imperative that we develop a will to live fully and positively. Sir Walter Scott, in *The Lady of the Lake*, writes: "Not in the clamor of the crowded street, not in the shouts and plaudits of the throng, but in ourselves is triumph and defeat." We will ourselves for a triumphant life when we strive to live positively, when we live by attitudes and values that prevent negative and destructive personality, when we seek to change the immature dimensions of our personality, realizing that many of the negative aspects we embody can be changed, and when we respond to the intellectual, social and purposeful community of the Church in helping us achieve a greater understanding of ourselves and our responsibilities.

Triumphant living is the spiritual act by which we cease to live unreflectively and live our lives with reverence. A triumphant life makes the most of the gift of life we each have been given.

Ralph Waldo Emerson, Welcome Back to Your Pulpit

MAY 2, 1982

(Concluding Service of Ralph Waldo Emerson Memorial Week)

RALPH WALDO EMERSON was the nineteenth century's greatest exponent of trusting the integrity of your own mind. The emphasis on the importance of the common man and woman is a special American contribution to human civilization. Emerson believed in the perfectibility of human nature. Trust your own self. Do not live secondhand through the insights of others, especially from the past, but live in the present. Strive to do your best, for the formation and force of character are cumulative. The power that resides in each of us is new in nature, and no one knows the extent of that power until we try! This is the essence of Emerson's philosophy.

Due to Emerson's belief that there is intelligence and good will at the heart of things, he is often mistaken as an easy optimist— one who sees only the pleasantries of life and ignores the grim realities, one who does not know hardship. Far from it! Emerson saw reality and knew hardship. His father, who was minister of the First Church in Boston, died when Ralph Waldo was seven years old. He was one of six children left fatherless in 1810. The Church granted his mother a small pension for seven years. Gay Wilson Allen, in his recent biography, writes that Emerson had an "ugly duckling childhood and a troubled adolescence." There were always financial difficulties. The circumstances of the real world made it necessary for the Emerson children to support each other through college. Ralph Waldo, who preferred to be called Waldo, worked to defray the college expenses of his oldest brother William. William, upon graduating, taught school in Kennebunk, Maine and helped financially to send Waldo through Harvard. Waldo, as did Thoreau, also received scholarship help from the First Church. He, in turn, taught school to render help to Edward, and so on down the line.

Emerson was a most penetrating, unfaltering critic of American society. In his journal during the panic days of 1837, he wrote: "The present generation is bankrupt of principles and hope as of property. . . . A person is a treadle of a wheel, a tassel at the apron-string of society. . . ." In 1841 he publicly stated: "The young man, on entering life, finds the way to lucrative employment blocked with abuses. The ways of trade are grown selfish to the borders of theft and supple to the borders of fraud." Wise, universal and clear sighted, Ralph Waldo Emerson never closed his eyes to the harsh and brutal facts of everyday living. He wrote so truly of himself: "I dip my pen in the blackest of ink because I am not afraid of falling into my ink pot." Facing the real as the prophet of the ideal, he calmly told the truth of whatever he saw. He was no Pollyanna, but it can be said that he was a discriminating optimist. This is clearly shown in his approach to the Church and religion.

When Emerson was called as minister to the Second Church in Boston in 1829, he felt the presence of the spiritual Puritan power of Cotton and Increase Mather. But it was not long before the ecclesiastical forms under which their spiritual values were encased became restrictive and shackling to him. The true religion of a Cotton Mather beset by dogmatic tests and Biblical literalism would come full circle with Emerson. He said, "Man's creeds are a disease of the intellect." He felt that the distrust of reason and the fear to think were suicidal: "The religion that is afraid of science dishonors God and commits suicide." It acknowledges that it is not equal to the whole of truth. His faith became exalted by the vision of a huge, natural universe that scientists were revealing. The God of Christian revelation must be also the God of the vast physical universe. Emerson thought of God as larger and greater than the human mind could conceive. Thus he would say: "The stationariness of revealed religion is the assumption that the Age of Inspiration is past, that the Bible is closed. . . . The fear of degrading the character of Jesus by representing him as a man, indicates the falsehood of theology. . . . God is, not was; God speaketh, not spake."

Emerson was a successful preacher. Preaching, to him, was the highest form of ministry. Although not caring for some pastoral duties, he was finding a growing response to his ideas. Margaret Fuller had started attending the Second Church. He questioned certain literalistic interpretations of the Christian faith. The Lord's Supper was a major stumbling block for him. This was the immediate background of his letter to the Second Church in May 1832 asking for modification in the communion service. He asked to dispense with the elements and make the service one of commemoration. Some of the members were shocked by this proposal. "Cold, Cold" he wrote in his journal when news of his proposal spread through the Church.

In June at a meeting in Emerson's home, Emerson stated his views respecting the communion service. He had four main points, which I will briefly summarize.

1. Jesus, in celebrating with his disciples the Jewish Passover, did not intend to institute a new and perpetual rite. Communion is to be esteemed as symbolic instruction and is no more binding on us than the washing of the feet of the disciples, which is followed today by the Church of Rome, though dropped by the Protestant Church.

2. The rite erroneously leads people to compare Jesus with the Deity as an object of worship instead of presenting him as a teacher and friend.

3. The eating of the bread and the drinking of the wine are to some an impediment to devotion. This incongruity between the act and the sentiment was Emerson's main objection to the rite.

4. The importance ascribed to communion as a means of religious improvement is not consistent with the spirit of the gospel that is at war with formal worship.

*   *   *

A committee was formed to consider Emerson's proposed change. On June 21 it reported that unanimously it was agreed that the proposed change could not be made. "It is expedient to maintain the celebration of the Lord's Supper in the present form; the church retains an undiminished regard to the pastor and entertains the hope that he will find it consistent with his sense of duty to continue the customary administration of the Lord's Supper." Emerson left for New Hampshire to think and to pray.

There are those who believe that Emerson was tired of the ministry. Following the death of his wife, Ellen, he was depressed. For months afterwards, he walked daily several miles to her grave. How much this loss entered into his decision nobody knows. On July 15 he made his decision. Since others regarded communion as "the most sacred of religious institutions" and he did not, he could only reaffirm his unwillingness to perform it. His sermon entitled "The Lord's Supper" was delivered on September 9. In closing this sermon, Emerson proposed to resign as the minister. Following this sermon he wrote his formal letter asking for dismissal from his pastoral charge.

Throughout this controversy, Emerson's conduct was mild and generous. No one was singled out and blamed. He refused to publish the sermon lest it be considered as a way of attracting proselytes to his view or as a cause of dividing the church. A grass roots movement, however, did develop to keep the minister on his own terms. A reading of the Church records of the year 1832 shows that actual minutes of meetings are missing and certain pages dealing with events after Emerson left have been cut out, indicating more discussion than history has revealed. Various meetings were called. On October 28 the matter came to a final vote. The proprietors voted 34 to 25 not to keep Emerson. A shift of 5 votes might have changed the future not only of Second Church but Unitarianism and perhaps other denominations as well. Emerson's future would have been decidedly different also. If he had continued as minister, he would not have had the time or the complete freedom to write and to lecture as he did.

Today we would broadly and warmly welcome Emerson's openness and discriminating optimism to his old pulpit. Theodore Parker once said, "Thank God for three things, the sun and the moon and Ralph Waldo Emerson." Welcome back, Ralph Waldo Emerson. We need your integrity in this world. The sun and the moon will remain for a long time, but will human beings? The greatness of nature can be brutalized by forces we have learned to unleash. The forces of nuclear fission can vaporize human beings. Today Emerson would remind us that survival does not rest on dogmas or rigid allegiance to authority. It requires us to face the present with courage, trusting ourselves! Welcome back, Ralph Waldo Emerson, to your pulpit!

Managing Your Life Creatively

MAY 23, 1982

TODAY IS CHILDREN'S SUNDAY, and so I have especially in mind young people. However, what I have to say is applicable to persons of any age. One of the strongest drives inside every healthy person is the desire to be independent. People grow in many ways, but one thing that is held in common is the wish to manage oneself. When children are tiny, of course, they have to be managed by someone else. But the desire for independence is there early in life, and as a person grows into the teenage years, it becomes one of the most powerful motivating forces. Far from being a bad thing, no child can develop his or her human potential who does not have this desire for independence. Parents make a mistake to place too many restraints and "don'ts" upon the developing child. Crushed children are ruined children. Children should be nurtured and encouraged, though some restraints are necessary. Children have a right to be prepared for independence. They need parental cooperation and balance to help them become ready to handle it. The goal is to have strong, independent people who are able to manage themselves.

How well do children, as well as adults, handle their independence? This strong desire to take charge of yourself is in all of us. People of all ages can mess up or even ruin their lives because of failure to handle this desire. Whether we like it or not, life has to be managed. Like an automobile if it is to run at all, someone has to take charge! To manage an automobile is simple compared to managing your own life. In the Bible it says, "He that ruleth his spirit is better than he that taketh a city." The late Dwight L. Moody remarked, "I have more trouble with myself than with any other man." Maybe everyone should say that of oneself. To manage your own life creatively, imaginatively, and positively is one of the greatest tasks in the world. "Oh God," replied Beethoven, "give me the power to conquer myself." Until a person has conquered the self, one will never be able to conquer anything else. Just to be free from someone else's management does not solve our problems. It is at this point that the real test commences. It comes down to this. Have I the wisdom, character, and stamina to competently manage myself?

A child growing up does hear many "do nots." The child wishes for the time when he or she may make decisions on his or her own without being told what should be done. Some tension in the home is natural. Parents have to start guiding their children and gradually pass responsibility over to them. Good parents understand this. They desire to see children grow up to be caring, independent men and women. They should feel about children managing themselves as they feel about young people driving the family automobile. It is fine, but the big issue arises—is he or she competent to drive it safely?

When the trees along the sidewalk in front of our church were planted, stakes were placed on each side of them so that they would grow straight. Today, there are no longer stakes, but the trees stand straight and tall. The early restraints were necessary so that the trunks would not bend or break with the forces of nature, while the roots were allowed to grow. Today the trees can flourish on their own without stakes. The same is true of children. They must be supported in a mature way so that they may grow straight and true. Given positive guidance, they gain the experience and wisdom necessary to intelligently and compassionately handle the many problems to be encountered throughout the rest of life.

Managing one's own life creatively requires freedom, but this freedom requires the substitution of one's own inner self control for someone else's control. Freedom is not escaping from control. Every creative life has to have some control. In the Moffatt translation of the Bible it says, "He that controls himself is better than a conqueror."

If we are going to live creatively, we must understand certain universal laws. There are certain aspects of the universe from which we can never be free. Take for example the law of gravitation that dictates certain things we may or may not do. If we want to live, we will not walk off a ten-story building. In a courthouse in Worcester, across its entrance are these words: "Obedience to law is liberty." Certainly that is true in science. We were not free to use electricity until we understood the laws of electricity. In every scientific laboratory, obedience to law is liberty.

In life as a whole, there are aspects from which we cannot be free—the law of habit, for example. All of us may be free to start a habit, but it is more difficult to stop one. We do something again and again until it becomes a habit. The person who manages his or her life creatively develops good habits. But we must remember that bad habits also may be formed. We have become conscious in recent years of the damage smoking does to our physical health, and yet we know individuals who find it almost impossible to stop smoking. There is an old saying concerning drinking: "A person takes a drink, a drink takes a drink, and then the drink takes the person." I had dinner this week with the Albanian Orthodox minister who conducted the funeral for John Belushi in Edgartown, Martha's Vineyard. He commended the accomplishments of Belushi but forthrightly condemned his inability to be in control of himself. John Belushi was a very accomplished actor. People admired him. Yet in his thirties, drugs destroyed him. Wrongdoing makes a slave of us. Right living liberates us. The business of managing your own life, of being free and independent, is more serious than many people think.

In the eighteenth century lived a man named Lord Northington, who became Lord Chancellor of England. But he started out in life on the wrong foot. In his early years he was self-indulgent, and as he became older, this self-indulgence caught up with him as he suffered extremely poor physical health. Though he lived two centuries ago, his insight is still valid. He said, "Had I known early in life that these legs of mine were to have carried a Lord Chancellor, I would have taken better care of them when I was young."

Another component in managing one's life creatively is the necessity to have an important aim in life. During World War II, children from Great Britain sailed to America to escape the dangers of Nazi bombing. An eight-year-old boy named Jack Keeley sailed to the U.S. in the steamship called *Benares*. It was torpedoed in the mid-Atlantic. The *Benares* sank. The boy clinging to a piece of wreckage kept himself afloat for an hour until, half frozen, he was picked up by a six-foot raft with three battered passengers on it. The first words that came out of his mouth as he clambered aboard were these: "Which way?" he said. "Which way is America?" Here was an eight-year-old with an aim and purpose and even in desperate circumstances this purpose held a grip on him. He was going somewhere and he was determined to get there—and he did.

Having an aim in life and managing it creatively does not have to wait until we graduate from high school or college or retire from an occupation. Mendelssohn was twelve years old when he went to work on his first published quartet. Michelangelo was thirteen years old when, rebelling against his family's determination to make him a businessman, he apprenticed himself to a painter. He dedicated his life to the study and creation of art. Joan of Arc was thirteen years old when her first vision came calling her to save France. Modern science goes back to an insight of Francis Bacon. He first saw clearly what the inductive method might mean when he was fifteen years old. Most people are and will not become as famous as the ones cited. But most of us may be like that eight-year-old child who was rescued in the mid-Atlantic. "Which way," he said. "Which way is America?"

Each one of us is like a boat. There can be three things said about a boat. First, it can be towed, and that is the way we all start in life. But we cannot go on that way forever. The next thing we can do, if we are not going to be towed, is to drift. This is to let the winds and the waves blow and push us one way or the other as they choose. Too many people live this way today. Too often we put our finger up to see which way the wind is blowing and then follow it. Hence we see so many people who are listless, without any aim or goals. They drift or are pulled or pushed by their friends or by the latest fad and not by some great purpose. But if you are not content either to be towed or to drift, you do have a final choice—to steer. You steer from within your own boat, from within your own being. And if you are going to do that well, you must have a course laid out, a port to reach, and an aim to achieve.

Inside each of us is a compass. Each of us can decide to use it or not. As it swings, it can take us over the shoals of life. We can be shipwrecked on the shores of bad habits or plunged into a whirlpool of destruction. But if we aim at a certain destination and, in spite of the storms we will meet in life, keep as true to our course as possible, we will not lose sight of our goal.

We see all around us people such as John Belushi or Richard Nixon who amounted to something in the eyes of other people but failed in the end because they were not being worthy of themselves. So much of the glitter and glamour of the world is external.

Suppose someone wanted to see your home. What would you show that person? You could show the chairs you sit in, the bed you sleep in, the kitchen—but these are material aspects. A good home is something else—a shelter where there is love, forgiveness, inspiration, and imagination.

So the Church too has a material side—the building where services of public worship, programs, and meetings are held. But it is the people that make a real Church—your learning and living by ethical and purposeful ideas and ideals and sharing them within and beyond this immediate congregation.

To manage life creatively is to aim for something beyond the self. William James said: "The great use of life is to spend it for something that will outlast it." Listen to the music of a great composer. How masterful that person is. The beauty which pours forth comes from a person who has fallen in love with music, who has surrendered to it, has wrestled with it, and dedicated a life to mastering it. This music outlasts the composer's physical existence. This, too, you may do in many areas of life.

Manage your life creatively by developing and using your self-control wisely. Think of the goals you wish to achieve and undergird them with your unique talents. Work for a better world—a more compassionate understanding between you and your family, between you and those that you associate with in daily life, between you and your community, between you and the nations of the world. Take on a great aim in life. Amount to something. Be something and stand for something greater than yourself that will outlast your life on this earth!

Dealing with
Unjust Realities

SEPTEMBER 30, 1984

WE SAILED INTO NAPLES this summer on a July morning. To the south was Mount Vesuvius covered by a hot haze, and on the port side of the ship loomed a large American aircraft carrier of the 6th Fleet. It was not only our first sight of something American for almost four weeks, but the sailors jogging around the deck indicated the American fitness consciousness that we had not observed in Eastern Europe.

Soon we were driving southeast towards Vesuvius. We chose not to visit the ruins of Pompeii but the better preserved ones of Herculaneum, the city of Greek origin. Unlike Pompeii with its regular stratification of eruptive material due to the ashes and fragments of lava transported by the wind, upon Herculaneum there descended a mass of erupted material and water in the form of an immense torrent of mud overturning and submerging all that stood in its path. This mud lava in its liquid state penetrated into every void. While Pompeii was covered by twenty feet of material, Herculaneum was buried under sixty feet in two eruptions—A.D. 79 and again in 1631. We joined the Commander of the 6th Fleet and his family to tour the ruins of this city. It was amazing to see the sophisticated system for plumbing and sewage, the advanced way of lighting, the artwork, and even the amount of wood used in their homes and still preserved. There were no human remains, but one can imagine the horror that befell that community. From a human point of view it was an unjust reality.

On Cyprus this past summer, scientists found the skeletal remains of a nine-year-old girl. They named her Camellia. She had died with her hands over her face. Radioactive carbon tests determined the year of her death, and the position of her hands sent these scientists to their history books for the month and day. Camellia had obviously been trying to protect her face and head. They found that Cyprus had been struck that year by an earthquake just after sunup July 21, A.D. 365. She had been killed by flying debris as the consequence of an earthquake. Why do bad things happen to innocent people?

Since ancient times people have sought to give answers to why bad things seem to happen to innocent people. The Greeks had the story of Zeus becoming angry because another god, Prometheus, gave men fire. "Men might become like the gods," said Zeus. So he sought revenge against all men and Prometheus. Zeus then made the first woman, Pandora, and gave her curiosity. Other gods gave her gifts of beauty and charm. Zeus sent her to live on earth. He gave her a mysterious chest filled with gifts but told her never to look inside. But her curiosity got the better of her, so she opened it up just enough to peak inside. Suddenly out of the chest came every type of trouble to flood the world: sickness, envy, hate, wars, pain, death. She shut it quickly, but it was too late. There was only one thing left in the chest and that was hope. To the ancient Greeks, that is why bad things happened and why people facing unjust setbacks could still maintain hope.

Many religions declare that bad, unexplained things occur because of the actions of a god or human beings at the beginning of existence. Consequently, all that are henceforth born must suffer. Many of us are familiar with the story of Adam and Eve and those two special trees in the Garden of Eden. One was the tree of life and the other the tree of the knowledge of good and evil. God tells Adam that he can eat from any tree in the Garden but the one containing the knowledge of good and evil. If he does, he will die. God then creates Eve. But soon a serpent is tempting Eve to eat the fruit from the tree. She does and gives some to Adam. They do not die as God had promised, but God seeks revenge on the whole human race. God says to Eve: "Because you have done this, you and all women, hereafter, shall suffer pain in childbirth, and husbands shall be the masters of their wives, and will rule their wives." Turning then to Adam, God says: "Because you have done this, I am cursing the earth so that thistles and thorns grow and you and all men, hereafter, shall have to work hard to grow food to eat. When you die, you shall turn back to the dust out of which I made you." They were then driven out of the Garden and prevented from eating from the tree of life. This Genesis myth, explaining suffering, hardship, pain and death, is not a satisfactory answer today.

The Book of Job deals with the issue of misfortune befalling the good. We read in the first chapter that, "There was a man in the land whose name was Job; and that man was perfect and upright." Then Job loses his wealth, his family and his health. We learn at the conclusion that despite all Job's goodness, God wants him to abhor himself and repent in dust and ashes. When Job does this, God restores to him twice as much as he had before. Here we have an explanation of why Job suffered and with a "silver lining" ending. There is a good purpose at the center of misfortune, but this good purpose may be beyond our human comprehension. God has a reason in what befalls us— even if to us it is unreasonable and unjust.

Now Archibald MacLeish has taken this story and put it into a modern idiom. But he leaves us with a different conclusion. He presents it as a play called *J.B.* One of the opening scenes shows J.B., the father, sitting at the dinner table carving a turkey for his five children. We hear his wife saying, "God doesn't give all this for nothing: a good home, good food, father, mother, brothers, sisters. We too have our part to play. If we do our part He will do His. He always has." During the conversation at dinner we hear J.B. exclaim: "Never since I learned to tell my shadow from my shirt have I doubted God was on my side . . . was good for me. It isn't luck when God is good to you. It's something more. . . . I've tried to show I knew it not only in words." Sarah, his wife, with conviction in her voice, exclaims: "God can reward and God can punish. Us he has rewarded. Wonderfully. Given us everything. Preserved us. Kept us from harm, each one . . . and why? Because of you J.B."

Next comes the bet between Nickles, symbolic of the Devil, and Zuss, symbolic of God. We hear Nickles say: "You know what talks when that man's talking . . . all that gravy on his plate . . . his cash . . . his pretty wife, his children! Lift the lot of them, he'd sing another canticle to different music." To which Mr. Zuss, who symbolizes God, says: "Of course he sickens you. He trusts the will of God. . . . Nothing this good man might suffer, nothing at all, would make him yelp as you do. He'd praise God no matter."

Then tragedy begins to plague J.B. First two drunken soldiers acting as messengers arrive, and after some time reveal that J.B.'s and Sarah's oldest son is dead. The war is over and his death is due to the stupidity of an officer. Finally the mother cries out— "David is our son, our son, our son. God won't let it happen to us! Can't be! Not to our kind, God won't."

Next we find J.B. and Sarah returning from the theater. Two people from the press are there with a neighbor woman. They ask the woman to divert their attention after they tell the couple some news so they can get a candid picture. "I'm from the press. There's been an accident. . . . Four kids in a car. They're dead. Two were yours. Your son. Your daughter." A look of horror and disbelief come across the parents' face as the camera flashes.

Later, still in shock, Sarah calls out to J.B., "Why did He do it to them? What had they done to Him—those children. . . . What had they done to Him and we—what had we done?" And

J.B. responds, "Don't Sarah. Don't! Shall we take the good and not the evil? We have to take the chances, Sarah: Evil with good. It doesn't mean there is no good!"

The next younger daughter is missing. Finally she is found behind a lumberyard, the victim of death from rape by a retarded teenager. The small child was found still clutching tightly her red parasol umbrella.

The tragedy accelerates. There is a massive explosion. J.B. is alive and his wife Sarah is knocked out as they fall into the cellar. A messenger comes by, incredulous that anyone is alive. He calls out, "You been down there? Whole block's gone. Bank block, all of it. J.B.'s bank. You know. Just gone. Nothing left to show it ever existed. Just a hole—J.B.'s millions gone. Plant went too—all of it—everything."

His wealth is gone but even worse, their eldest daughter, their only remaining child, is killed. J.B., turning to Sarah, says: "Even desperate we can't despair. God is there too, in the desperation. I do not know why God should strike. But God is what is stricken also: Life is what despairs in death and, desperate, is life still. Sarah! Say it after me: 'The Lord Giveth' . . . say it." And for the first time Sarah mechanically speaks after this seemingly final tragedy—"The Lord giveth." J.B. continues, "The Lord taketh away." But Sarah this time shrieks . . . "TAKES!—KILLS! KILLS! KILLS! KILLS!" and J.B. responds: "Blessed be the name of the Lord."

But J.B.'s ordeal is not over. We find him saying to Sarah, "If I knew why? What I can't bear is the blindness . . . the meaninglessness." And here Sarah interjects, "Has death no meaning?

Pain no meaning?" and pointing to his body says, "Even these suppurating sores—Have they no meaning for you?" To this J.B. says, "God will not punish without cause. God is just. God is God or we are nothing." Almost hysterically, before she leaves J.B., she cries, "God is just! If God is just our slaughtered children stank with sin, were rotten with it! Does God purchase His innocence by ours? Must we be guilty for him . . . ? Bear the burden of the world's malevolence for Him who made the world?"

Now alone, three so-called comforters come, trying to explain the why of their plight. They are a priest, a psychiatrist and a Marxist. J.B., explaining his condition, says, "The hand of God has touched me. Look at me! Every hope I ever had, every task I put my mind to, every work I've ever done annulled as though I had not done it. My children dead. Love too has left me. But God is just."

The Marxist responds, "God's justice! History is justice, not for one man. For humanity. One man's life won't measure on it. One man's suffering won't count, no matter what his suffering. At the end there will be justice. Justice for All! Justice for everyone! On the way it doesn't matter."

J.B. protests that guilt matters, and the psychiatrist jumps in, saying, "Guilt is an illusion, a disease, a sickness. There is no guilt." But J.B. cannot make "an irresponsible ignorance," as he says, "responsible for everything." He goes on saying: "I sit here such as you see me. In my soul I suffer what you guess I suffer. Tell me the wickedness that justifies it. Shall I repent of sins I have not sinned to understand? Till I die I will not violate my integrity."

The priest enters the picture, saying: "What integrity have you? A man, a miserable, mortal, sinful, venal man. . . . You squat there challenging the universe to tell you what your crime is called. Thinking, because your life was virtuous, it can't be called. It can. Your sin is simple. You were born a man!" J.B. protests, saying, "What is my fault? What have I done?" The priest replies: "What is your fault? Man's heart is evil! What have you done? Man's will is evil!" J.B. replies: "Yours is the cruelest comfort of them all, making the Creator of the universe the miscreator of mankind, a party to the crimes He punishes."

Unlike the Book of Job, where everything is restored with twice as much as Job had before, MacLeish has a different ending. He has, as in the book of Job, this perfect and upright man repent. But if God forgave Job, MacLeish has J.B., in spite of all he'd lost and suffered, forgive God.

Sarah, his wife, does return and J.B. questions her, saying, "Why did you leave me alone?" And she replies, "I loved you. I couldn't help you any more. You wanted justice and there was none, only love." J.B. responds, "He does not love, God Is."

And Sarah counters, "But we love. That's the wonder. . . . Blow on the coal of the heart."

Archibald MacLeish gives us insight for these modern times. The cosmos doesn't conform to our standards. There are questions that do not have ready answers. The Judaic Christian heritage that indicates that there must be some purpose to injustice or suffering, both personal and collective, may not be valid. Sakini, in *Tea House of the August Moon*, philosophizes, "Pain makes us think. Thought makes us wise. Wisdom makes life endurable."

But there is not always an adequate reason for the injustice or the suffering we incur. There simply may not be a good purpose at the center of it all.

One must simply start with the living reality. One should deal with that reality as openly and as honestly as one can in the hope, but not necessarily the expectation, that one can participate in making the reality meaningful. Rainer Maria Rilke writes, "I want to beg you, as much as I can to be patient toward all that is unsettled in your heart and to try to love the questions themselves . . . do not seek the answers, which cannot be given to you because you would not be able to live them. And the point is to live everything. Live the questions now. Perhaps, you will then gradually without noticing it, live along some distant day into the answer."

Lessons from Space

FEBRUARY 2, 1986

(After the Shuttle Challenger Explosion, January 28, 1986)

*T*ODAY I WANT TO BEGIN THE SERMON with a text from the words of the poet Robert Browning:

> *"Our reach should exceed our grasp*
> *Or what's a heaven for?"*

The shuttle exploded. As we watched the most horrifying of live images, we instantly knew the most human of astronauts, Christa McAuliffe, teacher, mother, an enthusiastic and articulate person whom we had gotten to know from T.V., was dead. There would be no classes taught from space. All seven astronauts were destroyed before our eyes.

Space shuttles had become routine. Only Cable Network News thought it worthy to carry them live on television. The three major networks retained their regular programming. We have seen twenty-five perfect launchings and landings. The reusable space vehicle is a scientific and technological marvel. We see them go to space and return. We have seen astronauts repair satellites in orbit. And we have seen them as they worked, ate and even slept. By so many successes, we had been lulled into that false security, forgetting that breaking free of the earth is a hazardous undertaking. Even the participants in this tragic real-life drama seemed relaxed and calm about the launch. Christa McAuliffe, in her verve, when asked about being an astronaut, replied, "It's neat." And there was certainly no tension in her voice or foreboding in her thoughts when in the farewell to her daughter she called out, "See ya later, alligator."

But one minute and twelve seconds into flight, the shuttle was engulfed in a massive explosion. Reviewing the pictures, one sees the right solid rocket booster leaking spurts of flame just before it was all consumed in a horrible fireball. To make matters more wrenching and haunting, the faces of her parents, which turn from pride to shock and anguish as *Challenger* disintegrates before them in the Florida skies, confront us. As Alison Curling of Concord, New Hampshire, remarked: "Everyone cheered at first. Someone said, 'That's a lot of flames.' Then no one said anything. It got really quiet."

What makes this terrible loss more moving for us and seemingly to touch so many lives is that for the first time there was a non-government employee among the astronauts. She was not a professional space person. What she did, teaching, is something to which each one of us can relate. For everyone has had schoolteachers. And in this case her children, her classes, and other school classes across the country were involved, and we know how this tragedy must deeply touch and confuse their lives. We were all also more involved with this particular space shuttle adventure because Christa McAuliffe was articulate. She had been on television over the past six months. She was able to express ideas clearly and dramatically, which has not always been the forte of some of the other astronauts trained in technical science.

Television last Tuesday brought tragic reality into classrooms and homes throughout our nation. Through the T.V. lens, the global village became the global family. How many hearts skipped, as a normal launch turned into devastating tragedy? How many clutched one another for emotional support? That Tuesday evening I had a call from a father with young children who said that his family was so distraught and emotionally exhausted that he was considering postponing a trip the next day. Dr. Elliot Wineburg of Mt. Sinai Medical School in New York City captures why this event was particularly moving for this nation. He observed that Christa McAuliffe, a "highly visible, energetic young woman whose family we came to know, suddenly disappeared. She was destroyed literally in people's homes."

There are religious lessons we can all learn from this. But before I develop this theme, I think it should be pointed out that we as people on this earth have a long history confirming at least the first part of Robert Browning's words, "Our reach should exceed our grasp. . . ." Human beings have always been fascinated with this universe. Montaigne, in the sixteenth century, wrote: "All the parts of the universe I have interest in; the earth serves me to walk upon; the sun to light me; the stars to have their influence upon me." From earliest recorded times we have had a fascination with space. Egyptians had winged men; Arabs had flying carpets; and the Teutons had a hero in a winged costume.

Now these imagined riders of the sky often became victims in flight. The Greek inventor Daedalus, imprisoned with his son Icarus, built two sets of wings. He held them together with wax. But when Icarus flew too close to the sun, the wax melted, causing him to fall into the sea and drown. A similar fate befell the eleventh-century Saracen, who hoped to fly over the hippodrome of Constantinople. He rose like a bird, only "the weight of his body had more power to drag him down than his artificial wings had to sustain him up."

When it comes to actual flights above the earth, the number of accidents increases. The French balloonist Jean Pierre Blanchard was first successful in 1793 in Philadelphia. He would make fifty-nine trips. On his sixtieth ascension he sustained injuries that led to his death. The most famous and seemingly invincible pioneer of flying in the nineteenth century was a German named Otto Lilienthal, who built a fixed winged glider in 1891. After making some 2,000 glides ranging in length from 300 to 750 feet, he died some five years later testing a wing flap he had devised for better control of flight. An Englishman named Percy Pilcher took up his work. But he died in a thirty-foot glider in stormy weather. The death of these two men put experimentation on hold in Europe for more than a decade. The next significant technical leap forward occurred in the United States with the Wright brothers.

When it comes to outer space, our first encounters did not use people. That came later. Our first tragedy happened nineteen years ago when Virgil Grissom, Edward H. White and Roger Chaffee were burned to death in a fire as their *Apollo* spacecraft was being pre-tested for flight on the launching pad. A few months later Vladimir Komarov died in the recovery phase of *Soyuz I.* And in 1971, three Soviet cosmonauts died in re-entry of *Soyuz XI.* The loss of *Challenger* and the seven astronauts underscores the fact that space flight remains a pioneering endeavor, using cutting-edge technology. But the history of human beings shows that we are not deterred by adversities. We may be slowed for a moment, as occurred in Europe after the two glider deaths in the late nineteenth century. But there is that inherent indomitable spirit of the pioneer in the human being that will take people aloft again and again to unlock more of the mysteries of this marvelous universe.

Of course we now hear voices such as the physicist Fritz Rohrlick, who would end the human exploration of space. He would pull us down from new heights to play it safe. His rationale goes like this: "The Shuttle is a very complicated piece of technology. There are many things about it that could go wrong. We are fortunate that we have not had accidents before. Now is the time to place our emphasis on unmanned missions. They are much easier and less expensive because you don't have the problems of creating and maintaining surroundings in which human beings can be comfortable."

But I believe human beings will not be frightened off in their personal quest of space, any more than occurred when the first plane flights experienced many crashes. Seventy-three percent of the American public, in a poll taken this week, believe that we should continue to use people in space exploration. There have been human triumphs in space—the crew of *Discovery*, for example, in November 1984, retrieved two satellites that failed to reach the correct orbit. This could not have been done without people. It meant a sixty million dollar savings. This indomitable spirit is summed up by a fifth grader named Chris Dodd from Concord, N.H., who, while holding in his hand a drawing which Christa McAuliffe had inscribed to him, "Reach for the stars," said, "I still want to be an astronaut even though the space shuttle blew up."

There is another important lesson that comes out of the aftermath of this tragedy. Consider that we human beings can live in a collegial or an adversarial atmosphere. There is always a tug of war going on between the two. The collegial one is where there is trust, sympathy, empathy, and good will. It is one where human emotions reach out to each other in times of joy and in moments of grief. It is where you want to do the right thing as you see it because it is the good thing, not just for yourself but also for those around you.

It is in this context that the reading from the Sermon on the Mount makes sense and does not sound so naively idealistic. "Blessed are those who mourn, for they shall be comforted. Blessed are those who hunger and thirst for righteousness, for they shall be satisfied. Blessed are the merciful for they shall obtain mercy." These words took on special meaning this past Tuesday.

Speaking with our son, Rhys, in Bologna, Italy, he said that the tragedy had received much news coverage and many Italians mourned with us. As people around the world mourn, they reach out to one another and express a common sense of loss, of grief, of sadness. Most of us, following the deaths in the sky, felt humanely human and not aggressively exploitive of one another. This is an important lesson to remember. Our most hopeful destiny is tied up to this feeling of collegiality, not only in moments of crisis and tragedy but in the daily scope of our living, with its times of joy and moments of hopeful expectations.

Now a survey of history, as well as observations about contemporary society, tells us that adversarial attitudes, and not collegial ones, can often be the dominant prevailing atmosphere of a person or a community. One who visits the countries where our spiritual traditions arose, such as Israel and Greece, is reminded of the truth of this. They are little countries. The people who once lived there had no swifter means of communication than a horse. They either made war on strangers or stayed at home. They shut themselves within walled towns. They were suspicious of all outsiders. Everything unfamiliar was indicative of an enemy—even the Good Samaritan that Jesus rescued from obscurity. To the Greeks, non-Greeks were barbarians; to the Jews, non-Jews were outlanders. So even our best spiritual traditions go back to a time when everything strange—strange speech, clothes, color, customs—denoted an enemy.

Today many of these walls have been broken down. But there are still many areas of adversarial barriers that need to be brought low and a new collegial environment encouraged. Race prejudice is one. Unfortunately it still exists. It is something that requires a commitment from each one of us to reach out and care, to see the spirit of each individual in light of that person's potential and need. International relations is another. Despite the United Nations, there is little trust and much suspicion between nations. Even Israel, which would not exist without billions of dollars of support from the U.S., felt the need to use espionage against us. And I often think that the people in power go out of the way to promote hostile feelings towards others.

The word "international" was never heard of in the English language until Jeremy Bentham used it in 1780. The word "international" never passed over from England to France until about 1840, where it appeared for the first time in the dictionary of the French Academy in 1877. Across numberless ages, humanity in segregated geographical localities grew and looked with suspicion on others, with all their accompanying prejudices of race, religion and custom. Today we are forced to live in close physical proximity. Our destiny cannot rest on adversarial relationships but must embrace collegial ones. The common concern expressed in the space tragedy of this week needs repetition in less dramatic times, in the daily routines of the future.

I believe one of the worst adversarial attitudes that is increasing in force, like a hurricane, in our society is that of suing everyone over anything and demanding compensation that is more like extortion than any semblance of fairness. While most of the nation wept, there were those unsentimental, greedy, adversarial people looking for that last dollar. It has been quoted that a lawyer in F. Lee Bailey's law firm remarked that the cause of the space shuttle disaster may be unclear, but one result is fairly certain: "Lawsuits will abound."

Unreasonable damages in lawsuits are driving physicians out of the state, may put a company like Texaco into bankruptcy and are creating a climate where almost everyone becomes a potential victim of a lawsuit. If you are at all involved in your community, as a trustee of a college, a company, a non-profit organization, you are a potential object of a lawsuit.

Blame is not collegial. It is adversarial. In a tongue-in-cheek column, Judy Markey writes: "From the very beginning of world history, we have always had someone to blame. Eve blamed it on the snake. The Egyptians blamed it on the gods. The Greeks blamed it on the Romans. The Romans blamed it on the Christians. The Christians blamed in on the Jews. And so it goes. If kids hadn't been able to blame their parents, we'd never have been able to be blessed with shrinks. And if the parents hadn't been able to blame it all on stress, we'd never have been blessed with Valium."

In spite of this week's tragedy, flights into space with people will continue. And most importantly the collegial attitude shown in the aftermath of the shuttle tragedy needs to be brought into the many facets of our daily living now and in the future. Let us each attempt to put our efforts on the collegial approach to life. This points the way to a greater future!

Washington and Our Founding Values

FEBRUARY 19, 1989

THIS PAST WEEK I overheard two men talking at Harvard. One was saying to the other: "Another three-day holiday. Isn't it wonderful." We all enjoy a three-day holiday, but how many of us consider that the extra day commemorates the birthday of presidents, most especially George Washington. Do we spend time thinking of the values he and his compatriots represented?

First of all, Washington, Adams, Jefferson, Hancock and Madison were not demigods. They were like any good citizens. They had their flaws and weaknesses. The president of the United States is, after all, first among equals. We have a tendency to deify our heroes, as has been done in the religious context. The early biographers of Washington, for example, did this. They attempted to create a legend about him, which was not always correct, including the cherry tree episode. It was said: "All pens wrote with reverence and veneration." Emerson said that Washington "absorbed all the serenity of America and left none for his restless hysterical rickety countrymen." Lincoln stated that on the name of Washington: "No eulogy is expected, it cannot be. To add brightness to the sun or glory to the name of Washington is alike impossible."

Jared Sparks of Harvard, in his biography of Washington, carefully removed any strong language that Washington was quite capable of using. More recently there have been other biographers who, in order to popularize Washington, have tried to make him into something he was not—an avid churchman, an engineer, or a businessman. Others have tried to bring psychological implications into his motives and his attitudes.

Admiral Morison, in his writings, brings some balance by humanizing Washington. He wrote, "He was direct, not adroit; stubborn rather than flexible; slow to reach decision rather than a man of quick perception. But with such handicaps, he was able to develop a philosophy of life and a way of living that enabled him through self-control to become a great leader and an eminent statesman. He was able to do innumerable kind acts for others. He was completely dedicated to a civil and not a military government. He gave others a sense of confidence. He used the abilities of people such as Alexander Hamilton and Thomas Jefferson, overlooking their faults."

Thomas Jefferson made a most fitting tribute to Washington's role in controlling the military when he observed, "The moderation and virtue of a single character had probably prevented this revolution from being closed as most others have been by subversion of that liberty it was intended to establish."

There are values and ideas that we associate with our founders that need recreating in every generation. It was Guizot of France who asked James Russell Lowell, "How long do you think the American Republic will endure?" And Lowell replied, "So long as the values and ideas of its founders continue to be dominant."

What values did Washington and other founders of our nation embody? First, they had faith in something larger and better than that which existed. An excerpt from Edwin D. Mead's "Epistle to the Americans" illustrates this. Mead paraphrases Paul's epistle to the Hebrews ("Faith is the substance of things hoped for, the evidence of things not seen. . . ."): "By faith the pilgrims, when they were called to go out into a place which they should afterward receive for an inheritance, obeyed; and they went out, not knowing whither they went. By faith they sojourned in a land of promise, as in a strange country, with John Winthrop, John Cotton and Roger Williams, heirs with them of the same promise. By faith Sam Adams refused to admit of bondage and was not afraid of the king. By faith Washington drew his sword and Jefferson saw that which was then invisible."

Second, our founders had a measure of ethical religion. The first four presidents appear to have been deists. They were not irrational about religion. They believed in reason to understand life and to improve it. Washington was christened in the Church of England and occasionally attended services. He was tolerant of other people's beliefs. In a letter to a Swedenborgian Church in Baltimore, he wrote, "In this enlightened age and in this land of liberty, it is our boast that a man's religious tenets will not forfeit the protection of the law or deprive him of the right of obtaining and holding the highest offices that are known in the United States." Washington was schooled in the Bible. He often used Biblical metaphor to illustrate a message. In his speeches you will find such as the man "who looked forward to the day when everyone could sit under his own vine and his fig tree and there shall be none to make him afraid." He hailed the west as "the second land of promise." Washington, Adams, Jefferson and many of our early leaders saw religion in a larger context. Washington gained inspiration from Marcus Aurelius and other stoic philosophers. The religious beliefs of our early leaders led them to value simplicity of living, a calm acceptance of life, duty to the nation, generosity to their fellow human beings and unfaltering courage.

How badly we need these religious values today. And how frightening is the existence of religious bigotry and hate. Khomeni's death threat to author Salman Rushdie for writing *The Satanic Verses* is a vivid example of religious terrorism.

Third, our founding leaders were lovers of liberty. Washington took undisciplined farmers and storekeepers and molded them into a force able to defeat the royal British army. We think of Yorktown, Philadelphia and Boston. These early Americans believed in freedom and this belief gave them an undeniable and invincible passion for self-government. That is why Paul Revere made his ride. That is why the farmers stood their ground on the Lexington Green and at the North Bridge.

That is why they worked on a Bill of Rights as well as upon the Constitution.

When we pledge allegiance to the flag of the United States of America, we refer to it as representing "one nation under God, indivisible, with liberty and justice for all." Sometimes in our history, people have enjoyed liberty and have forgotten its responsibilities.

A story goes that a bookie was to be brought before the court because of his illegal activities. A friend, trying to console him, said, "The judge that will hear your case is very fair-minded and known for his sense of justice." The bookie deject-edly responded, "I don't want justice, I need mercy." The values at the beginning of our nation were responsible liberty, justice, and often mercy.

A fourth value we need to mention is honesty. We associate honesty with our first president. I wish we could associate it with all our presidents. I do not believe that Washington, Jefferson or Lincoln would have lied to the nation about Cambodia or would have been involved in a situation such as Watergate. Society breaks down when you cannot trust people. Dishonesty and lying do not make a flourishing nation. Public office is a public trust. John Adams was in this spirit. He could not cast a hypo-critical vote. His integrity was most important to him. Quite unlike Frank Sinatra who, a few years ago when his honesty was questioned, said in Las Vegas that he did not feel accountable to any other person in the world.

A fifth value that Washington emulated was discipline. He embraced the Protestant work ethic. If the early settlers of this country had had an eight-hour day, this land would not have developed into a strong nation. The desire to dodge work, to get something for nothing, was not part of the make-up of those who fought for freedom in our Revolution. Washington, as I said, embraced more than a religion of ritual and form. He had the work ethic of a stoic. A stoic never evades responsibilities. The self-discipline of Washington came out of the totality of his life experiences. The handling of horses, which he learned at an early age, was a way of learning discipline. If you cannot control yourself, you can never control a spirited horse. This stoic self-disciplined philosophy enabled Washington to transform himself from a youthful person who was insecure, aggressive, headstrong, uninhibited and self-centered into a disciplined individual.

The English writer, Samuel T. Coleridge, said upon Washington's death: "Tranquil and firm, he moved with one pace in one path, and neither vaulted nor tottered. Among a people eminently querulous and already impregnated with the germs of discordant parties, he directed the executive position firmly and unostentatiously. He had no vain conceit of being himself all, and did those things only which he could do." It was self-discipline that stood him well in heading the armed forces and as the first president of this nation.

Washington gained from this self-discipline other qualities. Humility was one of these. Upon being elected president, Washington had no illusion about himself or a republic that had never worked on so large a scale. He wrote to General Knox that he faced "an ocean of difficulties without the competency of political skill, abilities and inclinations which are necessary to manage the helm." He was realistic then, as he had been throughout his life. The new government had to create its own machinery. Previous revolutions in Europe and Asia had taken over a corps of officials and a treasury. The American Confederation had left nothing but a dozen clerks with their pay in arrears, an empty treasury, and a burden of debt. The Army consisted of 672 men including officers. The Navy had ceased to exist.

Washington was sensitive to anti-federalist feelings. To show his simplicity, he appeared at his inauguration in a brown homespun suit instead of English broadcloth or military uniform.

One final value should be mentioned. Washington and his contemporaries had an exceptional cause. To what extent do most of the people in our country today feel concerned about any cause? To what would they give "their lives, their fortunes and their sacred honor?" The founders of this nation were inspired by the vision of a brave new world, which they thought it was their destiny to pursue. How many of us have such a vision and such a commitment? For Washington's contemporaries the birth of a nation produced excitement and responsibility. Are the values of our founders to perish because we do not care about them anymore? America's experiment has existed for 213 years. It can exist far into the future if we are true to our founders' values and the best that is in us.

Each one of us should remember what Washington did with his life. Although not the most talented or skilled, through self-discipline, through an openness to obtain knowledge and wisdom not only from books, including the Bible, but from people and experiences, he moved from being a narrow partisan individual to one who was magnanimous, inspirational and charismatic. He united an exploited people looking for hope.

The values of faith in something greater than what currently exists, a religion that is rational and open, liberty, honesty, self-discipline, and a sense of responsibility provide a moral foundation to build a great future. Edward Everett Hale, in his biography of Washington, wrote: "It is undoubtedly Washington's moral force which gave him his command and his influence. It is not that he wrote English as well as Fairfax. It is not that he understood the Constitution as well as John Adams. It is not that he was as skillful in tactics as Cornwallis. It is not that in compelling jarring factions to agree on a public policy he was stronger than any man of his time, or anyone since. It is, that in the efforts that he made in such directions . . . his intellectual and physical force were subordinated to his sense of duty. He did what he thought he ought to do."

More than a year before the Declaration of Independence was written, Washington wrote to his brother, ". . . it is my full intention to devote my life and fortune to the cause we are engaged in." The signers of the Declaration pledged "their lives, their fortunes and their sacred honour." Are we worthy of this heritage?

Developing a
Survivor Personality

JANUARY 7, 1990

$\mathcal{E}$NTERING THE LAST DECADE before a new century, like the cave of Aeolus of Greek legend where the winds were purportedly born, our minds are full of change. Whether it is joy over the dramatic changes in Eastern Europe or bewilderment over a nation with an expenditure of billions of dollars for the military or shock over Charles Stuart's apparent cold-blooded premeditated murder of his wife that has increased racial fears and animosities, who of us has not become aware during these recent days of the powerfully dominant importance of our emotions? Rather than dealing with some of the global issues, let us concentrate this morning on how we, on a personal level in these times of rapid change, may develop survivor personalities.

Emotions make life worth living. "The fruit of the spirit," wrote Paul, "is love, joy, peace." We exist for the hours when our feelings are touched responsively by happy issues. Yet emotions also can make life utterly intolerable: grief, despondency, hatred, guilt, jealousy, despair. Emotions are the driving power of life. From the fear engendered by being chased by a raging bull that could enable one to leap over a fence that normally could not be scaled, to those moved by love to self-sacrifice, the healthy emotional life of human beings releases energy that can create incalculable results. Fear, however, and other negative emotions such as rage, jealousy, and hatred may tear people to pieces.

Your religious and moral beliefs play an important role in your emotions. When your intellectual beliefs and spiritual life coincide, religion will be a powerful positive factor in handling your emotions and making you a survivor personality. When these beliefs say one thing and your dominant emotions are jealousy or anger, then your life is in conflict.

Jesus describes his life in emotional terms. He was not anti-intellectual, for great ideas permeated his thoughts. "Love your neighbor as yourself." Everywhere in the Gospels, Jesus faces the inner depths of people's emotions. Long before modern psychologists came along, Jesus showed that only an emotion could cure an emotion. You cannot drive out hate with an idea alone. You cannot eliminate despair with a logical concept. Only hope can rid you of despair. It takes one emotion to fully eliminate another emotion.

In Victor Frankl's *Man's Search for Meaning*, the psychiatrist recounts his experience in a concentration camp during World War II. At one point he was especially depressed. But then, in the midst of the horrors on which he was dwelling, he had a feeling of hope. "I turned my thoughts to another subject," he wrote. "Suddenly I saw myself standing on the platform of a well-lit, warm and pleasant lecture room. In front of me sat an attentive audience on comfortable upholstered seats. I was giving a lecture on the psychology of the concentration camp! All that oppressed me at that moment became objectively seen and described from the remote viewpoint of science. Both I and my troubles became the object of an interesting psycho-scientific study undertaken by myself." And so he survived another day. He chose to let a different attitude, a different emotion take control of his life. This is something you and I also may do.

But people do not always feel they have this option. Perhaps their personalities have been shaped by negative experiences in early life. These early experiences can have consequences for both mental and physical health. How people grow up psychologically will have an effect on what happens to them physiologically. The greatest emotion that needs to be affirmed from the time we are born is love. Lack of love in early childhood, resulting in psychological and sometimes physical abuse, may predispose us to a hopeless-helpless attitude and to physical disease later in life.

Dr. Ashley Montague, who wrote about the human condition in the 1950s and '60s once addressed a group of healthcare givers. He posed this question to his audience: "How can you demonstrate lack of love on an x-ray?" This anthropologist explained that when children are not loved, their physical growth might be severely hampered. He pointed out dense lines that can be seen in x-rays of their bones, indicating periods when love was lacking and growth did not occur.

If there is physical impairment from lack of love, there is a similar psychological burden which is often more devastating. Many of us have come to smile on the outside when we are hurting on the inside, but this may have a depressant effect on us later on in life.

When you express your feelings, you may heal inside. Many people, however, find this difficult to do. For it goes against life-long habits that, learned in childhood, enabled one to purportedly cope. The inexpressive emotional style is learned very early as a reaction to parents who do not respond to the infant's expressions of needs. When the emotions are either ignored or actively rejected or punished, the child may simply shut down emotionally and become withdrawn, blaming himself or herself for the lack of attention. This in turn lowers self-esteem and heightens the feeling of guilt. The message from childhood becomes "You are not worthy. No matter what you do, it is not enough." So you feel bad about yourself. That is why the Christening and dedication service is an important religious commitment by parents, godparents and other family members to affirm and nurture the child with love.

Unfortunately some religions have played on the strong emotion of guilt. The Bible describes an annual ceremony that the Jews still celebrate as their highest of holy days—Yom Kippur, the Day of Atonement. Back in Moses' time, they laid their sins literally on a goat that was then sacrificed. "Scapegoating" continues today in other forms, but it doesn't always work. Guilt does not transfer easily. Neither does the traditional Christian "Christ Atonement" have meaning for numerous individuals.

Many Christians, however, still believe atonement comes through faith in Jesus' dying on the cross for their sins.

Some people have never been satisfied with these standard theories. One of these was Peter Abelard, who in the twelfth century stated that the suffering on the cross was to change us, not God, by way of example. Jesus, he said, showed us how to overcome evil or sin by the emotion and act of love. This early twelfth-century idea influenced both the sixteenth century Socinians in Poland and the Unitarians in Transylvania, now mostly in Romania. It was the foundation idea for Hosea Ballou, the nineteenth-century Universalist, who believed not in the idea of saved and unsaved but in universal salvation.

The survivor personality of this decade needs to remember this! Are you carrying guilt imposed upon you by others? Is this guilt holding you back, making you feel bad about yourself, slowing you down, and taking the joy out of living? Here is a very simple question to test yourself. Someone asks you to do a favor. But you are tired, perhaps overwhelmed by commitments at the moment. You really do not want to do it. If you say "no," will you feel guilty? The survivor personality needs to come to the realization that compliance, conformity, constant self-sacrifice, denial of hostility and anger can breed guilt in your mind and danger for the health of your mind and body. This does not mean you should become a self-centered human being, refusing all requests from others. But it does indicate that you do not have to feel guilty if you do not want to do something that is requested of you.

Jesus understood that he could not reach the depths of human nature and transform it with just logical arguments.

Throughout his ministry he was trying to displace hate with love, fear with courage, envy with good will, covetousness with unselfishness, anxiety with peace.

For decades fear was a dominant emotion for most people in Romania. Typewriters were all registered. Several years ago in visiting Romanians in their homes, if they wanted to say anything critical of the government, they placed a pillow over the phone or would go outside. They could be taken from their home and if they disappeared, no one would know what happened to them. The freed Romanian Television showed this past week a torture chamber of the Securitate. The Securitate were Ceausescu's secret police, which for blind loyalty were given bountiful provisions and privileges. Many of them were orphans taken at birth or at a young age and indoctrinated to hate and kill anyone who opposed Ceausescu and his family. The television showed a charred corpse lying on a table in a concrete room, electric wires binding the wrists. All about were handfuls of human hair. It was the last panicky horror of brutes, seeking to terrify people back into submission. The Ceausescu regime was not merely oppressive, it was barbarous.

Most Romanians lived in tremendous fear. It was an emotion that was constantly with them. But this December in Transylvania when there was a protest against the regime, which was met by bullets, the people did not retreat. They traded the emotion of fear for the emotion of courage. They stood firm, though many were mowed down by the Securitate. Word of their bravery reached Bucharest and other parts of Romania. People everywhere cast aside the insidious fear of decades and with courage transformed a despotic nation into a freer one.

New emotions took hold of the Romanian people. If courage had driven out fear, another negative emotion came to the fore, revenge. The revolution of a degraded people called forth and inspired a response, which was in itself inevitably degrading. But if hate and revenge seemed to sweep through the Romanian people, it was exorcised by the quick secret trial and the death of the Ceausescus. Hope has entered into the lives of these people. The death penalty has been outlawed. Food has been made more available.

Today let us examine our emotions and choose those that enhance our ability to survive healthfully and happily. One factor in developing positive emotions is to have some measure of control over them. The Romanian people for so long did not have control over their lives. Thus they were swept by sadness, fear, resentment and anger. And under the circumstances in which they lived, they held these emotions inside. In a free nation and a free religious faith, you may control these negative emotions by releasing them. Replace them in your mind with a picture of what you truly want and enjoy in life. When negative images like resentment flash before you, do not make room for them. You can refocus on images that evoke feelings of peace and joy, love and happiness, as did Victor Frankl in the concentration camp. You bring control into your life by accepting and liking yourself, and by so doing, you will find that it is easier to like and appreciate the people with whom you associate.

A second factor in having positive emotions is having the right commitments. You have the freedom that the Romanians gave their blood to obtain. But in your freedom, is your commitment to excessive individualism, isolation and inevitable loneliness? Is it formulated in consumption, materialism and pervasive greed? By making a positive contribution to your church and community, through some form of work or service that you value and enjoy, by making a commitment to your health and well-being, by keeping abreast of the needs of the community and the issues of the day, you can fill your life with the emotions that elevate your well-being.

A third factor in having positive emotions is seeing life as a challenge but not hopeless. It is looking out with a perspective such that what others may find threatening, you find challenging. Augustine wrote, "Hope has two beautiful daughters. Their names are anger and courage: anger, the way things are and courage to see that they do not remain the way they are." The emotion of anger has its place as a starter to set things right. It can lead to courage to see that this is done. Fear held Eastern Europe captive for decades, but anger triggered the courage to change oppression to freedom. To see problems as a challenge and not as hopeless helplessness is your ticket to emotional health.

A teenager named Susan moved to a new community. Her mother encouraged her to do volunteer service before beginning school in the fall. She volunteered at a nursing home where she was asked to read to a resident. She introduced herself to a Mr. Jones and asked him how he was. "I'm all right so far," he told her. "What does that mean?" she asked him. "I'm like the man who falls out of a window at the top of a thirty-story building. Each floor you go by, people lean out and say, 'How are you?' and you say, 'I'm all right so far'." "I'm all right so far" can get you through many things.

The great issues of your life spring from and essentially involve your emotions. The survivor personality will use the control and the challenge to keep the positive emotions in focus. This will provide the inner peace that makes life worth living.

Let me close then with some suggestions that should help you develop a survivor personality:

1. Think and act more spontaneously rather than on fears based on past experience.
2. Replace worry with positive thoughts.
3. Think each day of something to enjoy.
4. Lessen your interest in constantly judging other people and in negatively interpreting their actions.
5. Express appreciation.
6. Smile.
7. Feel a connectedness with others and nature.
8. Accept acts of kindness extended to you by others and extend kindness to them.

When positive emotions become a part your life, your spirit is virtually indestructible. Its ability to rise from the ashes as we have seen in Eastern Europe remains as long as the body draws breath. May you possess a survivor personality for many years to come!

Loneliness vs.
Interdependence:
A Sunday in Romania

SEPTEMBER 23, 1990

THE HUMAN RACE IS MADE UP of people who live in different cultures, speak different languages and subscribe to different religious beliefs. But despite these differences, all humans struggle at some point in their lives with loneliness. Loneliness is as natural a part of being human as are hunger, joy and grief.

Looking at ancient societies where there was less knowledge and more interdependence, loneliness seems not to have been a major factor. This we deduce by the dearth of writings concerning loneliness. I can find, for example, only one reference to loneliness in the Old Testament. The 102nd Psalm contains this thought: "I cannot sleep, I mourn like a lonely bird on the roof; all day long my foes are taunting me, those who mock me call me the accursed." There are in the entire Bible a few episodes regarding being alone, but they do not often refer to being lonely. In Jeremiah we read of him talking to God and saying (15:17), "I never joined the festive band, I never rejoiced; I sat alone under thine hand, sharing all thine indignation." There are a few places in the New Testament where we learn that Jesus is alone, but the passages do not speak of loneliness. In Matthew, for example, we read, "After he had dismissed the crowds, he went up the hill to pray by himself." When Jesus wanted to be alone, it was more in the spirit of solitude. That is, to be alone, free to think one's own thoughts, to live in a world of one's own dreaming. When solitude is one's chosen desire, it may be a delight.

These thoughts concerning loneliness and the idea of interdependence versus loneliness, I expressed this past July, standing before the congregation of our sister church in Cluj, Romania. The twenty-minute sermon in English was edited down to nine minutes to allow for translation. Members of the Unitarian churches in Romania are Hungarians. They refer to the city of Cluj as Kolozsvar. The Hungarian language, which is used in these churches, requires more words than English to convey the same thoughts. Over the past fifty years, no one in this area has been encouraged to learn English; hence very few people including the clergy understand it. Bishop Lajos Kovacs, who is almost eighty years of age, but vigorous and proficient in English, translated to the Hungarian-speaking congregation.

The Unitarian churches in Romania are located in the western part of the country in the area known as Transylvania. This section was part of the Austro-Hungarian Empire until after World War I when it was given to Romania by the allies. During the past years, Romanians have been encouraged to settle there; hence the Hungarian population is now in the minority. Though the Hungarians have lived in Transylvania for centuries, many Romanians would like the Hungarians to leave this area and resettle in Hungary.

As I stand before this filled church in Cluj, while my opening remarks are being translated, my thoughts try to integrate the experiences of the past few days. I realize that when I speak about the interdependence of people in ancient societies, this also reflects on the current status of life in Romania. These people are interdependent, because basically, they only have each other; they need each other. The choices, the wealth, the independence with its ensuing loneliness we know in our country do not exist there. With the shelves empty of all types of goods, of food, of wine, with no sugar to preserve the fruits of the summer, with mile-long lines of cars waiting for gasoline (the drivers taking shifts before finally pushing the car up to a pump), it is obvious that they need each other to survive.

The previous day we had been driven to the town of Torda in the recently provided Volkswagen van given to the Unitarian Churches in Romania by the World Council of Churches. In Torda, in 1568, through the preaching of Francis David, the then King Sigismund, ruler of this Transylvania land, was so convinced by David's idea of religious toleration that he issued an edict allowing religious freedom. This was the first act in Europe to grant religious freedom of belief. Visiting in the home of the minister of one of the Unitarian churches of Torda, we were graciously entertained with conversation, with cakes and cookies, homemade wine and plum brandy, the only spirits available to the general population, and coffee with sugar, the latter two items officially unattainable. This was probably a community effort to show hospitality to western visitors.

Certainly the full church attendance in Cluj on Sunday was the result of the cooperative effort of the nearby Reformed Presbyterian Church whose minister held his service earlier so that he and his congregation could attend the service at which I was to preach. Not only because of scarcity of goods are these people interdependent; not only do they have a common community among the several Christian faiths, but also they are together because of fear.

The residue of fear that still exists from the dictatorial Ceausescu regime mars the ideal of religious freedom offered at Torda in 1568. We learned of this from the minister in whose home we visited in Torda. There, with his wife, grown children and grandchildren, we saw a man strung out to the limit of endurance. Bishop Kovacs translates and we hear that twice recently a Romanian who worked for the Securitate has visited him. The Securitate were the secret police of the fallen dictator, Ceausescu. Although officially banned by the new regime, this man and other former Securitate members are still using past practices of threats and intimidation. The conversation between the Bishop and this minister was tense and extended. The former Securitate man had asked him: "What are you preaching about? Why does your wife visit your daughter in Hungary? What do you talk about when your daughter visits you? Be careful. You are being watched." This minister and his family were obviously distraught and focused on the dangers set before them. "The Securitate is supposed to be disbanded," he said. "Why do they harass me? If this happens again I will make a complaint to the Hungarian press." These Hungarians in Romania are interdependent in order to survive physically and psychologically. They extend helping hands to one another.

That July morning on the way to church, Eleanor and I passed a cross at a street corner in Cluj. It marks the area where last December 22, forty citizens lost their lives in protest against the Ceausescu regime before the army deserted the dictator. Many of these people had the courage to master their own inner destiny. They possessed an inner spiritual citadel that was impregnable to outward attack. So when the opportunity arose, they seized it, becoming in the paraphrased words of Henley, "masters of their fate; captains of their souls." They threw over the outward yoke of oppression. Although we may question just how much freedom from fear of government they have now, life is certainly far more open and more hopeful than before last December 22.

I continued with my sermon that July morning, going on to say that loneliness and unhappiness are part of the human culture. Although common to all people, the nature of loneliness is a subjective experience and it varies from person to person. I asked them and I ask you to turn to loneliness and your own life. There are at least two different kinds of loneliness that touch the modern person. One kind is experienced by those people who are almost always lonely. I experienced this sense when I was growing up on Vancouver Island, British Columbia, Canada. My father was often away as a foreign correspondent. The twelve-grade school was housed in a wooden three-room building with no running water. I reached the school by walking for three miles along a gravel road. I was an only child and the only American in the school. Within one mile of my home, there was only one boy my age. He lived on a farm where the family barely made a living. He had many chores after school. And if there was to be any time to play, I learned to help him with such activities as the milking of cows. In the winter during storms, we evacuated the house for fear the trees would fall, crashing through the roof.

Several summers during droughts we were evacuated as forest fires neared and the direction of the wind could bring roaring flames across our escape route. After attending a high school in rural northern Vermont and college in rural northern New York State, I resolved that when I was in control of my life I would fix this isolated loneliness. I have lived in cities ever since and I have loved it.

A second kind of loneliness is the type that is triggered by some significant event in our lives; an event that makes us feel that something unique has happened to us and that no one else can really understand what we are facing. Such events may be of many sorts: bereavement, divorce, job loss, severe illness, and the last child going off on her or his own, leaving your home. These are events which require a change in your lifestyle, your daily routine. They may require a change of attitude or a re-evaluation of your personal value system. This second kind of loneliness, triggered by some major event, is universal because each one of us will experience it at some juncture of our lives. Loneliness in this context is the felt absence of one or more interpersonal relationships in an individual's life. Loneliness is the absence of another's trust and love.

We know that when we have anxiety or a vague unease about some unspecific threat to our sense of well-being, we can best relieve it by sharing it with someone we care about and trust. If we cannot share these feelings, they will cause loneliness. I contrast this with the very necessary and useful emotion we call fear, which is a reasonable concern over an identifiable and specific threat about which something may be done. We can get inoculations for certain diseases, which give us a better chance to live a long life. But against anxiety caused by some unspecific and imagined threat, it is necessary to reach out to someone you trust.

As I was preparing this sermon for today, I reflected on the warm reception of the extended families we had visited. Certainly this ministerial family of our sister church had opened their arms to us. From the booming voice of greeting by the Rev. Sandor Benedek to the exchange of pronouncements of friendship, the toasts made, the dinner with vegetables from their garden and chicken from their farm, the supper provided for our eight-hour train journey back to Budapest and the giving of gifts, I cannot help but feel moved and to sense both rapport and trust with these people. Having so little to give materially, they give of their collective selves. I made a note in my diary, "Regardless of the external problem, you are not alone when friendship is shared. In the Transylvanian homes we visited, in a country of shortages and repression, you sense the interdependence of family and generations."

There is certainly a rural isolation at night with minimal, if any, lighted streetlights. To arrive in Cluj at 1:30 in the morning, following blackouts in the train cars after crossing the border into Romania, to stumble down unlit stairwells and drive in a taxi that only uses its lights at intersections, is to sense isolation from your fellow human beings. There is also another type of isolation for these people—the difficulty of travel. Due to the strict border controls, and the impossibility of obtaining hard currency, people are unable to travel outside the country. Thus, if they travel, they are dependent on friends and relatives abroad.

They also have been isolated from the technical tools of modern societies. This shows up in their work habits. Around the free world there has been a growing sense of equality, an integration of skills. When I first came to Boston, I dictated my sermons. Today I use a computer. My capacities to do my job have expanded. After we decided on the sermon I was to deliver, Bishop Kovacs wanted a copy so he could translate it into Hungarian before the service. He triumphantly said, "We can copy it on the new Xerox given us by the IARF (International Association of Religious Freedom)." But then he frowned and remarked, "Since the revolution we don't have any office staff on Saturdays." He and the minister of our sister church looked at the machine in dismay.

Fortunately such machines have become part of the ministry of most of us in the United States. I made a copy for them. Because of the isolation from other nations, the technical tools and approaches used in Western nations are just beginning to find their way into the practices of the Romanian people. Hence they feel a certain loneliness due to status and compartmentalization of job expectations.

For us today in the United States, loneliness is more acute because of our modern, mobile Western society. Lifelong friends are scarce. There are more unsettling events making the experiences of those we trust different from our own. Thus there may be fewer people to whom we can turn, feeling they will truly empathize and understand us, for they have not walked in our shoes and we have not shared enough common experiences with them.

Any church is fulfilling a vital function if it has good caring people to provide the bridge out of loneliness. Establishing close relationships is among the most effective ways of coping with loneliness. Perhaps you are in the midst of a stressful change and you know the pathos of loneliness. Look for someone here to be a bridge for you. There are words of encouragement and poetry to be memorized and repeated as good friends when lonely moments sweep over you. Think of those you know who may be lonely; give them a helping hand.

We should not have to experience external hardships to feel an interdependence with and concern for our fellow human beings. What a great opportunity we have now to enlarge our circle of concern and community. Let us resolve to be as fully human as we can, reaching out to touch someone. Let us not "mourn like a lonely bird on a roof" but reach out to share our hopes and dreams with others and listen as well to them. For, as it has been said, "All that we give into the life of others comes back into our very own." Give, then, warmly and caringly to others, and you will not walk alone.

What Is
Religious Experience?

JANUARY 31, 1994

*R*ELIGIOUS EXPERIENCE IS UNIQUE with each person. Any definition cannot capture the pulsating aliveness that can exist in a personal experience. Though Unitarian Universalists treasure the rational approach to life, there is emotion that enters into our religious experience. Religious feeling is older than any historic culture and arose before it was given a name. Although feeling is important in a religious experience, it is only fully realized by creatures that have the capacity for and use logical thought. It includes a keen awareness of and response to reality and a haunting sense of something more, a mystery within and beyond.

In the childhood of the human race, feeling was a powerful factor in people's lives. In this postmodern era, religious experience has dimmed for many persons. The awe, the astonishment, and certainly the fear that our ancient ancestors felt are no longer part of many individual lives. We do not need a return to their perceived fears, but a little more appreciation and wonder in life today would make our lives richer.

We as a species can face the universe and stand in awe of the immense otherness. In the beginning among the human race, there was dread and terror mingled with the awe. A great swell of emotion arose with our early ancestors, who were over-whelmed by the external powers that changed their lives, threat-ened their destiny. We are distressed by damage from hurricanes and earthquakes, but to those ancient people the crashing of thunder, the disruption from earthquakes, and fathomless space sprinkled with stars were factors beyond their comprehension.

Every form of life has an environment in which it adapts to survive. Men and women are adaptable creatures. We extend our vital domain from desert to fertile valley, from river basin to mountain plateau, from the tropics to the polar regions and now even to space. But unlike other forms of life, our physical domain does not limit us.

In your mind you may visit countless places, talk with numerous people, including those close to you who are no longer physically with you. However you perceive the universe, your spirit cannot be restricted to a closed domain any more than your mind can be limited to your physical surroundings. A reli-gious experience is a sign that you possess a larger vision of the world beyond its physical dimensions.

I recall speaking with a professor from what was then called Leningrad in the summer of 1959. We were traveling in a ship on the Black Sea from Sochi to Odessa. The old Soviet Union had just opened to tourists the previous year and Americans were a great curiosity. This professor wanted to talk but not inside. "We would be bugged," he declared. So out on deck we went for our conversation. The gist of it was that he wished to speak about religion. He told me, "I would lose my professorship if I openly worshipped. So I breathe deeply and meditate to bring me into some religious focus with the larger universe around me." The religious experience is being able to face the universe, to feel part of it, to be at one with it. This is the basic religious experience from which the historic religions arose.

Modern life often isolates us from that sense of oneness with a larger purpose beyond our finiteness. From the artificial neon and streetlights hiding the stars, to the impersonal violence of modern means of destruction, we are separated from the religious experiences of our primitive past.

Religious experience may be a powerful feeling, a response to the tremendous mystery of the stupendous otherness that human beings confront. To some this has a dimension of dread and vastness, but to others it is a quieter and more prolonged contemplative experience. It may be an overwhelming and exalting tide of emotion that arises in our religious services. This happens to many who attend the Living Tradition Service at the UU General Assembly as the delegates rise to sing the processional hymn "Rank by Rank We Stand." These and others are fresh, personal experiences. No one may have them for anyone else. No one can truly convey them in words.

There are several aspects of religious experience. There is often a feeling of dependence. This occurs when our minds give consent that in the final instance we are dependent upon forces we do not totally control. There is a feeling of wonder, the kind of wonder which Socrates said is the beginning of wisdom. There is also awe, which says, "Let the earth keep silent," or that feels this and is speechless. Out of wonder and awe comes reverence in which the mystery that was feared can become loved. When love takes over from fear, you have what Schweitzer called the ethic of Reverence for Life. Out of this comes worship, which Carlyle called the transcendent wonder.

If there is a feeling of smallness before the majestic and the sublime, there is also a feeling of exaltation, of being touched with grandeur. "For thou has made man (woman) a little lower than the angels and have crowned (them) with glory and honor." A more modern voice expressed this after contemplating the stars on a clear night: "For I know that I am honored to be witness to so much majesty."

Reverence is a key word of religious experience. It was the center of Confucius' and Albert Schweitzer's philosophies. Plato in *The Laws* speaks of teaching children the spirit of reverence as being more important than all the gold in the world.

Reverence is also basic to the experience we call community with another or with many. Reverence often occurs in a setting where silence and not words establishes the mood. The silent meeting of a Friends Meeting is an example. Just being there and holding the hand of a patient in the hospital can become a religious experience for both individuals. Emerson wrote, "I like the silent church before the service begins . . . better than any preach-ing." In the silent church, as contrasted to a noisy togetherness, one can sense with awe that mystery in the otherness of persons and feel a kinship with them.

This feeling response to wonder, to the reverence of another human being, is in theological terms called the "Thou" of another person. Martin Buber, in his book *I and Thou* says that this experience is not constant. We do not face the universe and always encounter the same grandeur of our surroundings. Sometimes the feeling response is not there. Sometimes the world around us seems a great "it," a thing to be used or analyzed. "Twinkle, twinkle little star. We know precisely what you are. We've measured your size and found your mass; you're not a star, you are helium gas." But when we feel a relation to the universe in all its vastness and wonder, though often unexpressed, we have an intense feeling of the holy.

In our relationships with others, we do not always experience reverence. Sometimes that other person is an "it," hopefully a neutral "it" and not one to which violence might be done. Another person becomes a neutral "it" when one analyzes with-out compassion, concern, or reverence. When you turn to anoth-er inwardly and with your whole self, and when another person does the same thing towards you, then there is a living presence, one with the other. Martin Buber said that when this meeting takes place, a ray of the eternal "Thou" comes to the one through the other. There is that awareness of a mystery before which you stand in awe. This is the primary religious experience. It is reverence and awe towards the universe and towards others.

Since we can do little with the great universe except to be inspired by it, our primary religious experiences should focus on our fellow human beings. This is expressed in work done in the spirit of community; thus, social experiences can become religious ones.

A social experience becomes a religious experience when there is a reverential feeling towards the other. Religious togetherness is community in which people walk, not in goose-step under external compulsion, but willingly with one another. Within community we find comfort, guidance and support. In return we feel reverence, commitment and at times self-sacrifice.

Sacrifice is part of the religious experience. All people may sacrifice. The issue is: what is the sacrifice for? Sacrifice can lead to religious experience or to the dead end of self-serving gain, or worse, to destructiveness towards others. Appalling evil can come from self-sacrifice. Self-sacrifice in and of itself is not an ideal; rather the sacrifice that is made needs an ideal at its root. Too often sacrifice is commonly presented as a dour duty, phrased in the forbidding terms of a moral imperative. We ought to sacrifice, we say; it is our obligation. Only when the sacrifice has the element of love, of reverence and is an unselfish sacrifice does it take on dimensions of a religious experience.

Jesus remarked, "I came that they may have life and may have it more abundantly." What does this mean in terms of your daily life? It is to lose your life by embracing something greater than your present self. Devote yourself, therefore, to a task, to a cause, to a faith, to a person worth your love and service.

Today we think of nursing as a great art that reaches out to help people who are ill. At one time it was not considered an honorable profession any more than Hollywood enjoyed acceptability in the society of the 1920s. Florence Nightingale faced this dilemma. She was keenly aware of the pathos of human beings with health problems. She saw a need to reach out and embrace. Her family, on the other hand, highly disapproved of the nursing profession. Her family did not recognize the love or compassion that came with her commitment. Her biographer writes: "Florence felt that everything she said or did was a subject of vexation to her sister, a disappointment for her mother, a worry to her father." She wrote to her mother: "I should be as happy here as the day is long if I could hope that I had your smile, your blessing, your sympathy, without which I cannot be happy. Give me time, give me faith, trust me, help me. I feel within me so much that I could gladden your loving hearts which I now wound." Florence Nightingale felt that she must, if necessary, sacrifice family acceptance for a greater goal and calling of love and reverence towards a larger body of humanity.

The hallowing of an activity can be a religious experience: tending a garden, teaching a child, patiently observing and seeking to understand what is necessary to improve the human condition. It is in the hallowing of these and other everyday activities, through seeking to include them in your affections and aspirations, that you feel a religious experience. It is a personal experience. It occurs when you face another person and feel a reverential oneness between you. It occurs when you are deeply moved by music, art, and the colors and sounds of nature to contemplate with reverence the grandeur, mystery or ecstasy you feel. It occurs when you face the universe and feel with awe that you are an intrinsic part.

To Be Our Best

MAY 7, 1995

D R. CHRISTIAN BARNARD performed the first successful heart transplant in Cape Town, South Africa in the 1970s. There was a dramatic reaction worldwide. Doctors rushed to duplicate the feat. Enthusiasts began to predict that in time medical science would be able to overcome the negative results of any of our detrimental living habits. Consequently, the time was coming when we might eat anything, behave indulgently and pursue any undisciplined course because medical science would be there to save us. An organ breaks down, but surgical medicine is there to replace it. The heart could be like an automobile tire, replaceable after so many miles, or in human terms, after so many years. But the aura that everything is going to be all right began to pale. New organs, and there are too few for the demand, do not by themselves build better lives.

James L. Lynch, in his book *The Broken Heart*, says that the heart transplant operation made it clear that the physician, the human element, was in danger of being purged from medicine and being replaced by techniques, pumps, valves and drugs. Even if these are successful, something is still missing. Scientific skill does not drive away the hate, greed and exploitation that are part of human life. No matter how many organ transplants or new medical techniques we perform, human beings continue to behave in their own typical ways. Something more is needed in the human equation. It is a lifelong struggle to be our best, to lift ourselves out of life's tangles and troubles.

Eric Hoofer once warned, "It is easy to be full of rage. It is not so easy to go to work and build something." Albert Camus noted: "Like many today, I am weary of criticism, of belittling, of spite, in a word, 'nihilism.' That which deserves condemnation must be condemned. That which still deserves praise must be praised at length. No great work has been founded on hate or contempt."

Despite all that science has given us to ease our burdens, we see people in our society caught up in a high level of criticism, frustration and rage. We hear it in the media. We see it on our streets. We note it in our expectation of a new perfection from others, while exempting ourselves from the same scrutiny. We see it in intolerance of anybody who does not view life as we would like them to. There is too much self-centeredness and self-concern spanning this planet.

Human beings can portray both the best and the worst traits: compassion and bigotry, sensitivity and obtuseness, concern and arrogance, perceptive awareness and a total lack of understanding. People are torn between these forces. When we are at our best, we are neighborly; we feel responsible to others. But when narrow self-concern becomes the main focus in our lives, we complain and often exploit others.

Today we see so much of this narrow perspective that trust, respect, and acceptance are dangerously eroded. One hundred and twenty years ago, Mark Twain wrote: "It could probably be shown by fact and figure that there is no distinctly criminal class except Congress." The list has grown. Depending upon where we sit, the Wall Street broker, the union leader, the business person, the affluent, the poor, the welfare recipient, white Protestant males—have become in some measure victims of this insidious disease of mistrust, misinformation, antipathy, and often rage.

How then can we be our best? How can we move beyond all that I have mentioned to a life where people do not fear one another, where respect and tolerance emanate from one another, where trust is common and mistrust an aberration?

There is an old Latin proverb, "One man (or woman) is no man (or woman) at all." Though the worth of each personality is of primary significance, our worth is not in isolation; it is, also, community. There is an elemental need to have a community and a dialogue between persons; this has a profound medical and healthful effect on our lives.

To be our best means to be a friend, to be there for another in times of trouble. Sometimes what is needed is not so much our words as our presence. Recently I visited a man who suffered a devastating stroke. He could not speak. As I sat and held his hand, I could feel his whole body relax.

Someone has said that a friend is a person who comes when the world has crashed in. "The light of friendship is like the light of phosphorus; it is seen plainest when all around is dark."

Desmond Morris, in his book *Intimate Behavior*, says, "We laugh at educated adults who pay large sums to go and play childish games such as touch-and-hug in scientific institutes. . . . How much easier it would be if we could accept the fact that tender loving is not a weakly thing . . . only for infants and young lovers." The variety of group therapies, both scientifically and religiously oriented, point to the vital need of human beings to be caring and sharing with one another. It takes time to be a friend and be part of a caring community.

In spite of modern technology, there is a breakdown of communication due to differences in language, style, and attitude. We have radio talk show host J. Gordon Liddy telling how to shoot to kill federal agents. Lack of trust and respect for higher authority stem from the Vietnam War, Watergate, and presidential lifestyles. How do we respect and build community when we call the president a "crook, liar and thief"? This not only attacks an individual but also the office or position in the community. These are part of the causes that create emnity between the people and government, between genders, between young and old, between races, between citizens and immigrants, between those who work and those who do not.

Healthy communities focus on the real enemies: bigotry, hate, disease, ignorance and poverty. Healthy communities teach and nurture compassion and forgiveness. They promote a growing spirit of understanding that overcomes feelings of resentment and blame that now are too often fueled into rage and hate, such as that expressed in the tragic bombings of an abortion clinic in Brookline, Massachusetts or the Federal Building in Oklahoma.

In ancient scripture, we read in the 2nd chapter of Genesis: ". . . and God said: It is not good that man should be alone. I will make a helpmate for him." Aristotle said that a human being alone would be either a God or a brute. And Emerson said: "All are needed by each one; nothing is fair or good alone." Overcoming isolationism, finding dialogue and a respectful community, cannot be synthesized in a test tube or decided only by rhetoric. A caring relationship between people is not something that can be scientifically formulated. We need to return to a society that recognizes the healing power of human contact to help us overcome interpersonal difficulties, stress, grief, anger and depression.

On a person-to-person level, where can we turn in this technical age to position ourselves to be our best? I believe the church that remembers the past, speaks to the present and has a vision of a hopeful community for the future is the church that emulates a quality of trust that helps educate and inspire each of us to be our best. Emerson in 1841 said, "How many we sit by in church who though silent, we warmly rejoice to be with."

We can only be our best when we are nurtured in communities of respect and trust; where there is a sensitivity towards differences; where people of all ages, genders and races count;

where openness to change is not feared but tested, and if proven true, adopted without a sense of loss. This is our church—it is the place where we come together in sharing ways, where "mine" also includes "yours," and "ours" is created.

A church community should call for constructive and positive relationships. Our Unitarian Universalist faith is based on this premise. Our focus is not to separate and divide, not to dwell on brokenness and sin. But in acknowledging their existence, we strive to grow and develop beyond them; to seek commonality of interests, concerns, activities; to act commitedly, responsibly, compassionately within the circle we touch, and ever expanding this circle to bring diversity both to enrich us and to raise our level of tolerance toward that diversity.

To be our best we need to feel a relationship with something greater than ourselves. One God symbolizes our Unitarian Universalist faith. Monotheism came from the Old Testament, up from the Egyptian Akanaton, out of social struggle, racial antipathy and war. The great prophets, seeing such human alienation, sought to inspire people to be their best by saying that within them can be the flow of this eternal spirit. Though human beings can be abhorrent and evil, we realize the possibility of something better, something that drives us in positive ways towards being our best

I read recently of an American prisoner of war who always looked for good signs amidst his miserable situation. Torture was a good sign because it would end. Fridays were a good sign because fish was served instead of meat, but then meat was never on the menu at all. The approach of Christmas was always a good sign because prisoners of war might be released during the holiday. Seven Christmases passed before he was released. His perpetual optimism, his ability to see through the troubles probably saved his life and served as an inspiration to those around him. If there can be good signs in an almost unbearable prisoner of war camp, most of us should be able go beyond our difficulties to look with some hope towards the future. Hubert Humphrey once remarked, "The biggest mistake people make is giving up. Adversity is an experience, not a final act. Some people look upon any setback as the end. They are always looking for the benediction rather than the invocation."

To be our best means nurturing friendships and the caring dimension of our nature, being able to look through adversities to something more hopeful, feeling a relationship to the sense of divine in the universe and affirming all this together in gathered communities such as our Church. Caring is sharing. Living is giving. Remembering this, may we be inspired to be our best!

Sorrow and Joy

*A*CCORDING TO AN ANCIENT Greek legend, a woman came down to the River Styx to be ferried across to the region of the departed spirits. Charon, the thoughtful ferryman, reminded her that she had the right to drink from the waters of the river Lethe. This would erase her memory of the life she was leaving. Elated, she remarked, "I will forget how much I have suffered." Said the boatman, "Remember too, that you will forget how you have rejoiced." The woman exclaimed, "I will forget all my failures." But the remark came back, "And also your victories." She continued, "I will forget how I have been hated." Charon replied, "And also how you have been loved." At this point she stopped talking and reflected on the whole matter. She decided not to drink the water of total forgetfulness, preferring to retain the memory of her life experiences with both its sorrows and its joys. This is a wise choice. It is necessary if we are to understand the richness and challenges of being human.

I believe most of us would agree with her decision. Life provides mountain peaks of joy and valleys of depression for all of us. If we are fortunate, our peak experiences will predominate. Nevertheless, few of us would choose the fate of one who has amnesia. Memories are important to us. How many in the aging process would choose infirmity of mind over that of limb? As the poet wrote: "Now thieving time do what you must—quickness to move, to see, to hear—as dust is drawing near to dust such diminutions needs must be—but leave, Oh leave exempt from plunder my curiosity, my wonder!"

Two ingredients, hope and wonder, are almost always essential in giving us the zest for life that helps us leave our sorrows to find a measure of joy. Hope is needed not in our moments of great triumph but in times of challenge, in expectations of things to come, of progress to be made, of hills to climb beyond the ones already scaled. Hope has a powerful effect not only on our mental attitudes but also on the biological functioning of our bodies. Physicians have been known to give placebos to patients suffering from some maladies. Sometimes the ill person soon is well, not from any miracle drug, but from the miracle of the mind with hope affecting the biology of the body.

Consider that our existence is augmented by the ability to think things through and to think ahead. There is evidence showing that there is an advantage to those who think well of their future or of their immediate prospects. That is why religion has been such a powerful force in the past. Despite the mortality of our bodies, there was that promise of renewal in a heaven, a rein-carnation, a Nirvana, a Valhalla . . . some blessed place or state of being free from the ravages of mortal suffering.

William James, in his *Varieties of Religious Experience*, given as the Gifford lectures in 1901-1902 at Edinburgh, Scotland, pointed out that even if people were not absolutely sure of such immortality, the chance of salvation was enough. He said, "No fact in human nature is more characteristic than its willingness to live on a chance."

Though many people in this scientific era are not so sure of immortality, similar mind-sets of hope and optimism still have positive effects on our minds and bodies. Scientists today do say that it is in our genetic makeup to feel better if we have optimistic rather than despairing outlooks. Happy thoughts make us feel good. I cannot explain to you how optimistic thoughts can produce general feelings of well-being elsewhere in the bodily system, but they do! Biologically, they are as necessary as air.

Weston La Barre, in his book *The Ghost Dance, Origins of Religion*, writes, "The understanding of religion may be the key to an understanding of the nature and function of culture at large and the survival of the species. It is rooted in our human genes." If there is this common biological stimulus or root for religion, then it provides the logical basis for asserting the validity of religion. Some religions may be more ritualistic, colorful, militant or joyful than others. There may be different structures between professional leaders and lay people. However, all religions offer two things in common. First, they support communal social bonds including silent retreats. And second, they offer to individuals ways to organize and express their reservations or fears about their futures. The methods and the ideas may vary but the function is a common one. As a result people come to believe that their anxieties and fears are manageable, thus producing feelings of hope and optimism. That is why when orthodox Christianity was offering more fear than hope in the late nineteenth century, Universalism grew so phenomenally in rural areas of the United States, claiming at one time more than 800,000 adherents with its proclamation of Universal Salvation. That is why religion survives even in nations where people are persecuted for it. That is why religion survived and even grew in the former Soviet Union despite Communist oppression.

For all of Soviet officialdom's deliberate obscuring and relentless disparaging of religion, belief survived. Twelve years ago we found the Baptist Church in Moscow vibrantly alive with prayer, choir singing and the coming and going of many people. I felt a fervor and dedication among those people jamming the aisles for a two-hour service that would be repeated twice again each Sunday. When I gave the prayer, which was translated into Russian, you could see tears in people's eyes. In an interview with one of the English speaking Baptist pastors after the Sunday service, he told me of the growth of new churches in the outlying districts of Moscow and even the air-conditioning of one of their new churches in the southern desert region of the Soviet Union. We heard about the growth of religion in Tallinn, the capital of Estonia, where Lutheranism is the most dominant faith but where the Baptists are also flourishing by attracting young people. But these religions pale before the strength and growth of Russian

Orthodoxy. Having lunch with the Metropolitan of Kiev, he talked enthusiastically about the growth of all denominational churches but especially about the Orthodox Church in the Ukraine, where he presides. Today the Church is alive and thriving in the former Soviet Union.

Though religion is intertwined with our biological nature and need for hopeful expectations, that which religiously brings us hope and a sense of expectant optimism has changed across the centuries. From an emphasis on personal salvation promised in past centuries for believers, many religions today emphasize living our lives so as to bring hope to others for a better life on this planet.

With this in mind I was interested in the views of a number of church leaders as they looked to this New Year. What were the major challenges they perceived today? How could their congregations deal with them so as to bring greater hope and joy to their lives in a world filled with sorrows? A Methodist bishop from San Francisco saw the New Year in broad general terms. She saw people claiming to be Christians but failing to risk living the Christian way. She said: "The problems of hunger, poverty, racism and oppression could be alleviated if we could see the connections between the choices we make in our lifestyle and the way we act toward one another. We must continually gather our human and material resources to give leadership to political and social movements which reflect the teachings of Jesus."

In New York City we find a rabbi who feels we must grapple with how we define life. He points out that in a decade or two, there will be widespread use of artificial organs. He believes that these developments require a theological approach to the nature of life. He asks: "How do we define the sanctity of life as we technologically advance? When does life begin and cease? If you have artificial intelligence, what does it mean?"

The Episcopal Bishop of New York, on the other hand, was not so much interested in dealing with the definition of life and its theological implications but in the quality of life. He says, "The issue of world hunger, as well as peace and justice, should have top priority. Churches are in a unique position to enable government and the private sector to be in better communication and to work together in tackling these problems."

Going to the heartland of America, we find the Catholic Cardinal of Chicago believing that in wrestling with the issue of the separation of church and state, we may have a measure of hope. He writes: "Currently the toughest challenge is the issue of religion and politics. The role of the church in public policy discussion of 'the separation of church and state' has a crucial meaning. It holds that religious institutions are to expect neither discrimination nor favoritism in the exercise of their civic and religious responsibilities."

From a Fundamentalist Church in Missouri, the challenge and the hope is getting more people to accept Jesus as God and personal Savior. A Southern Baptist wants everyone to accept the Bible as the only true word of God. A Mormon in Salt Lake City tells us to "work more diligently to cultivate a spirit of love and charity in our homes." An African Baptist sees the great challenge as economic justice and with it will come a great spiritual awakening.

The director of the Islamic Center in Washington, D.C. sees hope in overcoming the ignorance one religion has about another. He writes, "Sometimes our judgments on other religions and nations are not based on deep research, understanding, and neutralism. I would like to see a unified effort for religious people to resist the trends to reject the idea of the one God." Here you have the views of a number of religious leaders on the challenges of today. Their perspectives, as well as their hopes, sorrows, and joys, differ.

How do I see things in 1996? Let me phrase it in this perspective. Here we are in the last five years of the twentieth century. Change is accelerating. Ten years ago polls proclaimed that we Americans foresaw a better life in the New Year. Five years ago I wrote: "At the opening of the last decade of this century, the United States may be entering one of the most promising periods of its history. We have before us images opposite those of the seventeenth and eighteenth century when civilization as we know it began to take shape in our country. Then Europeans headed west towards a continent that had no cities, industries or worldwide connections. Primarily we were a people who were rather 'out of it.' We were a conglomeration of idealists, frontier types seeking new beginnings. We cleared forests by hand, enslaved blacks, slaughtered Indians as a demonstration of natural selection, and at the same time we wrote tracts about human dignity and freedom, forging a Constitution and the Bill of Rights. Our new world looked back at the old one in Europe as the standard of life to emulate in the distant future. Now in 1990 with the demise of Communism in various places,

America looks out at the rest of the world that is rapidly changing. Now it is we who represent the standard of world power and order. Are we at our peak? Can we recognize this any more than Ming China, fifth-century Athens, the Ottoman Empire, and the Elizabethans who failed to see they were past the zenith of their power?" I concluded by remarking that we must capitalize on our eminence, we must turn our heads and wills toward the undereducated, underpaid, underfed and the overwhelmed.

So how are we faring? Recently, I heard a lecture where the speaker said that if you are over sixty, white, educated and have some investments, the next decade will be a bonanza for you, barring some personal catastrophe or illness. You will have social security, Medicare, and if you have investments, they will probably triple over the next ten years. Life for this group should seem hopeful and expectant. But today for many others, robots, downsizing, and bottom-line thinking are replacing jobs. This means a growing underclass. Can anyone be secure from the insecure and live on easy street while there is edge city? Will we allow these conditions to become the status quo for the future?

All, however, is not sorrow and loss. We need to come down to earth and see life in terms of its reality. We as a nation are healthier, live longer than ever before, and work at less exhausting jobs. The government in recent years has provided a safety net for the elderly, disabled and poor. Between 1945 and 1998 high school graduates have jumped from 25 percent to 81 percent; college graduates from 5 percent to 22 percent. Discrimination has diminished when compared to any past time. In 1945, 29 percent of the workforce were women, now it is 50 percent. The reality I see is progress and not perfection. Are we entitled to perfection when none of us is perfect?

Politicians in recent years have offered the vision of perfection, promises that in reality cannot be kept. As government has grown larger it has divided the population into those who have benefits and those who do not, with a growing resentment by both groups towards one another. What we need are not promises that are impossible to achieve but a vision of this nation as it is, with all its problems but also its vast possibilities. This will come about when we move past rigid ideologies and petty partisanship, when there is less emphasis on us winning and the other losing and more towards what will work for all. This will require more of running the office rather than running for office, making fewer speeches but making more sense, finding less fault and more answers, less growing apart and more growing up. Forty years ago three quarters of the people said they trusted government, today 23 percent do. But this attitude need not be final.

We should not be overwhelmed by the events of life, with the sorrows, burdens, and cares. Do not be passive with your expectations and hopes! Be active! Pursue those activities and ways of thinking that enable you to grapple with the challenges so that at some point a new attitude will lead to a positive breakthrough in your life. This is biologically sound, religiously valid, and uniquely human.

Let us remember President Abraham Lincoln's favorite quote from the Old Testament: "Where there is no vision the people perish." In all the talk about budgets and taxes, do not leave heart out of the deliberations. The vision that made this nation great was the vision that each of us has certain rights and potentials.

Together we may help lift those who are laid low by no fault of their own. This is to move beyond sorrow to joy. Joy and hope will enable America to stand tall in a most visionary way.

What are your challenges, hopes, and joys for the New Year? Whatever they are, wrestle with them at your brook of Jabbok. There may be sorrows for a time to lay you low, but strive to overcome them. Constantly continue your quest for the joys that will help to fulfill your life, for hope and joy are essential to our biological and spiritual well-being.

We must not be blind to the forces of evil or the world's wrongs. We must not put them aside or forget them, as would have been possible in the choice offered the woman in our opening story from Greek legend. We must not let those forces immobilize us, either. Take them on as challenges. Don't despair. Continue your quest for hope to help pass the midnight moments of sorrow, and embrace with appreciation the joys that do come into your life!

Unitarian Universalism

*I*N OUR UNITARIAN UNIVERSALIST churches across the country, most people will be worshipping today in services that use no creed, bond of fellowship, or declaration of faith. But this is not universally true. At All Souls Unitarian Church in New York City, their bond of fellowship will state, "In the love of truth and in the spirit of Jesus, we unite for the worship of God and the service of all." And once a year on Palm Sunday, in this church we repeat the Covenant that gathered the early Puritans together for worship in 1630.

At one time in many Unitarian churches, part of their worship included a statement written by James Freeman Clark: "The Fatherhood of God, the Brotherhood of Man, the Leadership of Jesus, Salvation by character and the Progress of man onward and upward forever." Some people, noting in the past the concentration of our churches in eastern Massachusetts, have shortened this in a joking way to read, "The Fatherhood of God, the Brotherhood of Man, and the Neighborhood of Boston."

In many Universalist churches during the earlier part of this century, the following affirmation was used:

"Love is the doctrine of this church;
The quest for truth is its sacrament;
And service is its prayer.
To dwell together in peace;
To seek knowledge in freedom;
To serve mankind in fellowship;
To the end that all souls shall grow into harmony with the Divine,
Thus do we covenant with each other and with God."

Some people, before the merger of the two denominations, defined Unitarians as those who believed man is too good to be damned by God, and defined Universalists as believing that God is too good to damn man.

In Charleston, South Carolina, many people still refer to the Unitarian Church as the "no-hell" church, because of our belief that people are punished by their sins and not for them.

Unitarian Universalism should be considered a religious gift. It is a gift to unfold, like a flower from the bud, to accept the freedom to exercise our intelligence and good will in experiencing greater love, beauty and justice in this world.

What are the roots of this Unitarian Universalist faith? In a broad perspective we can trace the roots of our current faith to Moses and the idea of moral law, to Socrates and the search for truth, and to Jesus' special, unique message of love.

After the death of Jesus, there developed various interpretations of the meaning of his life. To study church history is to see the gradual deification of him. At the Council of Nicea held in A.D. 325, there were two major conflicting views—one that supported Arias and the other that backed Athanasius. There was political strength behind both men. In the end, Athanasius, with his view of the Trinity, won. Jesus and God and the Holy Ghost were declared equal. The Arian view that Jesus was not equal to God did not prevail. However, for more than two centuries, there were churches that followed the Arian belief. Two of those churches still stand today in Ravena, Italy as museums with outstanding mosaics from the sixth century A.D.

Through the ensuing centuries there were occasional voices that spoke to the attitudes maintained today by Unitarian Universalists. In A.D. 440 Nestorius wrote that God could not have a human parent. In the fourth and fifth centuries, the Celtic monk Pelagius preached the essential goodness of human beings. Pelagius spoke strongly against the idea of original sin. Clement of Alexandria and Origen taught universal salvation. Later on there were the Waldensians and Albigensians, who were attached to the scriptures and a simple purity of life. None of these views prospered in the mainstream of the Christian Church.

We trace the modern roots of our faith to Michael Servetus, who was born in Spain in 1511 and burned as a heretic by Calvin in 1553. In the new era of communication resulting from the development of the printing press, he opened up the debate on the Trinity and the personhood of Jesus. Though Servetus became a medical doctor, he was intensely interested in religion. Christianity in the sixteenth century in Spain commingled with Judaism and Islam. The spirit of the Crusades had injected into Christianity an intense hostility toward these other two faiths. Servetus had a deep personal religion as well as a practical concern. Baptism at that time was believed to be essential for salvation. But Servetus noted that many from Judaism and Islam who accepted baptism often fell back into the practices of their former religions. Baptism that used the Trinitarian formula that conceived of a human being as being equal to God was just too foreign to have a lasting effect on these converts. They were treated as relapsed heretics and, if convicted by the Inquisition, were delivered to the secular authorities to be killed. In the early sixteenth century, the rigors of the Inquisition were being relaxed, but the problems and the possibilities were never absolutely absent from the Spanish mind.

Out of deep religious conviction, Servetus wondered why it was so hard to convert the Jews and the Moslems to Christianity, which claimed to be the one true saving faith. The most obvious difference between Christianity and the other religions was the Trinity. At that time the Trinity was depicted as three elderly men, sometimes with one body and three heads, other times with one head and three faces. Servetus raised the question of whether this doctrine, which had to be accepted on pain of banishment and even death, was actually essential to the Christian faith. He examined the New Testament and found that the doctrine of the Trinity, so vigorously required, was not formulated in the sacred scriptures. There is a mention of the Father, Son, and Holy Ghost, but the formulation required by the church was not found in the New Testament. Servetus noted in the Gospel of Mark evidence that Jesus did not believe he was equal to God: "Why callest me good. There is none good but one. That is God." In Matthew, Servetus felt that Jesus' statement, "My God, My God, Why hast thou forsaken me?" clearly delineated the fact that God was superior to Jesus. And even in the Gospel of John, which was written one hundred or more years after the death of Jesus, and at a time when there was a growing emphasis on deifying Jesus, Servetus pondered the statement, "My Father is greater than I." Thus Servetus concluded that every person is a child of God. He came to believe that the fall of the church occurred at the Council of Nicea in 325. He concluded that Jesus was greater than human beings but less than God. Through this concept he hoped to bring the many unconvinced friends in Islam and Judaism to Christianity. He never had the opportunity, as he was burned in effigy by the Catholics in Spain and after fleeing from Spain, literally burned as a heretic by John Calvin in Switzerland.

The only Unitarian monarch in history was King John Sigismund of Transylvania. He allowed free discussion and broad tolerance of religious viewpoints. It is there that the word Unitarian was first used. In 1568 King John Sigismund issued the Act of Religious Tolerance and Freedom of Conscience.

The first significant group of churches to become Unitarian was in Poland. An Italian by the name of Faustus Socinus united the Minor Reformed Church of that nation. He carried Servetus's idea about Jesus even further. Jesus saved people by setting an example for them, not by dying on the cross. The mission of Jesus was that of teacher—to show the way toward a better life. Socinus questioned the validity of original sin and predestination as meaningful religious concepts. The Polish Unitarian Church had a press in Krakow. Books from this press were brought to Holland and England and were instrumental in the formation of Unitarianism in Great Britain.

The first Unitarian congregation in England had among its worshippers Joseph Priestley and Benjamin Franklin. Priestley, whom most people know as the discoverer of oxygen, held strong Unitarian views on religion. He was persecuted for them. Eventually, he came to America to found in 1796 in Philadelphia the first congregation in the United States to bear the Unitarian name. Ten years prior to this, the First Episcopal Church in New England, King's Chapel, revised the Book of Common Prayer, eliminating references to the Trinity.

Today it is difficult for us to conceive of the fear of hell that existed in many people's minds due to the prevailing religions existing prior to the flowering of Unitarian Universalism, particularly here in New England. Caleb Rich left an orthodox Christian church and joined a Universalist church. He wrote of his early childhood, prior to his change of faith: "I often looked at the poison reptiles thinking how much better their lot in the world was than mine."

Hosea Ballou directed the Universalist movement towards Unitarian beliefs by affirming that God was Father, rather than Judge, that Jesus was an exalted man, rather than a person of the Trinity, and sin was personal rather than inherited.

In the early 1800s one hundred twenty-five churches in New England left orthodoxy to embrace the more hopeful, human approach to religion found in Unitarianism. This faith stood for human goodness, the unity of God, and the necessity of reason and free will to interpret religious life. It echoed the words of Charles Chauncy, minister of the First Church in Boston during our Revolutionary War, who advocated the "trustworthiness of reason and the right of private judgment." He, also, was a strong advocate of universal salvation.

From the early 1800s when William Ellery Channing insisted on the authority of the Old and New Testaments in proving the fallacy of the Trinitarian idea, there have been changes in emphasis and broader interpretations. With the passing of years and the development of historical Biblical criticism, we may add another belief not enunciated by Channing. The Bible is not the final authority in matters of religion. It is a wonderful book of the religious experiences of the Jewish people and of the early Christians, but not everything in it is inspired by God.

The latter part of the nineteenth century and the early part of the twentieth saw more people asserting the authority of human reason. Reason probed the secrets of the universe. At one time it was felt that almost everything could be worked out by reason. Even world peace could be attained through reason and no civilized nation could possibly have recourse to violence in a reasonable world.

Yet almost at the same time, with Sigmund Freud and others probing the irrational side of human nature and the age of violence through which we have lived in this century, we have come to realize that reason by itself is not the final answer. As a result of this, Unitarian Universalism has become, in the best sense, more mystical in the past few decades. We have begun to feel the mystery of existence. Many people had reasoned that any idea of God was unnecessary. Many Unitarians and Universalists called themselves humanists and some still do. Human reason was exalted. The mystery of life was denied. But to many of us this now appears to be inadequate. Those who felt that science was on their side in the denial of existence of anything beyond the human mind, find that the philosophical scientists have deserted them. The furthest probings of science have not found evidence of chaos in the physical world, but on the contrary, an incredible order, from the movement of the galaxies in space to the whirling of electrons around the protons in the smallest islands of matter. Science has also revised its concept of matter into one of energy. Einstein's equation is now generally accepted. What seems to be solid matter turns out to be energy.

Since we are not held together as a Church by a single creedal statement and since we permit a variety of interpretations, what unites us? We take people where they are and encourage them to move forward towards an expanded view of reality and truth. As Edwin Markham said,

> "He drew a circle that kept me out.
> Heretic, rebel, a thing to flout.
> But love and I had wit to win.
> We drew a circle that took him in."

We find common ground in our philosophy of life—the faith by which we live. What is this faith? First, we recognize religion as a natural characteristic of human beings. This includes the emergence of a science of religion born of spiritual law, rather than speculative theology, dogma, and creed. Our religion embraces the words of Emerson: "There will be a new church founded on moral science. The church to come will have heaven and earth for its beams and rafters, science for symbols and illustrations."

Second, we recognize the sacredness of truth. Gandhi once said that it doesn't matter that we take different roads as long as we reach the same goal. Truth is an expanding circle. It is sometimes avoided because it requires dedication and consecration on the part of each person. It is often easier to go the serpentine way of a river.

Third, we recognize the ethical and spiritual unity of all human beings. We look for common denominators with others. Thus we avoid creeds that separate and divide people or impose hierarchical authority.

A fourth aspect of our faith is reverence for personality, allowing each person to choose that which will be a positive influence in his or her life. There is the old Biblical story of Saul, Goliath and David. Saul gave David his armor, shield and sword to go out to do battle. But David felt uncomfortable with them. He put them aside and took instead his own slingshot. This he could trust. It was his own. It had been tested by his own experience. Thus we say to each person, have reverence for yourself, choose your own faith, one that you can test in your life, one that has terminology and ideas that make you feel comfortable, creating a constructive, positive difference in your life.

A fifth aspect of our faith is freedom to develop our potential. If you put a plant in a flower pot, it will be limited in growth, for the roots are not able to reach fresh, new soil. So we say to each of you, you should be free to attain your greatest spiritual potential. Channing phrased it, "I call the mind free which jealously guards its intellectual rights, calls no man master, contents itself with no hereditary faith, receives new truth as an angel from Heaven, and while consulting others, inquires still more of the oracle within itself."

There is a growing awareness that freedom with responsibility has been declining in the past few decades. Freedom has been used to escape both character and responsibility. De Tocqueville pondered the meaning of democracy and individual freedom and wrote, "The nations of our time cannot prevent the conditions of men from becoming equal, but it depends upon themselves whether the principle of equality is to lead them to freedom or servitude, to knowledge or barbarism, to prosperity or wretchedness." We can read about the impact of the selfish use of freedom in Christopher Lash's book, *The Culture of Narcissism,* or in Shirley Sugarman's *Sin and Madness: Studies in Narcissism.* These studies show that doing something for someone else is no longer in vogue. There are now whole generations illiterate in group experiences. They have never expressed loyalty or modified their own agenda for the achievement of a whole greater than the sum of its parts.

Freedom is vital to the Unitarian Universalist faith. But it requires freedom with character and responsibility. We have a heritage rich in those ingredients that will help us to use freedom wisely and which will give us an improved and hopeful society.

With our freedom comes a calling, a commitment to take the best in individuals and arrive at collective and communal decisions. We stand at the threshold of a new and finer society. Whether we cross this threshold is up to us!

When Life Tumbles In

*F*OR EACH OF US AT SOME TIME, life does tumble in. We suffer. Right now we may be afflicted with a physical problem or a threatening illness. If we are currently in good physical health, we know others, some of whom are close to us, who face such stressful situations. We, as individuals within this Church body, certainly want to use all our powers in supporting and affirming those who now face physical difficulties.

But it is not physical tragedy alone that may abruptly interrupt our lives without regard to our age, status or plans. People lose jobs through downsizing. Families split apart in these times of rapid change. Abuse, whether self-inflicted or imposed upon one by another, is on the rise.

We all have faced situations with some measure of dread because we were ill-prepared for a certain task or obligation. We have had circumstances imposed upon us that have disrupted our carefully laid plans and left us at loose ends. We have felt the pain of making a decision we do not wish to make. And we sometimes suffer in anticipation of some feared future.

There are times, too, when we suffer for no obvious reasons. We call this the blues or a depression. Sometimes we can do our own sleuthing in seeking the cause. In these days, many seek counsel from someone qualified to help, while others turn to something in pill, injection or liquid form to numb the pain, though not eliminating the cause. Then there are those who turn to self-help literature, assuming they will come out of the problem by right eating, new thinking or reflective introspection. Yet no matter how much we may read about self-help, troubles still come and life can tumble in on us, leaving us with an extra feeling of guilt because the self-help that was supposed to work did not.

When a government changes a policy on welfare, or a nation overthrows its form of government, or anarchy takes the place of order, life does tumble in on people. The former Soviet Union and Eastern Europe have had a dramatic change in their forms of government. This has brought great joy and opportunity to some people, but to others life has tumbled in.

Perhaps some of you remember Frieda Lurie who worshipped here a few times in the 1980s. For over twenty-five years she was head of the American Literature Section of the Soviet Writers' Union. This position afforded her the opportunity to meet every American writer who visited that land. From Robert Frost to John Updike, Frieda was their escort and guide. She knew the writers and was steeped in American literature. Our family was fortunate to come to know her and to be blessed by her many kindnesses on several visits to Moscow. She baby-sat our children when they were young and later found interesting places to take them. When our son Rhys was studying at the Pushkin Institute for foreign students, she was an oasis for a good meal at the Writers' Union and communications with us in the West. She interpreted for us, introduced us to Russian writers and eased our way in a complicated, highly socialized country. She would have loved to have been married, but her fiancé and most of the men of her age were killed in World War II. She threw herself into her work with zeal. She looked past the growing corruption in her country to speak about the sacrifice necessary to build a better society. She lived frugally and believed that someday the system would provide a life closer to the ideal for all its people. The fact that she never was permitted to travel west to any other country but the United States, and never alone when she came here, indicates she was not in the spoils system as were some Communists.

Now as freedom gives opportunity to many former Communists who also benefited greatly in the past, many retired persons who sacrificed for what they hoped would be a better society are in sad situations. Frieda is retired, she is sick and she does not have a sufficient pension to eat properly. Some of us who have known her for many years send medicine and money to help her along. She is a symbol of many whose life has tumbled in, with little or no hope for the future.

In all parts of the world, when unpleasant things happen, they need to be put into perspective. Some episodes that seem unpleasant at the moment, in reality pale before some ultimate catastrophe. Elisabeth Kübler-Ross, in one of her lectures, quotes a letter written by a young woman to her boyfriend: "Remember the day I borrowed your brand new car and I dented it. I thought you'd kill me but you didn't. And remember the time I dragged you to the beach and you said it would rain and it did. I thought you'd say: 'I told you so,' but you didn't. And the time I flirted with all the boys to make you jealous, and you were. I thought you'd leave me. But you didn't. There were many things I wanted to make up to you when you came back from Vietnam, But You Didn't."

There also is the problem in life for some people of climbing so high in the material realm only to be brought low, to lose face, and not to be able to cope. Back in 1923 there was a meeting held at the Edgewater Beach Hotel in Chicago. In attendance were eight leading successful financiers. They were: the president of the largest independent steel company, the president of the largest utility company, the president of the largest gas company, the largest speculator in wheat futures, the president of the New York Stock Exchange, a member of the president's cabinet, the head of the world's largest monopoly, and the president of the Bank of International Settlements. Here was a group of people who knew how to accumulate great amounts of money. But money is one of the quickest sources to bring life both up and down. Afterwards, what happened to these people? The president of the steel company, Charles Schwab, living on borrowed money for five years, died bankrupt. The largest utility's president, Samuel Insull, died a fugitive from justice and penniless in a foreign land. The head of the largest gas company, Howard Hopson, had an emotional breakdown. The great wheat speculator Arthur Cutten died abroad, insolvent. The head of the New York Stock Exchange, Richard Whitney, spent time in Sing Sing prison. The member of the president's cabinet, Albert Fall, was pardoned from prison so he could die of a terminal illness at home. The head of a great monopoly, Ivar Krueger, and the president of the Bank of International Settlements, Leon Fraser, both committed suicide. These people knew the art of making money, but when life tumbled in on them, they did not know how to live.

We in the West look upon suffering as a problem, if at all possible, to be solved. Suffering is a sign that we must be weak in some way or have failed. If we just "get right with God," if we just live right, we will not suffer, or at least we should not. That was the way Job's friends saw it. Remember? They said they were there to comfort him, urging him to think back to what he'd done to cause his problems. But, of course, they did not succeed. They were really trying to comfort themselves. They believed that suffering should be rationally understood. Somebody, or some action was to be blamed for it. Suffering was a punishment for some sin. Job, too, wished he could think of what he'd done wrong because it would make his suffering a form of punishment he could understand. We try to create a universe that is orderly, rational and understandable, but as yet, science has not come up with an equation that undergirds this wish with reality.

The causes of suffering sometimes can and have been eradicated. Often this takes the will and action of many people or of a whole community. But too often there is no justice as to who suffers. Innocent suffering is everywhere: in the floods in the west, the killings in Africa, the cold in Europe, the lack of health insurance for forty million in the United States. We know that suffering, often unexplainable and unjust, has always been part of life. We know this, but emotionally we try to resist this knowledge. Why does someone get a terrible disease? Many times there is no rational explanation that we can understand.

In his autobiography, Albert Schweitzer wrote: "Only at quiet rare moments have I felt truly glad to be alive. I could not but feel with sympathy, full of regret for all the pain I saw around me, not only of human beings but also of the whole of creation. From this community of suffering, I have never tried to withdraw myself. It seemed to me that we should all take our share of the burden of pain that lies upon the world. Even while I was a boy at school, it was clear to me that no explanation of the evil in the world could ever satisfy me. All explanations, I felt, ended in sophistries, and at the bottom had as the object to make it possible for people to share in the misery of those around them with less keen feelings." That's what Job's friends did. They sought to explain his sufferings so they could respond with less keen feelings.

Every response to suffering, whether in the name of religion or not, that tries to turn us from acceptance of suffering leads us to less, not more compassion. Schweitzer goes on to observe: "However much concerned I was at the problem of misery in the world, I never let myself get lost brooding over it. I always held firmly to the thought that each of us can do a little to bring some portion of it to an end. Thus I came gradually to rest content in the knowledge that there is only one thing we can understand about the problem and that is that each of us has to go our own way, but as one who means to bring about deliverance."

To feel pain is to be alive and respond to some of the reality of life around us. Suffering is part of living, as is joy and happiness. To be fully alive is to accept this. This does not mean we should wallow in suffering, but it is an inescapable part of life that we can never understand any more than we can understand those parts of life that are full of hope and joy. The factor that diminishes both is apathy.

When life tumbles in on us, we know that in many cases, "This too will pass." But we also know there are some things that will not easily and perhaps never go away. When this happens and we feel grief or sorrow, we may need to accept the condition as part of being human and, if possible, as a challenge.

You have watched children playing by the seashore. Here are two girls jumping in the surf. Along comes a huge wave that throws them over and pushes them to the bottom. They come up coughing, sand in their bathing suits. One runs back on the beach and sets up a loud cry for her mother. The other scrambles to her feet, takes a deep breath, and then plunges back into the water. One sees the ocean as an enemy to fear, a place of suffering. The second child did not suffer from the experience. She did not run crying to her mother. She went back in, enjoying the challenge of the sea.

In Carmel, California, I remember being on a horse when I was five years old. Suddenly it bolted and headed back to its stable. Holding on to the pommel of a western saddle, we careened down the road. Only my small size and holding my head against the horse allowed me to escape being swept off by a branch of a tree. I never enjoyed being on a horse again. Fear was my response. It is too bad, because later for a year I lived on a ranch in the Ojai Valley of California. There were many fine horses for riding. I never took advantage of a wonderful opportunity. When a wave of life knocks us over, if we can, we should pick ourselves up, take a deep breath and go forward.

How many times have you known of two people who experienced the same incident but had very different recollections of what happened? Our expectations, our strengths and insecurities and our prejudices shape what we see. Philip Kavanaugh, a psychiatrist, writes, "The most powerful system in our bodies, the one that controls all the other systems, is the actual belief system. More than anything else, more than what we eat or drink or feel, we are what we believe."

We are told that astrologers from the East saw a star that led them to look for a new king, the messiah, who would bring peace on earth. This is celebrated in orthodox churches as Epiphany on January 6. An epiphany is a revelation. It is a new way of seeing things.

When life tumbles in and you suffer, regardless of the circumstance, it may help to look at things in a new way. That is what Anne Frank did in Amsterdam, knowing death could take her at any time. In the darkness brought on by Hitler, Anne, hiding with her family in the attic of a warehouse, wrote in her diary: "I looked out of the window over a large area of

Amsterdam, over all the roofs and on to the horizon, which was such a pale blue that it was hard to see the dividing line. As long as I may live to see this sunshine, the cloudless skies, I cannot be unhappy." When life tumbles in, and you suffer, try to look for an epiphany, as did Anne Frank, and you, also, may find some happiness.

TRUSTING
THE
FUTURE

There Is No Death

APRIL 7, 1985

Easter Sunday

W E HAVE BEEN HEARING a great deal in our press concerning Star Wars. The answer as to whether it will prevent nuclear war or ignite it is almost as unclear as the events concerning the aftermath of Jesus' death. For as we heard from our readings this morning, there were those who were convinced Jesus rose physically from the sepulcher and there were those who held it in total disbelief. Then, as now, people came down on both sides of this issue. But returning to the idea of Star Wars, with this concern in mind, I was perusing my Easter file and came across a headline in the *New York Times* of twenty years ago. It read, "Galaxy Emissions May Come from Rational Beings." The article went on to explain that a certain regular radio signal was coming from a far distant galaxy named Pegasus and that the precise formula of signal occurred every 100 days.

It quoted a Russian astronomer, Professor Nicolai Kardaskev, who said that a super civilization had been discovered. But the next day in the press the affirmation had turned to caution and American and British astronomers proclaimed outright skepticism.

Regardless of the merits of the radio signal from another galaxy, there is a religious and philosophic implication to the pronouncement. Religion begins in wonder! And at the end, when religious thought has gone as far as we can go with it, the wonder remains. Whether we are religious conservatives or liberals, the Easter story of Jesus and his reported resurrection rests mostly on wonder.

Think of your own life for a moment. It is a miracle that human beings can see, hear, feel, and touch. A combination of molecules has created you as a living human being. You can philosophize, think abstractly, dream, show compassion, and sacrifice even your own physical life. This you, which is more than a physical body, is a miracle beyond explanation.

Today, in a world dominated by the rationalism of science, the wonder expressed in ancient scripture and by the Easter story is often shuffled to the side as myth and superstition. Though at times these stories may not stand the test of actual fact, the yearning behind them has humane and human validity. Wonder can only be expressed in the human community. It is something resting uniquely with human beings. It exists just as strongly for those who reject the literal interpretation of the Easter story.

The wonder of that scientist in Russia who projected a super civilization from a radio beam is the same type of wonder that took Jesus from the tomb and raised him to pervade the world. The super civilization at the end of the radio beam and the resurrection of Jesus expressed in hymns and scripture on Easter morning do not rest on complete facts. But they express the immortal yearnings of people through the centuries. Wonder pervades all religious belief and it is eternal.

The famous British Unitarian minister James Martineau wrote: "There is a sense in which nothing human ever perishes, nothing at least which proceeds from the higher and characteristic part of human nature; nothing which comes of one's conscience, nothing which one does as a subject of God's moral law. The good and ill live after you, an endless blessing or a lasting curse; a consideration which gives dignity to the humblest duty, and enormity to careless wrong. It is a mistake to suppose that any service rendered to humanity, any interrelation of human life, any exhibition of moral greatness can ever be lost; the form only disappears, their value remains, and their work is everlastingly performed. They exist as truly and perform their duty as actively a thousand years after their origin as on the day of birth."

From birth to death, we are surrounded by the presence of those persons who never served a lesser loyalty than the welfare of society. The spirit of moral greatness and of hope and progress running through civilizations and not destroyed by the pathos of daily events is in a sense immortal and divine. For this there is no death.

Easter, for most people in the Western world, is a focus on one person. In some liberal churches the focus is on spring as symbolic of life's renewal; or there may be vestiges of the

Passover commemorating the Exodus of the Jewish people from oppression to freedom. But beyond all this, it seems to me, is a central figure, Jesus of Nazareth, who for twenty centuries has not died in the hearts of people. What he means to us and what we choose to emulate from him depends on our own needs, hopes, and beliefs.

For some of us, Jesus is the absolute pacifist, calling for people to turn the other cheek. For others he is the prophetic crusader seeking to cleanse the world of its unrighteousness. Did he not drive out the moneychangers from the temple in a violent outburst? For still others, Jesus is a passionate social reformer, telling people it is harder for a rich person to inherit the kingdom of God than for a camel to go through the eye of a needle. But then again, for others he is the opposite of a strident reformer—he is pietistic though caring, concerned with the individual but fully believing the world is about to end and that people should leave politics alone, "rendering unto Caesar what is Caesar's and unto God what is God's." For some he brings a message of peace and comfort: "Come unto me, all ye that labor and are heavy laden, and I will give you rest." "Ask, and it will be given you; seek and you will find." But then for others, Jesus brings, and in his words, "not peace, but a sword." For those who wish to document their belief that Jesus considered himself to be God's only begotten son, there is a verse in John that reads, "I am the way, the truth and the light. No one comes unto the Father but by me." And for religious liberals who regard such verses as reading back into Jesus' life the theology of a later century, there is the reassuring text from the gospel of Mark, "Why callest thou me good? There is none good but one, that is God."

I like to think of Jesus not as a being going up to heaven but as one who attained heavenly heights by his insights and sensitivity to the needs of people in all their various conditions. He was not the God who worked on earth like a man but a human being who worked in godly ways on earth. He was not a God who lived humanely but a man who lived divinely. He was not a being who died that others might live, but a man who lived so others would no longer choose to live by narrow, selfish ways. This is the universality of Jesus. Regardless of your theology, regardless of which view of Jesus lives on in you today, he speaks still to the human needs unchanged by time. There has been no death in the qualities he espoused in his living.

In my life there have been a few persons with whom I have spoken on the subject of immortality who seem content with the idea that with bodily death, nothing continues. There are others who feel that individual spirits merge into a greater composite spirit. Although quite different, believers of both these ideas often quote Swinburne, who wrote:

> *"From too much love of living,*
> *From hope and fear yet free,*
> *We thank with brief Thanksgiving*
> *Whatever Gods may be*
> *That no life lives forever;*
> *That dead men rise up never;*
> *That even the weariest river*
> *Winds somewhere safe to sea."*

If we think objectively, we find there are certain ideas or laws upon which we will all agree there is no death. Consider first that $2 \times 2 = 4$. There is no death for this concept. A mathematician lives in a world that is far from mere transience and decay. If this is true with numbers, can it not be true with good deeds?

This past week marked the anniversary of the death of Martin Luther King. Often the ideals of Jesus marched with King on his way to Montgomery and Selma and on so many other occasions. When justice stood at the forefront, leaving bigotry behind, King's inspiration was the presence of Jesus after a physical death. This certainly is an indication of the immortality of justice, goodness and mercy. It is the enduring and vital spirit that lives on that is of essential importance.

It is neither the Jesus of ancient dogma nor the more modern Jesus of maudlin sentimentality that we so often observe on religious television, but Jesus the man, Jesus the courageous and compassionate prophet who is a fact of immortality on a life of reverence and good will. The experience of the eternal need not be limited to mathematics alone. A person is capable of living here and now in an imperishable way. Why should one suppose that this capacity, so profound and meaningful, cannot be as eternal as mathematics?

If I were to go into this congregation and ask each one of you who believes in some form of eternal life, "When does it begin?" I believe that the general answer would be that eternal life is something that happens after death rather than something that is occurring now. Reading the New Testament carefully we discover this central theme. Here and now we are in the presence of the eternal. According to the Biblical scholar Dr. Morton Enslin, Jesus brought good news about an impending kingdom where people would forsake their defiance of God's ways, would love good henceforth and would abhor evil. And this kingdom was imminent within the life of everyone listening to Jesus. The message was clear. Here and now we need not be fugitive and transitory creatures, for we have within ourselves eternal life.

Let us consider that this is a reasonable way of dealing with the idea of immortality. If our world is altogether transient, what possible reason is there for supposing that after death we may suddenly be ushered into an imperishable, permanent world? Many intelligent people have turned from the church that equates the spirit with another world and only materialism with this one. What we may believe on Easter morning is not the restoration to life of something that is transient but the re-dedication to the continuance of life that has always been, by its nature, eternal.

When approached in this way, immortality can become desirable. The great devotees of Indian religions (with their reincarnation, rebirth to rebirth in endless cycles) dreaded immortality. Buddha, who promised relief from the unending necessity of going on and on, became a welcome savior to millions. What makes life both desirable and immortal is not the quantity of it but its quality. Sir Wilfred Grenfell wrote, "I am very much in love with life. I want more of it after the incident called death, if there is any to be had."

There is something everlastingly worthwhile that can go on in our lives that we can share with others. The truly vital person allies the self with this creative purpose and wishes to go on with it—not for love of a reward—but for the love of sharing in something so infinitely worthwhile. A great artist does not necessarily look for a reward. Many of the great artists lived with rejection and poverty, though not desired. But what the artist strives for and desires is successful creativity. This is a quality of life that has no death.

Finally, on this Easter morning comes the challenge for our own personal consideration. We can speak about the birth of spring and the renewal of our spirit with it. But is this enough? With the great things men and women have done, they have also at times enclosed their lives with hate and envy, selfishness and greed. Do we want to give new life to this? These are not the deathless attributes of human beings. Let our life be filled with qualities of beauty, truth, faithfulness and love—these qualities that by their very nature can have no death.

The nails that pierced the hands and feet of Jesus did not pierce the truth that he sought to convey. The nails that drive pain into contemporary society need not hold us from the truth that spiritual quality must prevail in our society. No longer can we afford to have barriers between people. No longer can we ignore the cries of people who through no fault of their own are unable to cope with the reality of this world. No longer can we say it is not our business. Let us seek that quality for which there is no death on this Easter. Let us look out from any little prisons of our personal self, prisons dominated by prejudices and frustrations, out of dark tunnels of limited concepts of time and finiteness, to a larger world. The divinity that spoke in Jesus has grown brighter through the good deeds and acts of others across the centuries. This divinity can be a part of us now.

We cannot proclaim as fact that there is life after death, for this requires verifiable truth that overrides every doubt. But if we live now in eternal realms, why should that part of us, the most important part, stop because of bodily death? I believe that what is eternal stays eternal and that there is no death.

John Winthrop's Challenge to Us Today

MAY 5, 1991

New Member Sunday

*I*T WAS SAID OF JOHN WINTHROP that both the innocent and the guilty were glad to be judged by him—to the innocent he showed justice and to the guilty he displayed mercy. John Winthrop was largely responsible for starting this church in 1630. He was the first governor of the Massachusetts Bay Colony. At the Paul Revere Mall in Boston today, there is a plaque to John Winthrop stating: "The spirit of Winthrop is forever a challenge to America."

On this new member recognition Sunday, it seems appropriate to go back to our spiritual roots of 1630. Winthrop is famous for his sermon which carried this thought: "To provide for posterity, we must have affection for one another, we must delight in each other, rejoice together, mourn together, labor and suffer together." Certainly this idealism and this outreach,

231

one to another, is the type of community a church should be. And in turn the church should strive to develop this attitudinal climate in the larger community, something Winthrop tried to do in his time.

What do we know about John Winthrop? He was born at Groton, Suffolk, England in 1588. His early years were spent on his estate of Groton. He studied at Cambridge University and studied law in London. In 1627 he was appointed one of three attorneys in the King's Court of Wards. These wards were minors who fell heir to land held directly by the king. Winthrop saw at first hand the wickedness in this court as well as in government in general. Justice was a sham.

Winthrop wrote that England "was a sinful land." He saw both the social and the ecclesiastical evils. He listed the causes of his dissatisfaction. Some were religious in nature: ". . . the daily increase of the multitude of Papists, scandalous ministers, the suspensions and silencing of many learned ministers for not conforming in some points of ceremonies." But most of his complaints were social in nature. Referring to the affairs of the community: "The common scarcity of wood and timber; lewdness of bailiffs, inequitable taxation, the pitiful condition of the orphans, and the intolerable tax burden on farmers . . . people perish for want of sustenance and employment." These words paint a picture not unfamiliar in our own time.

In the late 1500s and early 1600s, the Puritans of England were primarily Calvinist in theology. The terminology that Winthrop used reflected the Calvinistic aura of his time. He saw in the effects of the economic and social conditions in England the depravity of human beings. He reflected in his writings on the utter dependence of people upon God in effecting their regeneration. He was not bound, however, by the logic of the theology he expressed. Indeed he often dismissed that logic. He believed that "You cannot will yourself into salvation." Yet basically, Winthrop was optimistic about building a godly society through the human effort of good works. He did believe that humans do possess the capacity to cooperate with and consent to God's will. Though a professed Calvinist in believing that everything is foreordained, he asked people to live a better life, one filled with mercy and justice.

We must remember that Winthrop was a person who had not been personally oppressed in English society. His conscience was moved by the evil he saw around him. But he dreamed of a better society. He came to the new world to try to establish a godly state that would provide justice and mercy.

Crossing on the ship *Arbella*, he gave a layman's sermon which he entitled "The Model of Christian Charity." John Winthrop had seen in England that people were a long way from living up to this ideal of Christian charity and brotherly and sisterly love. By bringing persons together in a common bond and making a covenant with God, he hoped to establish a model society in New England.

He asked charity of the settlers. He asked them to give of their abundance in ordinary times and to give beyond their means on extraordinary occasions. He asked them to temper the spirit of commerce with mercy, giving where it was necessary, lending only where feasible in terms of the capability of the recipient to repay, and forgiving a debt when the debtor could not pay.

But his idea of Christian love included more than mercy and charity. He had a deep wish for unity and stability in society. He worried about individuals who strove for their own good without thought of the well-being either of their fellow human beings or of society as a whole. Consequently—though generally he displayed mercy and compassion to the wayward—he was intolerant of persons such as Anne Hutchinson and Roger Williams, whose strong views threatened the well-being of the church and community. He allowed a variety of opinion as long as it did not threaten the existence of the church or the government. We should remember that for hundreds of years the church and state had been one. To threaten the church was to threaten the state. It is here that Winthrop would be most arrogant. When Anne Hutchinson was banished, she asked why—to which Winthrop replied, "There was sufficient reason unto the court." He was not a member of the General Court when Roger Williams was banished. It is believed that Roger Williams always held a warm feeling for Winthrop and was guided by Winthrop to Narragansett Bay, beyond the jurisdiction of Massachusetts Bay Colony.

However, the main thrust of Winthrop's life was to open up possibilities for people. He broadened the Massachusetts Bay Colony Charter in September 1630 so that all male church members could vote in the affairs of government. Previously only stockholders in the company had this right. He felt that if Christian love prevailed in a society, it would serve as a "ligament binding the individual members to one body." Individuality would remain, but all the parts of this body would be united. Winthrop exhorted the passengers on the *Arbella* that the care of the public must have preference over private concerns. "We must love one another with a pure heart. Fervently, we must bear one another's burdens . . . We must delight in each other. Make others' conditions our own." To this end, Winthrop continued, "We shall be as a City upon a Hill." This ideal of a godly society dominated Winthrop's thoughts. His thoughts and his actions were concerned with the real world. He was a deeply religious man; every day he sought to discover what he believed to be God's will. His guiding principle was that which he preached to others to follow—the counsel of Micah: "To do justly, to love mercy, and to walk humbly with thy God."

From the time of the fall of Rome throughout the Middle Ages, the religious quest of most religious people was for salvation. Many would retreat from the real world. Winthrop felt it was not possible to segregate a person's spiritual and civil life.

If society follows a course that one considers morally wrong, should a person withdraw and keep principles intact, or should he or she remain in that society? Americans have answered this down through the ages in different ways. Henry Thoreau did not hesitate to reject the society that made war on Mexico. William Lloyd Garrison called on the North to leave the Union in order to escape complicity in the sin of slaveholding. In more recent times, we have seen conscientious objectors and people escaping to the country, away from the complexities of the city.

John Winthrop clearly believed what he preached. He was an idealist and a self-disciplinarian. He felt that as a Puritan he must live in the world and not leave it. He was a person of simple tastes. He liked good food, good drink, and good company. He was married four times. His first two wives died at early ages. The letters between him and his third wife, Margaret, to whom he was married for almost thirty years, show his warm, affectionate nature. His letters to Margaret expressed great tenderness. He would call her, "my dearest friend and most heartily beloved." He often referred to his family: "I take thee now and my sweet children in mine arms, and kiss and embrace you all." He liked all the things that had been given to him, and he felt it was right to enjoy them because they were God-given. But he also recognized the perennial problem—that these aspects of the material world can be too fully enjoyed.

John Winthrop's view of marriage was typical of Puritan thought. Marriage was a good thing, but like everything else, it should not be enjoyed to excess. There must be love between husband and wife, but it should be kept within bounds. It must not exceed or diminish love for God. How do you love the world and still keep your mind on God?

After his first marriage, he disciplined himself to deny many of the things that he liked most. He gave up hunting, perhaps part of the reason being that he was a poor shot. He enjoyed eating, but when he did so excessively, he found it was difficult to turn to work. Consequently, he often moved between indulgence and restraint. He did not believe in putting temptations away, for this was not to live in the real world. On a business trip to

London which gave him the chance to enjoy God without the distractions and cares and pressures of home, he found that he had a spiritual deadness without any great sense of guilt or peace. From this experience he drew a Puritan conclusion. He said that to have sure peace and joy, a person must not retire from the world and be freed from temptations. The life that is most exercised with trials and temptations is the sweetest and will prove the most satisfactory.

It is quite obvious that John Winthrop felt very strongly that it was his obligation not to take the world as he found it. The world within limits was plastic, and each person bore the responsibility to shape it according to his or her ability. He would have agreed with Edward Everett Hale's famous verse:

> *"I am only one, but still I am one.*
> *I cannot do everything, but I can do something*
> *And because I cannot do everything,*
> *I will not refuse to do the something that I can do."*

Today many of the cities of our nation are in deep trouble. We have divisions between races and ethnic groups. People within a community are hunted on the streets in gang rivalry. Family togetherness is on the wane and violence on the increase. Children are suffering death by bullets fired by their peers. There is general fear and mistrust. Around the world the picture is even worse. Here in the United States some people who can afford it often escape from the tensions and turmoil of the inner city. If John Winthrop were alive today, he would be concerned for the overall good, aware that

237

one's talents must be used, not only for oneself but for the larger good of all people.

Though some Puritans tended to feel that New England was God's only residence, Winthrop strove against provincial self-righteousness. When Virginia asked Boston for ammunition to fend off a feared Indian attack, Winthrop wished to supply them with their needs. Some felt, however, that Virginia was not a godly society. The General Court refused the request, saying that Massachusetts needed the ammunition. Seven months later when the Boston powder house blew up, many felt this was a sign of God's displeasure with the selfishness in Massachusetts.

All of us, whether we live in this city or its suburbs, must become involved in the city. We must reconcile our differences. We must be willing to give up some of our special privileges in an attempt to recreate a climate of trust. We must follow Winthrop's advice to make each other's conditions our own. Today the words of Winthrop are as relevant a challenge as ever: "To provide for posterity, we must have affection for one another, we must delight in each other, rejoice together, mourn together, labor and suffer together." By becoming a member of this Church you are taking a positive step beyond yourself. Before us as a Church is the gargantuan task of making a difference. The difference will be that justice and mercy will emerge as the prevailing mood in this city and eventually throughout the world. This is Winthrop's challenge for us today.

A New Vision

APRIL 4, 1993

Palm Sunday

ONE OF THE PURPOSES of organized religion is to remind us of those people whose visions have offered hope and purpose for creative, adventurous and spiritual living. It serves our purpose in this regard to re-look at Jesus of Nazareth and also to Martin Luther King, who was killed twenty-five years ago today. Dr. King called for all people to regard strangers in the same spirit of acceptance as they would their friends.

Palm Sunday marks in the Christian Church the beginning of Holy Week. It is the last week in the drama of the earthly career of Jesus. No other person has touched and changed so many lives for so many centuries in so many ways. In light of the difficulties we each face, the deterioration of how government governs and how people treat each other, it behooves us to re-examine the personality of one who brought to people a new vision. Who was Jesus? What can Jesus bring to brighten our current conditions? Was he a human being in our guise—"flesh as our flesh and spirit as our spirit"—or should we regard him as belonging to a different order of life?

When human beings enter into the dawn of consciousness, they find themselves pushed and pulled in two directions. I shall refer to these directions as "liberalism" and "orthodoxy." Liberalism is a word used to describe the quality in women and men who seek to depart from the old and venture into new territory to seek new truths. Orthodoxy is a word used to describe that quality in people that tries to protect the old traditions in order to ensure security and to prevent the fear that often comes with change. Liberalism is identified with new visions and adventurous spirits.

In the realm of religious and ethical ideas, there has been no greater adventurer with a new vision than Jesus. Many different groups have exclusively claimed him. In fact, however, he did not start a church or found a religion. It was Paul and some of the early church leaders who formulated the theology of Christianity. The early church was a sect within the general framework of Judaism. Paul, as he traveled on his missionary program, often used synagogues as his headquarters. It was among the Jews that Christianity had its start. The theological emphasis of Paul moved the Christian sect out of Judaism as it began to deify Jesus. The first Christians stressed the ethical religious ideas taught by Jesus, but the religion taught by Paul developed into Christianity about Jesus.

During the first four centuries, there were both liberal and orthodox elements in Christianity. Then during the latter part of the fourth century, the doors closed, keeping out the more open spirit. It happened this way. Emperor Constantine converted to Christianity. He sought to bring unity to the church. A series of councils were called to settle all the doctrinal differences. Constantine wanted a strong united church with one doctrine. This he then could use to restore unity to his empire.

A council was called at Nicea in A.D. 325. It lasted six weeks. There were two schools of thought. Bishop Arius advocated the belief that Jesus was of the nature of a human being. Bishop Athanasius held that God and Jesus were one. After great debate, Constantine joined the Athanasian Trinitarian forces. The vote was called. The Emperor's political power assured victory for religious orthodoxy and Bishop Athanasius. The Nicean Creed and the Trinity were accepted by the majority and established as the truth for the Christian Church. Only Arius and two others refused to sign it. They were sent into exile. Their books and writings were burned. Arius was condemned as an enemy of Christianity. Remnants of the Arian approach were still practiced in certain churches until A.D. 381 when the Trinity became the only accepted form for Christian worship as decreed by the Pope.

The initial ideas of religious liberalism of the first four centuries did not die with Arius. They lived on in the minds of a few people. But for eleven centuries they were not revived in a church body. Then as the Reformation swept Europe, an Italian named Faustus Socinus became the head of the Minor

Reformed Church in Poland. He began stressing the humanity of Jesus and shied away from the Trinity, saying Jesus was greater than other human beings, but not equal to God. Jesus' message needed interpretation in new times with new knowledge. Socinus's influence went west, with a printing press in Krakow turning out tracts and books proclaiming this new vision of Jesus. This helped to convert a Francis David in Transylvania who in turn convinced his king, John Sigismund, to adopt what we now call Unitarianism. King Sigismund issued an edict of toleration for all religious faiths in 1568.

I would like to emphasize the Unitarian Universalist view of Jesus, as it began with Arius, changed with Socinus, progressed with Francis David and Sigismund and evolved to its present state. For Jesus to be a major source in helping us create a new vision, we need to go beyond the doctrines of old.

Who is Jesus? Let me express it in a personal way. First, I believe in the human Jesus because the evidence in the earliest Gospels in the New Testament indicates that he regarded himself in human terms. Here are three examples from the writings closest to his time. A young man comes to Jesus saying, "Good master, what shall I do to inherit eternal life?" This was the forthright answer: "Why callest me good? There is none good but one and that is God." This is a human and not a divine answer. Consider again that when Jesus went into the Garden of Gethsemane, he uttered this prayer: "Father, if it is possible, let this cup pass away from me. Nevertheless, not as I will, but thy will be done." Does this sound like equals talking? Take that frightening time on the cross. We feel the mood of abandonment and loneliness as Jesus cries out in complete agony and desolation: "My God, my God, why hast thou forsaken me?" Are not these the words of one conscious of being human, indicating despair at impending death?

Second, I believe in the human Jesus because the evidence shows that the idea of Jesus as God evolved through time. As I mentioned, this later idea was not finalized in Church doctrine until the fourth century at the Council of Nicea. It is similar to what took place in Buddhism. Guatama, who became known as the Buddha, would have condemned any adulation paid to him as a god. But over time his adherents gathered around his memory a wealth of miracle and legend, leading to the conclusion that to worship him is the supreme revelation of the most high.

We can point out that Jesus did make unusual claims for himself. We read in the Gospel of John: "I am the way, the truth and the light. No one cometh unto God but by me." But this illustrates the point that the idea of equating God and Jesus was something that developed in the minds of people over a period of time. Biblical scholarship is clear in stating that the Gospel of John is not an historical account of the life of Jesus. It is a second century interpretation. John was probably written to reconcile the life of Jesus with a certain school of Greek philosophy that exerted a strong influence upon the early church. The basic idea of the Greek thinking was that of logos, or the word. Jesus was portrayed as the Word.

The Gospel of John is similar to a modern work called "The Prophet," written by the poet Kahlil Gibran. Gibran gives an interpretation of Jesus that puts into the mouth of Jesus all sorts of sayings. The language is beautiful, but these are interpretations of what Jesus might have said, not what he did say.

My third reason for a human view of Jesus is that only a human being can be a real source of inspiration. The only tools I have are human tools. They can be used for good or evil. And it is the example of the good that can cause one to progress ethically, spiritually, and humanely. If Jesus were more than human, his example would be hopeless for others to attain. But if as a human, he overcame the trials and vicissitudes of life, if his courage and fortitude, his patience and forbearance, his ability to see life with a new vision were derived from sources open to all of us, then his way is a challenge as well as an inspiration for each of us.

The human Jesus represents the liberal spirit. He was a person open in lifestyle and ideas. He did not limit his vision to the old concepts of the day. He based his teachings on the conviction that people can lead a new, more compassionate way of life. Despite human waywardness, there is also much promise in each of us to become a child not of evil but of good. When Jesus entered Jerusalem, he challenged the people. That most of them drifted back into their old ways does not mean that we cannot accept his challenge now. Our faith calls us to a new vision in our personal lives. This is sorely needed in an era where commitment, search for truth, and a common unity are not universally accepted.

A new vision calls for people to pull together for the common good. Palm Sunday is a good time to look into our lives to see where we might be undercutting one another in narrow and selfish ways, where we might be self-righteous instead of righteous. These are not the attributes that our world needs today. They may be part of our lives, but they can be reduced and replaced, with positive attributes coming to the forefront. John Henry Newman said, "We perfect our nature not by undoing it, but by adding to it what is more than nature and directing it toward aims higher than its own."

A new vision, based on the teachings of Jesus, calls for us to broaden our concepts and concerns. In the endeavors we decide to undertake, may we have the courage and perseverance to do the best we can. Let us remember the words of Thoreau: "That which is done well once, is done forever." This in turn creates the power of the imperishable example. Thus we can proceed to move towards the vision of the good life of Jesus that has been expressed across the centuries by many fine human insights and examples. It is the combination of love and necessity in our outlook, of loving what we need to do as we work out our destiny on this temporary stage of earth.

We are all kin to all that lives. We draw our nourishment from the same spring that sustains the flowers and the wheat fields. The adventurous spirit, the new vision, will take us on a journey towards the underlying unity of life. For human beings, Palm Sunday is a perfect time to begin to bring more humor and joy, love and beauty, and a commitment of concern and compassion into our lives. This requires thinking and acting big.

There is a story of a small girl who was bothering her father while he was reading the paper. To quiet her he gave the child a piece of paper and told her to draw something. Said she, "What shall I draw?" He replied: "A horse." She drew what she thought was a horse in a very few minutes. Realizing that similar suggestions would result in quick solutions, he handed his daughter a large piece of paper and asked her to draw God. She sat down with the paper. Peace for the father. A long period of silence. The father looked up and saw the paper still blank. "What is wrong?" he asked. She replied, "If I'm going to draw big, I have to think big." A new vision requires thinking big, thinking creatively, using imagination and ingenuity.

Let Palm Sunday be a time of committing ourselves to a new vision! May our commitment not become a passing fancy. May everything that separates and divides, all theologies, doctrines and ideologies that separate our natures from the vision that Jesus had, be overcome by the nurturing of our very best. How in the end can Humanity and Divinity be separate?

Trust the Future

APRIL 11, 1993

Easter Sunday

COLLECTIVELY, WE HAVE ALL experienced a long, seemingly endless winter. Individually, each of us now or at some other time has had our own personal wintertime experiences. This individual darkness can translate into collective problems for communities, institutions and nations. Today, we need a turning point away from dark times towards hope and promise.

There are a few occasions that can be said conclusively to represent a turning point. Easter is one of them. But in Unitarian Universalist circles this is not always the case. The literal story of the resurrection does not have meaning for most of our members. Some of us may be confused about what metaphors and meaning we gain from Easter Sunday. We are not as confused, however, as some of the pupils in Mrs. Rogers's first-grade class. She asked her young students the meaning of

Easter. The hand of an Episcopalian boy went up. Eagerly, he exclaimed, "It is when we buy a tree, put lights on it, give presents and sing about baby Jesus." "That's not it," said the teacher, "you have Easter confused with Christmas. Is there anyone else who can tell me?" Another hand went up . . . a Roman Catholic girl. She proudly said, "Easter is when you have a big turkey, and your father sits before the T.V. all day watching football." "No," said Mrs. Rogers. "Someone must understand what Easter is." A Southern Baptist announced in no uncertain terms, "It is when you shoot off fireworks, have a picnic." "No! No!" cried the teacher, becoming exasperated. "Doesn't anyone know?" The Unitarian in the class raised her hand. "I know," she said. "After a ministry of three years, Jesus rode into Jerusalem on a donkey. He is a troublemaker to the authorities. They arrest him and place him on a cross between two thieves. When he is dead they bring him down and put him in a cave." "Wonderful," exclaimed the relieved teacher. "Go on, Jane." "Then after a couple of days the stone is rolled away. Jesus comes out. He sees his shadow, goes back into the cave and there will be six more weeks of winter."

Though we may not be as confused as Mrs. Rogers's class, Easter has different meanings to many of us. It combines time, theology, legend, and customs from many lands and places. Today I will attempt to cover the broad spectrum of belief that is associated with Easter.

Easter has venerable origins, all of which are related to the beginning of life, to the rising sun of the new day. Some say the word Easter is derived from the Norse Eostre, meaning the festival of spring at the vernal equinox. The word also has its origins in Sanskrit, where it meant dawn in the East. Easter not only includes the idea of dawn, but it also encompasses the idea of the resurrection of nature. With the disappearing of snow, we are greeted by crocuses, the return of migrant birds—life quickening after a long dormancy. Some, seeing this, view Easter as some vague, cheerful neo-pagan lunar celebration of the predictable return of tulips and robins after a weary winter.

But many people have felt the need to go further than celebrating earth's seasons. This year is no exception. People feel the need for something more life sustaining than the brief existence of a daffodil. They want to live life more fully and courageously even when there is difficulty in this world and in one's life. Easter also is associated with people and their renewal. While many people have been mainly concerned with leading better lives, others have either hoped for or believed in some aspect of immortality.

Looking at the ancient world religions, we see in other faiths symbolic saviors who lived to help humanity, who died as martyrs and who rose triumphant over death. I refer to Orpheus, Krishna, Osirus of Egypt, Marduk of Babylon, Persephone of the Greeks, Baldur of the Teutons. All these ancient figures depict the descent of the spirit, the struggle with evil and selfishness and then triumph.

We cannot think of Easter without noting the traditional Christian approach that mirrors so closely these ancient scenarios. In the *Christian Century*, there appeared an editorial by the dean of a highly respected, deeply Christian-oriented divinity school. "Who was responsible for the death of Jesus?" asked this dean.

After he pointed out many who might be held responsible, including the temple authorities, Judas and Pilate, he answered: "Jesus was not delivered up by his generation alone. He was delivered according to the definite plan of God. Who then was responsible? In the last analysis God was the responsible one, since God so proposed and accomplished the redemption of man."

This type of Christian theology echoes the instincts of primitive people. Some primitive persons, in order to atone for their mistakes or to be on the good side of deity, sacrificed a person as a blood offering. In a strict interpretation this is what Christian theology has done with Jesus. We read in John 3:16 that God gave his only son as a sacrifice so that individuals accepting this sacrifice and accepting Jesus as Lord and savior might have eternal life. How did this primitive concept of salvation become associated with such an ethical leader? Reading the Gospels we cannot fail to be impressed with the impact of Jesus upon his immediate followers. Paul wrote that they saw "the light of knowledge of the glory of God in his presence." Then Jesus was crucified. His followers did what all people tend to do. They began to rationalize their experiences. They were steeped in the Jewish heritage of sacrifice. They were saturated, both through custom and inherited ideas, with this tradition. They believed that without the shedding of blood there was no remission of sin, no salvation, no reconciliation with God. Thus Jesus became the perfect sacrificial victim as the church developed its doctrine and theology in the early centuries.

Here in the twentieth century, we can see the close relationship between the idea of God sacrificing Jesus and the primitive concepts of blood sacrifice. Many of us see this belief of God's sac-rificing Jesus as both unethical and unreal. We have a concept of deity that is much broader. Those who can no longer accept this old theology find in Jesus an exemplar of a style of life that can give people a sense of renewal and purpose in their daily tasks. Jesus illuminates the way for a fuller life, an open road available to all of us. To Jesus a meaningful life was shown by the father of the Prodigal Son watching and waiting for the moment when his son would understand himself and would say, "I will rise and go to my father and will say I have sinned against heaven and before you and am not worthy to be called your son." The father would reply, "Rejoice with me for my son was dead and is alive again. He was lost and is found." A renewed life was one lived by the good shep-herd who searched the hills and valleys until the lost sheep was found. When he found it, he laid it on his shoulder rejoicing, and arriving home he called together his friends and neighbors saying, "Rejoice with me, for I have found my sheep which was lost."

We see in the teachings of Jesus no shedding of blood for the remission of sins, no blood atonements, no sacrifice of death arranged before the world as a moral spectacle, no mediator between the soul of a person and one's deity in order that one might be forgiven.

With this quick review of Easter—its origins, history, theology—we can come to two overarching conclusions that are relevant today. First, people have always felt the need for person-al renewal and spiritual renewal with the end of winter and the arrival of spring. That is not to say that renewal cannot occur at other times. But with spring's arrival, we do think about life's restorative powers. What we see in nature, we know exists with human beings—renewal, change, and growth. Second, we see growth in life from infancy to adulthood. Infancy means our needs are met by others. But it cannot last. We will want to move out and explore our world, experiment with independence, discovering our individuality and the joy of creating and giving. Of course there are moments throughout our lives when thoughts of dependency seem appealing to us. When life confronts us with pain, disappointment, loss, there is the temptation to return to infancy's narcissistic state of self-centeredness. Yet if we want to grow up and experience the rewards of maturity, we must give up this past and learn to take care of ourselves. It is a type of death, this letting go of infancy, but we survive it by moving beyond it and by trusting the future. A little later our childhood comes to an end. We add more responsibility, and take our place in the world of home, school and community. No more endless play. Saying goodbye to your childhood is another kind of death, but unless you want to stop growing, the only direction is forward towards increasing responsibilities. The realization that you are fulfilling your life brings a special kind of happiness reserved for using your talents. What then can these little deaths teach us? They can teach us to face and accept the passing stages of life. They teach us to let go of our outgrown pasts and to trust the future.

Symbolically, Easter is a time of moving from darkness to light, from a lesser self to the visibility of a better one. It is a time of spiritual resurrection for each of us. Let us ponder then, this day, those things that keep us in darkness. Let us resolve to overcome them so that we move beyond the routines and the dark times of our lives to reach towards our greater potential.

Here is a widow finding new life and relationships after losing her husband of forty-six years; the alcoholic rediscovering freedom and hope in sobriety; the fifty-year-old man uncovering new purpose and joy as he, with a physician's help, controls a stubborn depression; the paraplegic, from a wheelchair, building self-worth and identity by serving others in need; an ex-prisoner starting over on the outside with a new job and determination to be a responsible and productive citizen; the victim of childhood abuse slowly finding personal peace and the ability to trust again; a person downed with a disease, yet rising to reconnect with hope with those who are close. These are people removing the blocks away from the traps and tombs in which they find themselves.

Easter, besides carrying the thrust of personal and spiritual renewal, signifies to some people the idea that in some way life does not end in death. This is where honest differences of belief may be focused. No one will disagree with the idea that what you give to others goes on into the future with them. Some believe that assurance of eternal life comes from accepting the concept of salvation based on the sacrifice of someone else. Some, realizing the inconsistency of the literal Easter story with the ordering of the universe and the process of nature, are turning elsewhere for affirmation.

Many of us feel that life is an unfinished symphony. Schubert died at thirty-one, leaving an unfinished symphony. There is an unfinished symphony in every life. Ralph Waldo Emerson said,

"The blazing evidence of immortality is our dissatisfaction with any other solution. What is excellent as God lives is permanent." Voltaire, Descartes, Kant rejected the literal Bible story of a physical resurrection and yet firmly held to the belief of life after death. There are many of us who would like to believe this, but as the English clergyman Dean Inge remarked, "The evidence is not there. I will have to wait and see."

In the last seventy-five years people have been looking into new areas of consciousness that speak of dimensions of existence beyond the body. They go from altered states of consciousness, near-death experience where the spirit seems to be outside the body, to meditation. There is growing evidence that we have touched upon a whole realm of existence that is just as real as our bodily one. There is Kirelian photography, which uses high-energy fields to help photograph the human aura. There is bio-energy, which is a form of energy that allows for telepathic communication. Psychic research is being done at Duke and the University of California. There was research in this field in the former Soviet Union. We should realize that we are only at the dawn of understanding human personality, what its true nature is and what its final destiny will be.

Whether the significance of Easter to you is the renewal of a better self or an affirmation of some dimension of immortality, each one of us can trust the future if we are committed to making our lives worthy of immortality. We live in a world that runs by principle. The greatest principle is the capacity to grow in love and communion with one another, to have courage and to sacrifice when it is demanded. Regardless of certain talents and certain deficiencies, each of us has the ability to see through darkness in order to discover a way toward nobleness and acts of greatness.

Regardless of our beliefs, life is not defeated by seeming death any more than nature is defeated by winter. Life is to be lived not as if it has a beginning and an end but as if we are on an eternal stream. Let this Easter then be a turning point—from darkness and incompleteness to light and hope, renewal, development and affirmation. In this spirit let us trust the future: "To lose the earth you know for greater knowing; to lose the life you have for greater life; to leave the friends you loved for greater loving; to find a land more kind than home, more large than earth whereon the pillars of this earth are found."

Beliefs That Matter

OCTOBER 17, 1993

(Reflections from three trips to China)

*L*ET ME BEGIN BY DEFINING what I mean by beliefs that matter. A belief is the conviction of the truth or reality of an idea. Beliefs that matter enable us to cope in our environment regardless of the external circumstances and internal turmoil. They do not include, however, actions and thinking that bring harm and ill to others. Beliefs that matter are influential but not authoritarian. Some beliefs are like walled gardens, as Sophia Fahs put it: "They encourage exclusiveness and the feeling of being especially privileged. . . . These beliefs are divisive, separating the saved from the unsaved, shutting off the power to choose one's own direction. . . . Some beliefs are rigid like the body of death." Just imagine the mind power that has been wasted across the history of the human race because people were stifled in their thinking, were kept entombed by authority.

Most people over the centuries have lived under threats by some controlling authority. This has certainly been the case in the Far East. This past summer Eleanor and I spent four weeks in two nations where authoritarian practice has been the way of life across recorded history and still exists today—Indonesia and China. Traveling in these Pacific Rim nations, you quickly become aware of the influence of religion in people's lives—perhaps as a counterweight to the authoritarian power of the state. It was a religion or a combination of religions that gave people inner meaning in a world that was externally controlled by others. Today the influence of religion is in a transitional stage. Beliefs are taking on new forms, leaving behind some tenets and attitudes that had helped people survive in ruthless societies.

Let us take a look back for a moment at the Chinese philosophical tradition and religions and their influence with the people as a background for understanding what seems to be taking place today. Let us look at Confucianism, Taoism and Buddhism as against the twentieth-century imports of Christianity, Marxism and entrepreneurial capitalism.

In the Chinese tradition, there is no Supreme Being or creator. There is a myth, which describes how the supernatural being Pan Gu created the earth, but this is a late addition to the Chinese canon. According to more ancient beliefs, primordial chaos was transformed into order through the continuous interaction of the cosmic forces of yin and yang. Yin, the female principle, is represented in the darkness, night, moisture and the moon; yang, the male principle, is found in their opposites: light, day, dryness and the sun. The harmonious interaction of these opposing but complementary forces results in the pattern of life known as Dao, the way.

The Chinese social order and the moral justification for an authoritarian, hierarchical government in imperial China were based on the ideas attributed to Confucius, who lived Before the Common Era (551–479). In an ideal Confucian society, order is maintained by ensuring that all people know their place in society and act appropriately. Confucius defined relationships of apparent mutual responsibility but actual dominance and subservience between ruler and subject, father and son, elder and younger brother, husband and wife. Books attributed to Confucius, although probably compiled after his death, include the *Analects* or sayings, *The Book of Songs* and the manual of divination called *The Book of Changes,* which we in the West refer to as the *I Ching.* This last book has been used for over two thousand years as a guide to human action. The reader throws three coins, and the way they fall directs the individual to a particular passage which, when correctly interpreted, indicates an appropriate course of action.

Confucianism has been a conservative influence on the Chinese throughout their history, asserting the primacy of the past over the present and the old over the young. It has been particularly oppressive towards women, whose position demanded obedience to the father, then to the husband and finally to the son. The importance Confucianism places on maintaining outward composure may be good for authoritarian government but must take its toll on people who are told to suppress their wants, their feelings, their dreams.

In the twentieth century, Confucianism has come under attack. But despite the criticism, the Chinese retain many of the ideas of Confucianism, most notably the respect of children for their parents. Authoritarian Chinese leadership, whether imperial or communist, stands to gain from perpetuating a belief which aims at keeping society orderly. The communists do not attribute this so much to Confucian beliefs but to the traditional morality of China.

Our picture changes when we bring in another strand of Chinese philosophy and religion—Taoism. Taoism rejects the constraints that define Confucianism. Where Confucianism is hierarchical and emphasizes responsibilities and duties depending upon one's place in the social order, Taoism stresses spontaneity and the need to be at one with nature, that is, the natural world and one's natural self, somewhat in the spirit of Emerson and Thoreau. Though seemingly contradictory, Confucianism and Taoism have complemented each other in the Chinese tradition. Together, they appeal to two sides of the human personality. Mandarins of the past might have been model Confucians in their official dealings, but they still could have adopted a Taoist approach in private life.

In the book *The Way and the Power* by the supposed founder of Taoism, Lao-tse, a contemporary of Confucius, there is a summary of Taoist thinking. Lao-tse regarded civilization and learning as enemies of nature. Perhaps this was a background for Mao's Cultural Revolution, as Mao persecuted all religions during his dictatorship. In Taoism, the ideal person is an uncut block. Ideal behavior consists of nonintervention with the natural functioning of the world. Freedom and integrity are qualities to be prized and the pursuit of power is disdained.

Taoism began as a refined and quiet philosophy. Over the centuries, it blended with other folk beliefs and practices to form an elaborate religion with many sects and with innumerable gods and spirits. Popular Taoism as practiced in the rural Chinese villages involves the power of the shamans and ritual offerings to ancestors and household gods.

Buddhism came from India and took a strong hold in the third century A.D. with the chaos that followed the fall of the Han dynasty. Buddhism is regarded, with Confucianism and Taoism, as one of the three fundamental religions of ancient China. Buddhism teaches that life is painful, but the pain and sorrow may be eliminated by suppression of the self through meditation or performance of rituals. The believer attempts to achieve enlightenment and attain nirvana, an escape from the world. It has held and still does hold a strong influence on popular imagination, especially with the peasants in interior China. In the ancient capital of Xian, the eastern point of the Silk Road, you can still see today processions of the faithful praying and offering incense at shrines and temples. But along the coast and south China with its booming economic development, Buddhism seems relegated to the past.

These three belief systems have combined over the centuries to produce patterns of behavior that can be seen in Chinese communities everywhere. Their influence has been instrumental in helping people accept authority with its recurring ruthlessness. They have enabled people to withdraw from worldly expectations. Confucianism has had a most obvious effect. Its powerful sense of family loyalty and respect for elders has been a force holding Chinese society together but unfortunately suppressing initiative, especially of the young. Taoism's influence has been more on private than public life, but many Chinese intellectuals commonly express a Taoist's posture of disdain for worldly affairs. Buddhist influence is seen in the fatalism of the Chinese people, the peasantry most of all, in enduring centuries of tyranny with little active resistance.

An attack on the influence of these three traditions, seemingly in conflict at some points yet existing harmoniously in people's lives, commenced with the Cultural Revolution of 1966–76. The young were turned against their past so that a new order might replace it. Brutal attacks by youth on their teachers and on anyone tainted by bourgeois thinking, religion or foreign connections were commonplace in the late 1960s. Families were torn apart as children denounced their parents, and wives and husbands repudiated one another, divorcing partners who came under suspicion or attack. Colleagues attacked one another, both to settle personal scores and to save themselves from condemnation. The only way to survive in that atmosphere of mutual betrayal and suspicion was to maintain a public face that was enthusiastic about the achievements of socialism and the policies of the Communist party.

The ancient blend of the religious past was jolted by the Cultural Revolution and is fast losing its persuasiveness and influence in coastal and southern China. Although the Cultural Revolution was tragic and is now discredited, it did set in motion new forces that are influencing the Chinese in ways foreign to their religious heritage of accepting poverty and authority.

The most recent factor influencing Chinese attitudes and behavior is the national experiment with entrepreneurial capitalism, or market socialism, as it is sometimes called. The economic liberalization of the 1980s renewed personal ambition and initiative and has created considerable wealth for the successful. It also has led to rising consumer expectations and intense jealousy of the newly rich at a time when inflation has reduced living standards for those who have not participated in the upward economic spiral. These new pressures combined with the abiding problem of overcrowding and the abandonment by many of their religious heritage lead to great stress.

The Chinese leadership believes in Western technology. A sign at the city of Yantai's Economic and Technological Development Zone reads in bold English letters: "God is the Investor." But they believe other Western ideas cause many of the problems in their contemporary society including exploitation, corruption and tax evasion. These vices, however, are not foreign; they are universal, existing in every nation.

But if China is adopting Western entrepreneurial capitalism, it does not have to adopt exploitation and corruption with it. They have existed in China for centuries. We, as a culture and nation offer other alternatives sometimes neglected among ourselves. We offer the idea that human beings can be good and positive as well as evil and negative. Our Emersons, Hales, and Parkers talked about beliefs that mattered. Among them were the full use of the mind in taming our passions and opening our potentials. They reminded us that a mind is like a parachute—it has to be open to function properly.

The open mind will lead each of us to the less traveled road in life called the second mile. This leads us to civility. Civility means much more than politeness. It is all-embracing, an awareness that personal well-being cannot be separated from the well-being of the groups to which we belong—our families, our associations, our churches, our businesses, our nation, our world.

Lack of civility is tied to unreasonable, mindless expectations and beliefs, seen in recent decades by a demand for constant happiness and comfort. When real life presents us with painful experiences, when we feel unfulfilled, we feel cheated. Too many of us too often reach for instant happiness by means that disregard the interests of other people. If we have lost some of our civility as a society, there is a road back.

In today's world, perhaps the belief that matters most is civility. This is what we need to export along with our entrepreneurship. But first we need to redefine it and bring it to the fore at home. An open mind tells us that to improve civility we must follow a route that begins with greater awareness of our shortcomings and our tendencies to manipulate others. We should expect some difficulties and pain in the short run, but we should achieve long-term gain in having a sense of well-being, of having warmer and more meaningful relationships with those close to us and with society as a whole.

Civility requires two-way communication, not the building of walls. Some of its principles are these: Do your best and learn from your mistakes; don't expect perfection. Set aside time for real in-depth communication. Clear your mind at times from your point of view and listen to the other person. Don't be so fragile that you cannot listen to another viewpoint. Be honest with yourself and with others. Judge yourself first; look into your real motives. Take time to think and respond; don't be afraid of silence. Try to be as gentle as possible; don't make unnecessarily painful statements, yet don't be so subtle that the point is completely missed. These are ways of communicating ideas and beliefs that can help free you from environments and influences that negatively affect you and the well-being of others.

History shows us that at times there is a shift of consciousness from a diversity that is antagonistic, to finding a more common purpose despite diversity. Beliefs that matter affect this goal. Most recently the fall of Communism in the East has opened up the minds of millions. And at present the threat of a global confrontation has gone. The fighting in Somalia, Haiti and Bosnia are countered by the attempt at resolution taking place between the PLO and Israel. May we each play a part in bringing civility to the diversities in this land, that it may shine as an example to be followed by others throughout the world.

Making Change Work

MAY 21, 1995

*(Joint service of the First and Second Church in Boston and
delegates to the Triennial of the Society of the Cincinnati)*

THE LUTHERANS STARTED the Protestant
Reformation. They and the Anglicans changed the orientation
of their religious beliefs from an infallible Pope and his advis-
ers to the writings of the Holy Bible. The Puritans offered a
cohesive covenanted community of Christians working together as one. The Methodists deformalized religion, making it
more understandable to the masses and more sensitive to the
social issues. The Baptists focused on separation of Church
and State. The Congregationalists moved supreme ecclesiastical power from a hierarchy to the members of each church. All
these denominations and others have contributed to the development of our country. The strength of each denomination
has come from the commitment of its members working
together.

There is a story about a certain Puritan family who, before coming to the Massachusetts Bay Colony, were riding in a public carriage near Manchester, England. As they bounced along the road, a mosquito landed on the nose of the horse. The father, looking at his children, became fearful that the mosquito would bite, the horse bolt, and they might be in a terrible accident. Gaining the attention of the driver, the father asked if he could do something about the situation. "No problem," said the driver, and picking up his whip, he flipped the lash, removing the mosquito without disturbing the horse's nose. Soon a fly landed on the nose, and the same scenario was enacted. Then a hornet alighted. When the request came to remove the hornet, nothing happened. Again the driver was asked but still no response. "Why won't you do to the hornet what you did to the mosquito and fly?" the father asked. The driver finally turned around and said, "The situation is entirely different. The mosquito and fly are individuals. The hornet belongs to an organization."

Each one of you here this morning in this sanctuary is, of course, an individual. But each of you also realizes the importance of being part of an organization. Organizations at their best help inspire people. They free people from their lesser selves, enabling them to work with others to gain their finer potentials, even helping to change a community and transform a nation.

Highly effective people create and develop such organizations. Their intrepid devotion and inner fire give others a vision of a fairer, more humane world. They often come forth in times of tyranny. The Puritans came to the Massachusetts Bay Colony because of religious tyranny in England. Efforts to achieve a harmonious community require a unique and creative leadership. To be knit together as one for a higher cause, larger than the self, is not an easy task. It requires a large measure of self-discipline.

One of the founders of this church, John Winthrop, whose statue stands to the right as you approach the entrance to this church, captured the imagination of the Puritans in 1630. He preached a sermon entitled "A Model of Christian Charity" to the group of Puritans who were on board the sailing ship *Arbella* on their way to establishing this new colony. He said in part: "We must love one another with a pure heart. Fervently, we must bear one another's burdens. . . . We must be willing to abridge ourselves of our superfluities for the supply of others' necessities. We must delight in each other, make others' condition our own, rejoice together, mourn together, labor and suffer together, always having before our eyes our community as members of the same body."

This need of community is an opportunity always before us. Each generation should relive it, refocus this need in terms of the understanding and knowledge of the times. We should remember that John Winthrop meant this for a small homogeneous Puritan society, but these sentiments are not outdated spiritual values.

By the time of the American Revolution, there were actions and attitudes that were tearing people apart. The thirteen colonies were certainly different. Taken as a whole they did not constitute a homogeneous society in the old Puritan sense. But if tyranny was to be defeated, there was the need to pull the diverse elements then existing into a cohesive force for freedom.

Paul Revere was deeply moved by the fiery revolutionary preaching of John Lathrop, who was minister of the Second Church in Boston, then known as the "Old North." The night of April 18, 1775, Revere made his famous ride to Lexington, warning that the British were coming.

On April 19 the British attacked; on April 20, the Continental Congress in Philadelphia appointed Artemas Ward of Shrewsbury, Massachusetts, General of the Continental Army. His commission called for him to raise an army of 22,000. He exceeded this goal. But under Ward, discipline was lax. Some of the troops would disappear, returning home to plough; others exploited the situation, requisitioning supplies for nonexistent troops. Here was an army of independent and undisciplined men. They were not knit together as one, yet they were to go up against a disciplined European armed force.

While the Battle of Bunker Hill was being fought on June 15, 1775, the Continental Congress appointed George Washington to be Commander in Chief. He arrived in Cambridge on July 3, taking over command of the army. During the ten weeks under General Ward's command, there had been one court-martial and a measure of confusion among the 25,000 troops. After ten weeks under General Washington's command, there were eighty-four court-martials, and the size of the army was reduced to 6,000. But under Washington, those troops were knit together more as a community. This in the end made all the difference in the eventual winning of the Revolution.

The Society of the Cincinnati provides a living link to the American Revolution. Organized on May 10, 1783, at Fishkill, New York by the Continental Army officers, George Washington served as its first president until his death in 1799. The Society's charter states three purposes for its establishment: to preserve the rights and liberties for which its founders had fought, to promote the national honor and dignity of the American Empire, and to reinforce the "cordial affection" among its members by providing aid and assistance to them and their families when in need.

With the early Puritans, this Church, and the Society of the Cincinnati, there is the common thread of being knit together in friendship around an ideal, a vision of a better world. What happened in each case was, as Whitehead described, "to adventure beyond the safeties of the past."

To be able to inspire people to work together in a great cause takes a certain type of individual. All Americans should be grateful that a large measure of the characteristics necessary were embodied by George Washington. One of the qualities necessary in a leader is self-discipline. This was one of Washington's outstanding characteristics. Working at personal discipline and self-improvement, Washington transformed himself from a youthful person who was insecure, aggressive, headstrong, and self-centered into a very disciplined individual.

Discipline is not a popular subject these days. Often we think of it as being thrust upon us by external forces. Washington's discipline was not external. His parents, superiors, or institutions were not the primary catalysts for his lifelong duty to discipline. Through his own experience, he realized that you cannot control a spirited horse if you cannot first control yourself. He came to the conclusion that one can only be free by mastering oneself. To maintain a free and just society requires constant personal and collective discipline.

Today, we face in the U.S. a larger and more diverse body of people. George Washington needs to be reintroduced to Americans of today. It is his disciplined example that could give fresh vitality to the quality of life in this nation. He was a strong, effective, balanced and inspirational leader. He made change work. The English writer Samuel Coleridge, knowing of Washington's discipline and sense of control over base emotions, said: "Tranquil and firm, he moved with one pace in one path, and neither vaulted nor tottered. Among a people eminently querulous and already impregnated with the germs of discordant parties, he directed the executive power firmly and unostentatiously."

To make change work requires not only self-discipline but also forgiveness, steadfastness of purpose, and at times, compromise and humility. When the British evacuated Boston in 1776, many "Tories" who supported the British sailed on the British ships as they left the harbor, but many Tories were left behind. Washington wrote: "Deluded mortals! Would it not be good policy to grant a generous amnesty, to conquer these people by a generous forgiveness." By the end of the Revolution it is estimated that 80,000 people had left this newly founded nation to remain loyal to the British Crown. Many did not return, but those who did were accepted, and many gave credit to the new nation. As an example, Cadwallader Colden returned from a self-imposed exile and was elected mayor of New York. Dr. John Jefferies of Boston, a surgeon in the British Army, returned to Boston and built up a large practice.

To make change work, steadfastness of purpose is required. In the early months of his command of the Continental Army, Washington had nightly toasted King George III. This stopped in January 1776 when, after reading Thomas Paine's *Common Sense*, Washington realized that there was no turning back from the cause of freedom that had begun. He was converted completely to the goal of independence from Britain. Even with battle losses and Britain's attempt in 1779 to make peace with the colonies by offering dominion home rule as existed in Canada until 1867, George Washington remained steadfast to the cause of the Revolution.

The example of Washington in knitting together a new nation through the dimensions of self-discipline and sacrifice has continued to be a catalyst for the peoples of this country in times of crisis. This heritage helped to bring us together to defeat the forces of Nazism. We recently have been reminded of this in our celebration of the fiftieth anniversary of V. E. Day this past May 9.

We would do well today, in working for solutions to current problems, to consider the words of Washington in his first Inaugural Address. He urged a spirit of compromise and the pursuit in public matters of "private morality." He said, "There exists an indissoluble union between virtue and happiness, between duty and advantage, between an honest and magnanimous policy and the solid rewards of public prosperity and felicity."

We acknowledge that nothing left loose is ever a creative force. No horse is useful to us until harnessed. Gasoline is useless until it enters a carburetor. No life becomes great or inspires until it is disciplined and focused, yet tolerant and to a degree humble.

Our nation came into existence because the leadership and the people had both spurs and bridles. They adventured into the unknown, but they kept the concept of liberty before them as their goal. They made changes, but they kept change in perspective and in balance by self-discipline, by steadfastness of purpose, by decisiveness in action and by loyalty to an ideal larger than any person.

We can make change work today if we apply ourselves to specific organizations that speak and act ideally while embracing responsible freedom. We must cherish the uniqueness of each individual. But we know the power and the strength when, together in our organizations, we reach out to improve the quality of life in our American society.

Look at your watch. It is telling you that the time to end this service is at hand. Your watch works because its individual parts are working together. How much greater our individualty can be developed by working with others. Commitment and involvement with organizations that value the heritage of responsible freedom elevate our hopes for the future—a future where life, liberty and the pursuit of happiness will become reality for increasing numbers of the world's peoples.

Millennium Challenges

SEPTEMBER 20, 1998

TODAY AS WE COMMENCE A NEW CHURCH
year, I hope we will discover a measure of optimism for the
future.

Each millennium gives us the special opportunity to look
forward and backward over a thousand years. Although we have
not quite reached the year 2000, we are so close that it is tempting to speculate about this milestone in human history. In sharing some thoughts on this subject, I hope not to be like the com-
mencement speaker this year at Johns Hopkins University. He
opened his remarks by saying: "My job is to bore you, and to let
the hardness of your seat and the warmth of your robe prepare
you for what is to come." What a pessimist! At least here you do
not have hard seats and academic robes do not overheat you.
That should give you some optimism.

The world we know today was unimagined 1,000 years ago. The world then was thought to be flat. Western European culture knew little about the cultures of Asia and of Africa. Democracy was untried. Kingdoms and tribes dominated, and the feudal system kept people in virtual slavery. The printing press was unknown. Book knowledge was primarily limited to the clergy, who set the tone of civil and spiritual belief. Religious wars were an accepted practice. Superstition was the cornerstone of faith. Diseases such as smallpox and the bubonic plague decimated populations. The greatest invention of the time was the large plow that enabled people to increase the food supply and ward off famine. The measure of fear was high; the expectation of joy was low. The unknown loomed large and dangerous. A person's lifespan was short.

A major scenario dominated the thoughts of Europeans who faced the year 1000. It was that God would come to earth to judge the saved and unsaved, ending human life on earth. A minority thought that God would bring forth an era of universal peace for the peoples of the earth.

As the centuries progressed, there were a few who speculated about the future on this earth. Roger Bacon, living in the thirteenth century, proved to have a fairly accurate vision of the future. He foresaw the magnifying glass, microscope, telescope, balloon flights, diving gear, high-speed ocean travel, the automobile and global circumnavigation by ship. He foresaw this 200 years before Columbus risked all to find that the earth is not flat. Bacon also foresaw bombs and modern warfare. The wars of the twentieth century certainly have replaced disease as the biggest destroyer of human lives.

Leonardo da Vinci of the fifteenth and sixteenth centuries, halfway through the millennium, was a virtual genius in predicting the coming achievements of the human race. Before their actual discovery, he spoke of parachutes, life jackets, contact lenses, planes, bicycles, water turbines, odometers, tanks and mass production.

Edward Everett Hale, one of our former ministers in the nineteenth century, predicted people walking on the moon in one of his books entitled *The Brick Moon*. Hale might not have been surprised that in less than 100 years, millions of people would view Neil Armstrong actually walking on the moon.

No one can imagine the strides that will be achieved in the next 1,000 years. Expertise is a matter of cumulative learning and experience. Look at the expertise the human race has to build upon today. Since 1960 more scientific knowledge has been acquired than in the previous 5,000 years. Today scientific knowledge doubles every decade, and the number of library volumes doubles every thirteen years. Most technology is obsolete in six years. In both electronics and computers, obsolescence occurs at around two years.

Catherine the Great of Russia, reflecting on her own changing times, said: "A great wind is blowing, and that gives you either imagination or a headache." Individuals, even at a young age, have achieved breakthroughs in widening the body of knowledge. Darwin began his work on evolution at the age of twenty-seven. At the age of twenty-one, Michael Faraday invented the electric motor. Einstein, in his twenties, began his work on space-time relativity and realized that mass can be converted into energy, leading to the atomic age and space travel.

It is not unreasonable to assume that if we do not destroy ourselves as a human race, the healthy and productive lifespan of human beings will be dramatically extended. This will come about through genetic engineering, greater understanding of nutrition, and control of diseases. We may not be limited to living on the earth and moon but may be able to colonize elsewhere in space.

I believe we will move towards a global multicultural civilization. Already up and down the Pacific coast, the first multicultural civilization is taking form. There is a blending of European, Asian, African and Hispanic cultures. The August issue of the *Atlantic Monthly* devotes its feature story to this fact. The article says that just over the horizon is "a land in which the dominant culture is an internationalized one at every level; in which the political units that really matter are confederations of city-states; in which loyalty is an economic concept, in which the United States exists chiefly to provide military protection."

We could all write down our dreams for the next thousand years and then wonder how we might put foundations under them. I think, however, that first we must deal with the same issues our ancestors did 1,000 years ago—optimism and pessimism. Optimism was voiced at the beginning of the last millennium by those who saw an endless era of peace. Pessimism was felt by those who saw the end of life on earth with Armageddon.

The church in the year 1000 offered the pessimism of Armageddon, with optimism open only to those who accepted the church's formula for salvation. It was a religion that shunned reason and individual interpretation and held people in ignorance by the power of fear and promises of salvation through unquestioning obedience. Its vision was narrow and self-centered.

Although this approach to religion, with its pessimism about the future, still exists as we come to the year 2000, it is by no means the dominant force in the actual belief system of most people. Pessimism today stems more from the misuse of the achievements developed over the last millennium by the human race. Look at technology. Atomic weapons could destroy life in a flash, just as the ancients 1,000 years ago thought God would do. Today, terrorists in their fanaticism could use these weapons or germ warfare to destroy much or all of life on earth.

Genetic engineering portends extended life spans and control over diseases. The pessimistic consequences might be in eugenics, creating a master race with vast discrimination among people.

If there is optimism about raising the standard of living in the Third World, there is pessimism in watching affluent nations overindulge with materialism and excessive lifestyles leading to premature deaths. Continued undisciplined use of natural resources, especially by mature nations, will portend the future collapse of civilization. I am not speaking about 1,000 years from now but maybe 50 years ahead.

Here in Boston we take for granted plenty of clean fresh water, free of disease-bearing microbes. Today one-fifth of the world population has no access to safe drinking water. It is predicted that in twenty-seven years, two-thirds of the people on earth will face either water shortage or water pollution.

The problems we face in these changing times and those that the human race will meet over the next 1,000 years are solvable.

They can be positively dealt with if, as the Bible states, we, the human race, get both wisdom and understanding.

Materialism and physical inventions are not the sole ingredients for a successful future. What is more important is what kind of human attitudes we bring to the mix of life. Attitudes are contagious; are yours worth catching?

Religion is supposed to be the source of our ethical compass. The Church needs to remove its focus upon the past, its reliance on blind faith, and instead challenge each of us to do our utmost in making this a humane world for the human race.

Someone asked Mahatma Gandhi why, since he admired Jesus so much, he didn't become a Christian. He replied, "I have yet to discover anyone living by his teachings." The Church of the future needs to help us overcome our indifference to the ethical life.

Gandhi also warned of the dangers of living in an age characterized by:

> "Politics without principle
> Wealth without morality
> Pleasure without conscience
> Education without character
> Science without humanity
> Worship without sacrifice."

And I would like to add: Power without responsibility.

On this continent, so richly blessed just now with material prosperity, outward signs of prosperity are deceiving us. Unless a person's faith and character include good will, there will not be real progress in the new millennium.

If there is growing animosity on all levels, indifference and even laziness have too often overtaken pride and loyalty in what we do. Leonard Read of the Foundation for Economic Education tells of a shopper in a crowded department store during the Christmas rush. After buying some gifts, she forges her way to the gift-wrap counter, remarking to the clerk that the store is so jammed. "Yes," said the clerk, "it's our best day so far." Then the shopper goes to the post office to mail her gifts, remarking to the postal clerk on the crowd in the post office. With a sigh, she hears, "It's our worst day so far."

Added to our animosities, indifference, indulgence and laziness is our growing obsession with celebrity in determining the worth and values of our society. The way the media handled Princess Diana's and Mother Theresa's deaths indicate the public is more enamored with glitz and glamour than with sacrificial living for others. With multi-million-dollar athletic contracts and some CEO salaries at astronomical levels, will such values help us through the next millennium?

I have indicated that we may be optimistic about the future if wisdom and understanding become the foundation of our living. One aspect of wisdom is education. In early America, there were some like Governor Berkeley of Virginia who detested public education. "I thank God," he wrote, "that we have not free schools nor printing and I hope we shall not have these for a hundred years. For learning has brought disobedience and heresy into the world."

It is partly due to the efforts of the Puritans that Massachusetts is such a center for education. Despite their reputation for Biblical legalism and joyless religion, the Puritans maintained that education was essential. They strongly believed that literacy was a road to salvation and that ignorance played into the hands of Satan. Good schools support the economy, improve behavior and advance civilization.

We know, however, that education is not sufficient for the attainment of wisdom and understanding. Knowledge can be used so that it is detrimental to an individual, a nation, and a race. Wisdom is understanding and knowledge and being the best we can be. This is our highest calling. It is the vision religion should inspire us to follow. It requires us to take our talents, both great and small, and use them to advance, not just our own good but the good of all. In receiving the Nobel Prize in 1970, Alexander Solzhenitsyn said: "The salvation of humanity lies only in making everything the concern for all." That is a big undertaking for the coming millennium.

Think of the vastness and miraculous wonder of the universe. We now measure the speed of light at 186,000 miles per second. Measured by the speed of light, the sun is eight minutes away, the planet Pluto five hours, and some galaxies in the universe are billions of light-years from earth. Wow! We can contemplate this vastness with wonder, but realistically, it is not out there that we may make a difference but within ourselves and how we interact with life on our earth. The world we touch with our lives may become one of human dignity and respect. The success in our lifetimes of peace movements, civil rights rallies, and environmental campaigns show there are powerful positive and constructive ideas that are changing our lives.

When people ask, "What can we do to be positive in the new millennium?" there is an answer. There are ideas that need our attention: the idea that war is wrong; that humankind in all its diversity is actually one family, brought ever closer through advances of science; that just as democracy could not exist with an illiterate population, neither in the end will it prosper if millions of people are without adequate food, housing and health care. Therefore, it makes sense to develop a more humane, responsible, cooperative society. A mob could kill Jesus but could not kill his idea of love. Once a great idea begins, nothing can stop it. Try to kill it and you glorify it.

The challenge for the new millennium is to optimistically perceive the wonder that is here and to be stirred by the desire to integrate the self into a holy order of living. Our Unitarian Universalist faith requires us to think and reason. It is opposed not to knowledge but to indifferent aloofness. Our faith calls us not only to enjoy but to act and not only to accept but to change. Our faith means adherence to ideas that enhance and deepen our lives and the lives of others. In this way we may look to the coming millennium with optimism.

Peacemakers

*P*ERUSE THE BIBLE and you will find more than 500
references to peace. Some focus on rest. Some refer to peace in
terms of going forth with a blessing, as in Exodus (4:18): "And
Jethro said to Moses, 'go in peace.'" There is peace that means
unity and concord such as in Luke (2:14): ". . . and on earth
peace and good will." You also will see references to peace as a
state of being. In Job (22:21) you find: "Be at peace, thereby
good shall come to you." And Job includes species other than
human beings: "The beasts of the field shall be at peace." There
is the peace of not speaking or silence, vividly portrayed by Jesus
in Mark (14:61): To questions from the high priests we read
"He held his peace and answered not." There are several references in the Bible to making peace, such as this found in 2nd
Samuel: "They made peace with Israel." There is, however, only

one reference to peacemakers. You find it stated by Jesus in the Sermon on the Mount (Matt. 5:9): "Blessed are the peacemakers for they shall be called the children of God." This last statement forms the context for our thoughts this morning.

Peace on earth calls for human relationships that are friendly, not hostile and strained. When people manage to get along with one another, in the home or outside of it, there is peace. When they do not get along with others, there is tension that leads often to mental and/or physical violence. If there is to be peace on earth, if the human race is to move hopefully into a new millennium, we must double our efforts to understand and to get along sensitively with one another. We need to be committed peacemakers. Yet in practice this is so very difficult.

The human race carries within it certain propensities that when encouraged or uncontrolled may lead easily to hostilities. Many people seem unwilling to curb and control these feelings, to the detriment of all! Every morning we pick up the newspaper to read of some tragedy: a highway death from drunken driving, a teenage death pact suicide, domestic violence, robberies, stabbings, and embezzlement. Similar feelings of hostility are felt by unacceptable numbers of people whose stories do not reach the media, but nevertheless are tragic. Misunderstandings and thoughtlessness lead to mistrust and the weakening and even destruction of relationships. This happens across all races and classes, and as we know, touches the highest places.

Constantly we see violence in latent or active form as the way some people handle living. Violence takes center stage on television, in newspaper headlines, and it certainly is abundant on the Internet. Violence becomes so common that we forget what it actually does to human beings.

Today I will not focus on latent violence, which is the violence of hurtful words or acts that destroy trust, but upon the physical violence that besets this world. We have become numb to the realities of violence; that is, until we are physically or mentally attacked or we are drafted and shipped off to war. Violence means pain. Violence can become life-threatening. Violence can destroy individual or collective good.

While we were rebuilding this church in 1971, I was walking down Chestnut Street to the church. It was shortly before 7:00 at night. One person passed me, and then another figure stepped out from behind a parked car. He stood directly in my path. From a large manila envelope he pulled a long knife. I sensed the person who passed me was coming back behind me. Adrenaline copiously flowed through my body. Ducking my head to miss the outstretched arm, I bolted across the street. My usual slow pace was replaced by a frantic run. My loud cries and neighbors calling 911 resulted in the capture and arrest of my would-be attackers. All of us have met crises where some form of violence did or could have occured in our personal lives.

What becomes more tragic is when violence engulfs groups of people; when nations hold grudges not only from some current felt grievance but also from some episode in the distant past. For example, violent history matters in the Balkans. In the former Yugoslavia, the conflict in Kosovo erupted this past February. What was the trigger event? You might think it was some contemporary wound. Actually we have to go back six centuries. At the scenes of recent ethnic cleansing, in explanations given by perpetrators of atrocities, the one constant, obsessive reference is to a military event of 1389. Yes, the year 1389. It was the battle of Kosovo Polje. "We must avenge Kosovo Polje."

The battle pitted Serbs led by Prince Lazar against Turks led by Sultan Murat. The factual outcome of the battle does not coincide with Serbian legend. It was neither a straightforward defeat for the Serbs nor did it mark the end of the Serbian Empire. It is interesting to note that the defining moment of nationhood should be a trumped up defeat. In 1987 the Serb Leader Slobodan Milosevic converted the myth into a rallying cry of defiant nationalism that ultimately turned his country into an international outcast. Are there not enough current misconceptions that lead to violence? What a tragedy to commute back six centuries to restart a feud that today leads to atrocities and death!

The catalyst for this sermon was the summer movie *Saving Private Ryan.* The entire film, and particularly the first thirty minutes, vividly and dramatically portrays the horrors of war. The filming of that thirty-minute opening is so realistic that you might think it a well-edited sequence of documentary clips from the initial invasion at Omaha Beach on the coast of Normandy, France, June 6, 1944. The Allies put 170,000 soldiers ashore with two million more to follow. That first day, 2,500 men were wounded or killed. From that day until the war ended in Europe in May 1945, 586,628 American military became war casualties; 135,576 died.

Each split-second image is seen as if it is out of the corner of the camera's eye. The men are preoccupied, not with the context of the horizon, but with the few hundred yards in front of them. Bullets, bodies, panic, and confusion mark the disorder of the scenes. Through the chaos of bewildered soldiers, a man lurches across the sand carrying his severed arm. If German machine-gun fire did not shred them, artillery shells blew them apart; many simply drowned. The Americans were caught between the cold waters of the English Channel and the entrenched Nazis firing down upon them as their landing crafts touched the beach. It is a credible vision of hell. The din is augmented by the digital sound that separates every skull-blasting thud and whine. You see the water lapping red on the sand. One soldier feels and hears a clang on his helmet. He removes it, and dumbfounded, rubs his unscathed head, thanking his lucky stars that he is alive just as a new bullet goes through his forehead. These scenes capture the smell, taste, and sense of utter futility of trying to get out of the conflict.

Following the scenes of devastation and raw violence, of life destroyed by a faceless enemy, the theme of the movie moves to eight men who survived out of a battalion of 200. They are assigned on orders of General George C. Marshall to find Private Ryan so that he may be sent home to his Iowa farm. His three brothers have been killed in action in various theaters of war. This last brother, James Francis Ryan, who parachuted into France with the 101st Airborne, is now somewhere in Normandy. Making their way through enemy territory, these eight carry on an intense debate about why one person's life is so important that they should risk all of theirs. "Ryan better be worth it," said the Captain at one point in the search. "He better go home and cure some disease or invent a longer-lasting light bulb."

While they are looking for Private Ryan, we are shown a series of wrenching episodes: a hidden sniper, a machine-gun emplacement, a crashed glider. Ryan is finally located, but he refuses to go home. Those remaining of the eight who were sent to find Ryan, join what is left of Ryan's unit in defending a crucial bridge against a Nazi tank unit counter attack. What we gain from this movie is the fact that war is hell; that the use of violence to solve human problems is not acceptable.

As we come to a new millennium, we as individuals and as nations must grow up and approach our problems in ways that do not destroy, put others down, or raise tensions through a win-lose attitude.

Contempt for others is paramount in this old approach to solving problems. "As soon as you have contempt," Eli Siegel writes in his poem "James and the Children," "you don't want to see another person as having the fullness that you have, you can rob that person, hurt that person, kill that person."

The novel and film *Sophie's Choice* epitomize the violence that contempt can cause. Sophie is taken with her two children to Auschwitz. She is a Polish Christian. Speaking perfect German, she pleads for her children's lives. She tells the S.S. officers that she is not a Jew or a Communist as are the others in the death camp. Her children have a blond Aryan look. She points out how beautiful they are. "You're a believer?" the officer asks. Sophie nods her head, showing him the cross around her neck. Then he asks, "Didn't Jesus say 'Suffer little children to come unto me'?" He tells her to choose which child will live and which one is to die. Sophie looks at both of them. Her knees weaken. The choice is impossible. She refuses, pleading, crying out in anguish. Then the officer steps forward and seizes both of the girls. And Sophie cries, "No, take the baby. Take my little girl." It was too late. Here is extreme contempt of others, leading to death.

Contempt need not be active; it also may be witnessed in latent indifference, in people who never question, never wonder, never feel involved or responsible to do the right thing. Elie Wiesel likened such people to the Swiss who lived a mile from occupied France: "I could never understand, and I cannot understand now how those people in Switzerland, who were free, could remain free and eat in the morning, and at lunch and at dinner, while looking at the other side to occupied France. . . . Any frontier is made by human beings, and yet, on one side people died while on the other side they went on living as though the others didn't die."

Today we desperately need peacemakers, people who see humanity in other human beings. This is no small undertaking. Mahatma Gandhi thought perhaps this was too difficult a task for the adults of his time. He wrote: "If we are to teach real peace in this world and if we are to carry on a real war against war, we all have to begin with children; and if they grow up in their natural innocence, we won't have to struggle, we won't have to pass fruitless, idle resolutions, but we shall go from love to love and peace to peace, until at last all the corners of the world are covered with that peace and love for which, consciously or unconsciously, the whole world is hungering."

I am not sure all young children have a propensity only for goodness, but I am sure that the mature adult, one who desires to see the world on an honest or accurate basis, can be a peacemaker. If we look through the eyes of that great ethical teacher Jesus of Nazareth, we have such an example. He had no illusion about the human potential for combative attitudes. He saw, as we see today, certain people who look upon life and upon others with contempt. These people use their negative experiences as excuses to justify their own ill will. They fail to recognize that other people are not immune from these same bad experiences. They use unjust economics and their disappointments in love, in the family, at school, and on the job, to justify their contempt for everything. These people make the mistake of believing that because they have suffered, they have an excuse to make others suffer. Feeling they are the victims of injustice, they feel they owe nothing to another human being.

In contrast Jesus had a mature outlook, realizing the importance of love rather than contempt. His Sermon on the Mount is a guide for each of us to live up to the potential in ourselves, to hold to a moral purpose that stops at no obstacle and balks at no sacrifice to establish a humane society. We are called to see people as they are and also as they might be, since they are all the Children of God. Our first reading, the parable of the Good Samaritan, is an illustration. Our second reading, "the light that creates harmony between people," says the same thing from a Buddhist perspective. What if we were to look at one another through similar eyes—seeing others as people not to exploit and put down but as people like ourselves who may need encouragement and a helping hand?

Today we encounter people with different languages, customs, political and economic institutions, historical and racial backgrounds, mores and religions. If we are realistic, we shall see that they have similar needs and hopes and dreams. If we perceive some bad intent on their part, perhaps it stems from negative circumstances in their lives. By coming from the perspective that they have more in common with us than differences, we are more likely to be peacemakers. Being peacemakers means assisting people entering the modern era, not exploiting them or their lands. We should ask the question, "What can I do for you?" instead of "What can I make you do for me?"

Peacemakers remember and act on the lesson taught in Dickens's *A Christmas Carol*. Scrooge, when visited by the miserable chain-ridden ghost of his dead partner, says, "But you were always a good man of business, Jacob." Jacob Marley's ghost, wringing his hands, cries: "Business! Mankind was my business. The common welfare was my business—charity, forbearance, benevolence, were all my business."

Peacemakers know that they do not have to live at the level of the jungle. They do not have to look out on life with contempt but with an honest, accurate understanding of the world and its people. Our progressive religion gives us this challenge! May it also give us the tools to be peacemakers with one another along the way.

Positive Assumptions

NOVEMBER 1, 1998

A PRIEST WAS RIDING IN A SUBWAY when a disheveled man staggered towards him, smelling like a brewery. He sat in the seat next to the priest and started reading the newspaper. After a few minutes, the man turned to the priest and asked, "Excuse me, Father, what causes arthritis?" The priest, tired of smelling the liquor and saddened by the man's apparent self-indulgent lifestyle, said roughly, "Drink, dissipation, contempt for your fellow human beings and spending time with loose women!" "That's amazing," said the drunk and returned to his newspaper. A while later the priest, feeling a bit guilty over his harshness, turned to the man and asked, "How long have you had arthritis?" "Oh," said the drunk, "I don't have arthritis, I was just reading that the Pope did."

This story is a lesson in assumptions. We live our lives by assumptions. Assumptions are essential in both our personal lives and in public policy. Plato said: "We all live in the same world. But it is one kind of a world for the person asleep and it is another to the person awake." Our world has trash piles and rose gardens. A shallow pessimist sees only the trash pile. A shallow optimist sees only a rose garden. The perspective and assumptions are quite different for the pessimist and the optimist.

Some demographic information recently was brought to my attention. It stated that if we were to shrink the world's population of 5.7 billion to a village of 100 people . . . with all existing human ratios remaining the same . . . this would be the resulting profile: "Of the 100 people, 57 would be Asian, 21 European, 14 from North and South America and 8 from Africa. Fifty-one would be female, 49 would be male. Eighty would live in substandard housing. Seventy could not read. Half would suffer from malnutrition. Seventy-five would never have made a phone call. Less than one would be on the Internet. Half the entire village's wealth would be in the hands of six people. Only one in the hundred would have a college education."

We in the United States, compared with the rest of the world, live in the rose garden. The assumptions we carry in the United States are based on a common belief. Unless we are extreme pessimists, we assume that if we are healthy, we will stay healthy; if sick, that we will return to health. We assume that our family will stay healthy, our jobs secure, and our standard of living will not fall dramatically. We assume that in our lives there will not be major disruptions.

Certainly we in this nation have lived in an environment of stability. When there is genocide in Bosnia, Kosovo, Sudan and

Sierra Leone, and when there is economic meltdown in Thailand, Indonesia, Russia, and Brazil, where a new, though small, middle class finds itself without jobs, we definitely should have no complaint. Still, it appears that the slightest bad news concerning lower corporate earnings may throw the stock market into a panic, with a majority of workers looking with dismay at their retirement 401k and 403b plans, as occurred with the recent downward erosion of portfolio values.

We need to examine public policies that touch the whole society. One assumption in the public realm that I wish to examine with you is that innocence is evaporating in our society, especially among children. Our church is involved with the *Promise the Children* program that is working for constructive legislative action. It is trying to help the 320,000 children in Massachusetts who do not fall within the safety net of society. Many are facing the end of welfare after being on it for two years.

On the other hand, on the surface and in contrast, the majority of children in the United States enjoy lives of luxury and safety. The widespread pestilent children-killers of the past such as diphtheria, polio and smallpox have been virtually eradicated. Millions of middle-class children play with computers that give instant information. Scholars of previous decades would weep with envy at the scope of information and the speed at which it can be accessed. Companies vie to entertain and capture the loyalties of the young. It is a world of carseats and bike helmets, baby monitors and parenting classes.

The assumptions concerning young people today are all over the place. Since World War II, we have had three different generations of children who took certain attitudes into adulthood. First there were the baby boomers. They were the activists against the Vietnam War and for the legalization of marijuana who met with opposition from many of their parents.

Next came Generation X, those 52 million people born between 1965 and 1978. William Strauss, co-author of *The Fourth Turning*, says that Generation X came of age in one of the most anti-child periods of modern history. He cites the soaring divorce rates, the devastation in families from drug use and the disparaging of parenting. Generation X also struggled in an early 1990s economy burdened by dead-end jobs, layoffs and recession.

Now we have Generation Y, referring to those people born since 1982. Strauss calls them the millennialists. Their youthful times are surrounded by the hottest U.S. economy in memory. According to research, each week teenagers spend on average 94 dollars. This coming year, teens are expected to spend 141 million dollars. Generation Y has more clout with their parents than any other previous one. Children under sixteen have unprecedented say in family decisions. Texas A&M marketing Professor James Moyes says 48 percent of kids weigh in on family purchases from paper towels to vacation destinations. Pre-teenagers are telling their parents what kind of computer they should purchase. Beyond unprecedented affluence, Generation Y is "one of the most healthy to come along," according to the Executive Editor of the *Marketing to Kids* report.

Strauss spells out some other characteristics of the millennial generation. He says, "Though they see some of the worst things in life: schoolyard shootings, drug use, sex scandals, they are far more optimistic than the baby boomers and Generation X. They have a cocoonlike upbringing with protective mini-vans and 'baby on board' signs, and they are raised to feel that they are something special since they are consulted by adults for their advice and help in the technological world." Cell phones and beepers are all part of their personal lives. In a world of preaching boomers and fatalistic Xers, the Millennials "rebel by being upbeat," according to Strauss. Their morality is more activist, embracing environmentalism with their parents.

Media critic Jon Katz says, "This information age is a great time in which to be a child who can take advantage of the best of what is available." Such a generalization and other assumptions that shine with an optimistic glow speak to the safe reality of middle-class children but not to the harsh existence of the children in the underclass, which is too often riddled with violence, fear and family dysfunction.

What it comes down to is this: we of all ages live in a materialistic, media-saturated culture. Is it realistic to believe young people are going to live finer lives than their parents' and grandparents' generations?

There are those who see the same scenario but arrive at different assumptions. A college professor from Mt. Holyoke College, a mother of two boys, age six and nine writes: "As a parent I'm dealing with things my parents never had to deal with. Everything is much more on the table these days." Such parents despair that their children's lives differ dramatically from the childhood they remember. Even allowing for rose-colored recollections, there is demonstrable change. The world they recall had more neighbors and fewer marketers. It had more stay-at-home mothers and fewer babysitters. It had more innocuous sitcoms and fewer sexual innuendoes. It had more time and fewer pressures.

Harvard's Sissela Bok, in her new book, *Mayhem: Violence as Public Entertainment*, writes: "Is it alarmist or merely sensible to ask about what happens to the souls of children nurtured, as in no past society, on rape, torture, bombings and massacres that are channeled into their homes from infancy?" A newspaper poll, underscored by experts, shows the deep dismay and sense of hopelessness that many people have about the cultural environment in which they are raising children. Fifty-one percent of those polled agree with this discouraging assessment: "There are so many bad interests out there. Even for parents who do a good job, there is a good chance their children will get into serious trouble."

On the issue of children today, then, we have contradictory assumptions. There are those who view the current conditions positively and see hope, and others who look at the past with nostalgia and see only a downward slope in the current climate.

In all areas of our lives, we hold assumptions. We have them about many of our public policies. Some assume that the United States has a divine destiny, meaning that the U.S. is especially blessed, or as the adage goes: "God watches out for drunks, fools and the United States of America." The U.S. is a great place, but so were at one time Rome, Greece and the British Empire. At one point it was said that the sun never set on the British Empire. We cannot assume there is some special force out there that will keep us at the top. We shall always have to earn our prosperity, our greatness and our spiritual humanity.

A second assumption concerning public policy is that our governmental institutions are equal to the problems we face. Fifty years ago the average age of an American was twenty. Soon it will be forty. In 1900 the average lifespan for men was forty-seven, and for women forty-nine. In 2000 it will be seventy-four for men, eighty for women. Wonderful! More time and leisure! But does the status quo in government and other institutions have the resiliency to meet the needs of an aging population and an overexploited environment?

Another assumption is that democracy is sustainable. We must pay more attention to diminishing the growing trend towards self-gratification and civic ignorance. E. J. Dionne notes, "A democracy that hates politics can't remain long a democracy."

There are steps we should take as religious people to give a positive spin to our assumptions. First, we need to expand our empathy towards and understanding of other religions and cultures. They are no longer overseas but are growing substantially within our borders. Twenty-five percent of the people living in Boston today are foreign born. English, I am told, is a second language in Miami and many parts of Southern California. Even our concepts of what is happening abroad need constantly to be updated with new facts.

A decade ago there was fear that Asia was going to take over the economy of the world, that we in America were passé. Now the United States is in an economic upcycle. We need to remember that there is not one final overall truth for all times. We can say our ideals are what the world needs; that our democracy holds the answer for everyone and that other countries should follow us now. But is this correct?

There is a Zen saying: "In a beginner's mind there are many possibilities, in the expert's there is just one." That is the trouble with detailed contracts; there is no room for growth and change. One of the ways toward growth and change is to compare our values, our culture with that of others. We will discover that there is also validity to some of the concepts embraced by others. We as a society have become distrustful of one another. We are a litigious nation. There are other cultures where trust and friendships play an important and positive role in the behavior of people. If we think of ourselves as students and not experts, we can find opportunities to give positive dimensions to our assumptions.

Another way to enhance our positive assumptions is to pay close attention to our highest personal values. Our values are comprised of not just what we say but how we spend our time each day. Compromising our personal values weakens our ability to affirm our assumptions and goals. We end up defending our weaknesses while the great tasks and opportunities presented by our assumptions languish. Individuals who have strong personal values can learn from other people and from other cultures. Similarly, they may have their values enhanced by seeing some of the inadequacies of those same cultures.

There is some merit in the eight-fold path of Buddhism and the Middle Way it teaches, but there are some practices that are found wanting in this faith—striving for inner peace without any particular concern for fellow human beings. In the book, also made into a movie, *The Bridge over the River Kwai,* we learn of Buddhist monks passing by a Japanese prison of war camp in Southeast Asia during WW II. We learn of the torture and indecencies meted out to the American prisoners, while the monks, with their begging bowls, showed neither interest nor compassion for the plight of the Americans.

Personal values that better an institution, a community and the world help to fulfill positive assumptions. A survey was made recently that indicated that a politician will do anything for a vote, a businessperson for money, and a journalist for a story. Fortunately this is not true for all. There are many people in those professions and others whose strong sense of personal values uphold this society.

A helpful step to take in seeing that the positive assumptions that are important to you may be realized is to experience leadership. You may study great leaders, but the only way to really learn is to experience. Don't be satisfied with being close to leadership and power. Experience it yourself: introduce a speaker, volunteer to lead a committee, be the scribe. There are multiple opportunities to take leadership roles. They will give you greater confidence to persevere for the success of your assumptions.

Let us remember that it is often our assumptions that influence our attitudes and actions. Let us overcome the prejudices of our times and help create an environment for healthy, spiritual growth with greater understanding, encompassing people of all ages and different backgrounds.

A Woman for All Seasons

FEBRUARY 7, 1999

$\mathcal{E}$VERY CENTURY BRINGS some major shift or transition in the life of a nation. Often one person symbolizes the dramatic change more than any other person. In the case of the United States, I think of George Washington for the eighteenth century. More than any other person, he captured the spirit and the success of the American Revolution that overthrew a monarchy and established a government that (to the white male) was more representative. The nineteenth century brought us Abraham Lincoln as the catalyst in abolishing slavery. The twentieth century has opened up more opportunity for more people than any time in the history of any nation. The diminishing of segregation is one of the great strides of this century. But even more universal, because it touches more than half the population, is the expansion of opportunities for women of all races and ages.

Early in this century women obtained the franchise to vote. World War II enlarged the scope of job opportunities for women in old and new fields. Post-war America saw the acceleration of this, with the breaking of glass ceilings in heretofore exclusively male territories. There were certain pioneers, both female and male, who were out in front for their times in the pursuit of women's rights and opportunities. To me, the person in this century who was the most inclusive pioneer for women's rights, who broke down the barriers for women and for people of color, and who established a level playing field for all people was Eleanor Roosevelt.

Those of you who lived and read the papers during the presidency of Franklin D. Roosevelt will remember that his wife, Eleanor, was literally everywhere. Even after his death she continued at a frenetic pace. She could be found giving encouragement and material help to the unemployed and the hopeless. She would go up the sling of a great crane at a Tennessee Valley Authority dam site, down into the slums where the Resettlement Administration was constructing hospitals and feeding children, and underground into the coal mines where the machinery was idle and the miners starkly desperate. As Archibald MacLeish said, "She became an American legend of ubiquity (being everywhere at once), of ceaseless movement, running, flying, an American myth of measureless energy and an inexhaustible theme for the wisecrack." Some, like Jack Benny, who in one skit had Mrs. Roosevelt saying: "I'm very happy to buy this ticket from you, Mr. Benny. How much do I owe you?" and Jack Benny replies, "Well, that's twenty-five cents for one ticket."

Mrs. Roosevelt: "Can you give me change for a dollar?" Jack Benny replies: "Well, I haven't the change with me just now, but I'll be glad to send it to you if you'll just stay in one place."

There is a story of two Eskimos hunting seal. Just as one was about to cast a harpoon at his quarry, a swishing noise overhead distracted him and he missed. The seal immediately slipped into the water and disappeared. The day's effort was wasted. "What was in the clouds?" one of the Eskimos irritably asked his companion. "Must have been Eleanor," came the response!

To have an overview of the life of Eleanor Roosevelt is to see the social and attitudinal changes across a century. In the 1930s, Eleanor's public identification with black causes brought hope and energy to that community. She opened the White House doors to them as visitors, not servants. She fundraised for schools and organizations. She pioneered in the spirit of what should be done rather than being restrained by what typically had been done.

Refugees were another dimension of her focus. In August 1940 a Jewish refugee ship arrived in New York Harbor. Three hundred did not have visas. They were to be sent back to sure death. Eleanor Roosevelt's intervention gained their admittance to this country. One of them remarked later: "She saved my life."

Her life best reflects, I believe, the changes of thought and the increase of opportunities for women over this twentieth century. Her life demonstrates that the needs and desires of human beings remain in many ways constant. In examining the life of Eleanor Roosevelt, we will touch on these issues.

This past October 11 marked the 115th anniversary of her birth. She was not a beautiful child. She was considered by her mother an ugly duckling. Later in life when she was the president's wife, cartoons regularly denigrated her looks and her energetic living. One artist likened her to a horse, showing her using her protruding teeth to eat an apple on the other side of a picket fence. This cruel treatment was not new to Eleanor, for she had experienced it early in life and at home.

Her grandmother, with whom she went to live at eight years of age after her mother died of diphtheria, brought up her grandchildren upon the principle that "no" was easier to say than "yes." Eleanor was forbidden to eat sweets and therefore stole them, lied, got caught and was subsequently disgraced and shamed. To keep her from catching colds, she alone of the family was obliged to take a cold bath every morning. Her clothes were a constant embarrassment to her. She was tall, thin and shy and was dressed in skirts which were above her knees while other girls her size wore them longer. Thick underwear was worn and prescribed by the calendar date and not the actual temperature.

From the very beginning she encountered rejection from her mother, who was considered a beauty. Her mother lavished her affection on the two sons. Eleanor writes, "I felt a curious barrier between myself and these three. And still I can remember standing in the door, very often with my finger in my mouth—which was, of course, forbidden—and I can see the look in her eyes and hear the tone of her voice as she said: 'Come in, Granny.' If a visitor was there she might turn and say: 'She is such a funny child, so old-fashioned, that we always call her Granny.' I wanted to sink through the floor in shame."

At two and a half years of age, Eleanor was on a ship, the *Britannic*, with her parents, heading for Europe. The *S.S. Celtic* rammed the *Britannic* when she was one day out at sea. Several passengers were killed, a child was beheaded and many were injured. Although her mother made light of it, the crash made an indelible impact on Eleanor's attitude towards the sea. Eleanor's recollection of it was quite in tune with the reality. A passenger described what happened in a newspaper: "The sea foamed, iron bars and belts snapped, and above the din could be heard the moans of the dying and injured. Grownups panicked. Stokers and boiler men emerging from the depths of the *Britannic* made a wild rush for the lifeboats until the captain forced them back at the point of his revolver. The air was filled with the cries of terror." Eleanor clung frantically to the men who were trying to drop her overboard to the outstretched arms of her father Elliot in a lifeboat. From that time forward she feared the sea.

Although she did not lack material things, she was deprived of affection. She was placed in a convent school when she was six. She was the only Protestant and was treated as an outsider. One day a girl swallowed a penny. There was much fuss made over her by the sisters. Eleanor writes: "I longed to be in her place. One day I went to one of the sisters and told her that I had swallowed a penny. It must have been evident that my story was not true, so they sent for my mother. She looked at me in disgrace. . . . My mother did not understand that a child may lie from fear or want of affection."

Rejection and the absence of love would literally follow her all the days of her life. In her autobiography, *This is My Story,* she tells how badly she played sports and danced. She felt like an outsider and interloper when people her age seemed to enjoy such activities. The one person whom she felt gave her love was her father, Elliot Roosevelt, the brother of President Theodore Roosevelt. In contrast to the cool and uncomfortable relationship with her mother, she delighted in a closeness to her father, who provided warmth and tenderness. He had welcomed her as "a miracle from heaven," later naming her "Little Nell" after a Dickens character. He seemed to find her in all ways charming, amusing and companionable. She writes: "I remember my father acting as a gondolier, taking me out on the Venice canals, singing with the other boatmen to my intense joy. . . . I loved his voice, however, and above all I loved the way he treated me. He called me 'Little Nell.' I only knew it was a term of affection, and I never doubted that I stood first in his heart." The greatest blow came into her life when he fell from a horse and died when she was ten. She was not permitted to go to the funeral.

There was marriage to her fifth cousin, Franklin D. Roosevelt. Between 1906 and 1916 six children were born. Her personality could not emerge in the midst of so many children. The dominance of others over her in childhood continued into her young adult years, only with different players; chief among them being her mother-in-law Sara Delano Roosevelt, a dominating mother-in-law who knew what was best for her boy Franklin, even deciding how his home should be decorated.

Eleanor was beginning to realize that there was something colorless and lacking in her personality: "I was simply absorbing the personalities of those about me and letting their tastes and interests dominate me."

Her exposure to people outside the social set into which she was born, due to her husband's politics, began to bring about a transformation in her life and thinking. Franklin Roosevelt went to Albany as a state senator. He became an advocate of women's suffrage. She writes; "I was shocked, as I had never given the question serious thought, for I took it for granted that men were superior creatures and knew more about politics than women."

Her husband became assistant secretary of the Navy, giving her greater exposure to the larger world, and her shyness began to wear off. When her grandmother suggested that her brother, who was called to serve in WW I, pay a substitute to take his place, as was the custom of the wealthy who were born during the Civil War, Eleanor made her first outspoken protest against the privileges of the society into which she had been born.

Even as she emerged into a personality in her own right, she had to wrestle with rejection and tragedy. The romantic relationship between her social secretary, Lucy Mercer, and her husband was a battle in which her will combined with that of her mother-in-law triumphed. 1921 found her husband badly crippled by polio. Again it was a battle to make him regain muscle strength against the wishes of a mother who knew what was best and wanted her boy to return to a life of ease at Hyde Park.

Eleanor would experience personal attack and rejection throughout the rest of her life. The cartoons, the columnists such as Westbrook Pegler, the politicians such as Senator Joseph McCarthy, all tried to destroy her image. But she wrestled with the forces of evil and separation, pride and prejudice, selfishness and greed and was a strong force in the emancipation not only of women but of all people.

Because she had been wounded by rejection in younger life, she found it difficult to exude the warmth that a husband and children might need and even expect. I think she recognized this inability when she wrote her autobiography. "All human beings have failings, all human beings have needs and temptations and stresses. Men and women who live together through long years get to know one another's failings; but they also come to know what is worthy of respect and admiration in those they live with and in themselves. Franklin might have been happier with a wife who was completely uncritical. That I was never able to be, and he had to find it in some other people. Nevertheless, I think I sometimes acted as a spur, even though the spurring was not always wanted or welcomed."

The last part of her autobiography is entitled "On My Own." What were her aims? Though she warmly supported many causes, her essential purpose focused on two issues. First: equality. There should be equality between women and men in their involvement in public affairs; equality between individuals in a classless society; equality of rights and opportunities for all races, classes and creeds—these rights to be won in the service of human dignity. She resigned from the Daughters of the American Revolution after the black singer Marian Anderson was banned from its auditorium. Second: peace. She firmly believed that war is no solution to problems between nations and people. Her appointment as member of the American Delegation to the United Nations from 1945 to 1953 gave her an ideal setting in which to pursue this aim. She also was the U.S. Representative to the Commission on Human Rights for seven years.

She was interested in exposing young people to this new world, and in working towards human dignity for all. The summer that Eleanor Williams, my wife, was an intern at the United Nations, Eleanor Roosevelt graciously entertained at Hyde Park the forty interns who came from all over the world.

We need to hear again her words from a ringing speech: "It seems to me that we must have the courage to face ourselves in this crisis. We must regain a vision of ourselves as leaders of the world. We must join in an effort to use all knowledge for the good of all human beings. When we do that we shall have nothing to fear."

Eleanor Roosevelt carried the wounds of early life throughout all her years. But she overcame that which would have made her a colorless dependent person. She developed her personality. She reached out to others. She showed that women are as strong as men, able to emblazon hopes and help others to expand their horizons.

She points to each one of us here today. Reflect upon your own life. What have been the ingredients that made you suffer, that stifled your joy and your hopes? You know that at some point, adversity has been with you. Eleanor Roosevelt should speak to you. Something of worth in you can triumph, some affirmation can take hold of you. Eleanor Roosevelt became a woman for all seasons. She calls to you today as a woman, as a man, as a child, to affirm yourself and to affirm the humanity surrounding you. This is the positive vision to take into the twenty-first century.

Great Expectations

JANUARY 30, 2000

*(Last sermon preached by Rhys Williams
as minister, before retirement.)*

WHEN WINSTON CHURCHILL was defeated as prime minister of Great Britain following World War II, the king offered him a dukedom and the coveted Order of the Garter. Said Churchill, "Why should I accept the Order of the Garter from his Majesty when the people have just given me the Order of the Boot." I am happy that in my official retirement, which begins on Tuesday, that you as a Congregation have given me neither a garter nor the boot.

As Eleanor and I step down, neither of us feels like the wild-eyed man during the French Revolution who rushed up to a citizen on the street corner. "Where is the mob?" he shouted. "I am its leader." The point of this illustration is that in transitions, due to time and age, an organization is sometimes carried into an entirely different direction from that of the past leadership. We do not feel separate from your future destiny but hope to be a part of it, though in new roles.

In this church the leadership involves many people working together. The chairs of the Standing Committee deserve tremendous accolades for the tireless hours they have given for the well-being of our Church over the past forty years. The trustees, committee chairs and so many of you who have been unstinting in your efforts and interest on behalf of this church need to be enthusiastically thanked. What a privilege to have been supported by an administrator, Susan Twist, and a music director, Leo Collins, each for more than thirty years. Like a functioning watch, a congregation works well only if all parts work harmoniously together as you have done. All of us together, in sharing a common destiny and sense of community, have created an atmosphere of hope and optimism that has moved us more quickly towards our goals. We have traveled on the positive thrust of one another. It gives credence to Margaret Mead's statement: "Never doubt that a small group of thoughtful and committed people can change the world. Indeed it is the only thing that ever has."

We still have a long way to go before the ideal dominates in the global human community. Yet, I have great expectations that we shall make important strides in reaching a freer, more compassionate and healthier global community. The task is not easy, but life without challenge leaves us unfulfilled as human beings.

People have always been torn between the forces of good and evil. The ideal toward which we strive is to be a community of people who are not tramplers or slaves but friends and neighbors. The way of life shall be not fear and hate but courage and love.

We must consider, also, the ugly aspects of human nature that still persist. Cain is that symbolic person who is the antithesis of those qualities that make human beings great and which create both civilization and culture. He is consumed by jealousy. He wants. He takes. He becomes violent and murders for his desires. He cannot give generously of his means or talents. He is not sensitive or reflective; he does not love.

Scott Peck observed the following in his book *The Road Less Traveled*: "Most (people) do not fully see the truth that life is difficult. Instead they moan more or less incessantly, noisily or subtly, about the enormity of their problems, their burdens, and their difficulties as if life were generally easy, as if life should be easy. They voice their belief noisily or subtly, that their problems represent a unique kind of affliction that should not be and that has somehow been especially visited upon them . . . and not upon others." They see life as a series of problems. Yet life offers great opportunities.

Religion, in my view, should help people seize opportunities that make life on this planet, for increasing numbers of people, more just and humane. It should open up less traveled but better roads. Religion should offer hope and guidance in enriching and enhancing the potential of individual lives. It should challenge us to have great expectations and strive for the best.

Over the past forty-nine years that I have served Unitarian and Universalist Churches, we have witnessed a tremendous move from isolationism and hierarchy in many situations to diversity and globalization. This has brought about a new understanding of the uniqueness and worth of different cultures, races, genders and religions. Let me share with you a few highlights of the changes in the United States during my half-century ministry.

Two issues have been dominant: race and gender inequality. Over time there has been positive value enhancement for both people of color and for women. The formal ending to segregation was a giant step towards justice for people of color. Although racism itself is a long way from being eradicated here and around the world, the formal segregation that existed in this country when I started my ministry is gone.

When I stepped off the train in North Charleston in September 1953 to candidate for the ministry of the oldest Unitarian Church in the South, there were two waiting rooms at the station—an up-to-date one for white people, and a small run-down one for colored people. Having lived on the West Coast and in the Northeast, the artificial barriers between the colored and the white in the South were very foreign to me. There were separate schools; the people of color rode in the back of the bus; there were churches for blacks and churches for whites. On May 17, 1954 the Supreme Court held segregation in the public schools to be unequal and therefore unconstitutional. Segregation, however, persisted in Charleston throughout that decade. Racism is still a problem, but great strides have been made in reducing the opportunity gap in education and in the opportunity to enjoy the privileges of a free society.

Besides the reduction of racial segregation, this past century saw a reduction in gender inequality. One of the most important steps was the amendment to our Constitution giving women the right to vote. The male framers of the Declaration of Independence should have heeded the advice of Abigail Adams, who wrote in a letter to her husband on March 31, 1776: "If particular care and attention is not paid to the ladies, we are determined to foment a rebellion and will not hold ourselves bound by any laws in which we have no voice or representation."

Early in the twentieth century, Margaret Sanger wrote: "A woman must not accept, she must challenge. She must not be awed by that which has been built up around her. She must reverence that within her which struggles for expression. Her eyes must be less upon what is and more clearly upon what should be." This requires freedom from all harassment.

Certainly as we enter the twenty-first century, great strides have been made in the cause of women's rights and opportunities. There is a way to go, but the glass ceiling has some sunshine coming through.

The expansion of freedom in many dimensions has been a dominant occurrence during the course of my half-century ministry. Freedom has not moved, however, in a smooth linear progression. Fear of communism fomented much of our thinking in the '50s, '60s and '70s. One of the forces that diminished freedom in our country in the '50s and early '60s was the character assassination led by Senator Joseph McCarthy of Wisconsin. He became so powerful that even presidents were questioned as to their complete loyalty. His innuendoes resulted in people losing jobs and whole groups of people being defamed, including Hollywood writers and Protestant clergy. This episode fed the bitterness of hatred and suspicion in our land.

The Republican senator from Maine at that time, Margaret Chase Smith, summed up the counterattitude that restored freedom of thought to our country. She wrote: "Those of us who shout the loudest about Americanism in making character assassinations are all too frequently those who, by our own words and acts ignore some of the basic principles of Americanism: the right to criticize; the right to hold unpopular beliefs; the right to protest; the right of independent thought." If we do not continually test our limits, we would never walk, we would never grow, we would never fly.

Another change that began in the '60s was a shift away from valuing some superficial aspects of life. The 1960s started with some parishioners disturbed that students wore jeans to church, but the vast majority welcomed them as a commitment to our future. It is not on the surface but in the attitudes and sensitivity of the inner soul where true value and richness lie. Today we are much more accepting of diversity whether in clothing styles or expressed ideals. Herman Hesse writes about the transitional times of the '60s and '70s. He says: "Human life is reduced to a real suffering, to hell, when two ages, two cultures, and religions overlap. There are times when a whole generation is caught in this way between two ages, two modes of life, with the consequences that it loses all power to understand itself, and has no standard, no security, no simple acquiescence."

In the '60s and '70s there was much unrest: Woodstock, Vietnam, the assassination of Robert and John F. Kennedy, Martin Luther King, Kent State and draftcard burning. Abroad there was Pope John XXIII and the Berlin Wall. Surely Pope

John was a light in this time of transition and change. He took Catholicism off the throne so that, for example, today a Catholic priest and a Protestant minister may jointly perform a wedding ceremony. The transitions and changes of the late '60s and '70s were on the whole, tumultuous.

The First Church did not escape the violence of that transition. Our fifth church building burned in March of 1968. The cause? It has never been determined. Old BX electrical wiring gone bad or retribution against us for having two controversial speakers that month—a black power woman, and an antiwar Vietnam activist and Yale chaplain, Henry Sloane Coffin. After soul searching and much study, the First Church in Boston and the Second Church of Boston merged. Together we raised the money to rebuild on the First Church site. Immediately after obtaining the funds, we were presented with non-negotiable demands to put the money elsewhere and not rebuild. We were a united congregation and did not fold before words or even physical threats of hostility. By rebuilding, we continued our outreach in the community with the John Winthrop School, Hale House and the Barnard Services. It is through this latter connection that the seed money was given to establish the Peter Faneuil housing, consisting of low-cost single-room residences, and AIDS housing on Beacon Hill.

Our intern program with Harvard Divinity School is unique in its scope and numbers. We as a congregation have helped train over 60 men and women for the ministry.

Our Church continues to serve as a nurturing and stimulating place for fledgling musical groups and for the establishment of theater groups such as the Boston Rep and Boston Shakespeare, and for numerous activities that enhance the lives of individuals and the community.

The past decades have seen tremendous changes in our world: space exploration, biotechnology, cloning and instant communication, just to name a few of the dramatic changes in many areas.

I have great expectations for the future of the world, our local community and especially this Church. First, as a Church we do not hand you unwarranted doctrinal guilt from the past. You are not free from responsibility, but you do not have to carry the religious baggage of guilt imposed upon you from an ancient age. To illustrate, Charlie Brown says to Lucy, "I think my trouble is that I feel guilty all the time." Lucy looks around, back and forth, and then with a shout yells, "Not guilty!"

Second, you are allowed to free your imagination in all areas of life . . . from the mundane to the most vital. Human beings are the only species that can cry, laugh, and come to new realities through imagination. We can move past attitudes such as, "But we've always done it this way." With imagination we may move beyond long held truths about ourselves, our religion, and our world, to discover fresh realities.

How infinitely superior to our physical senses are those of our spirit and mind. As Stephen Spender poetically expressed it: "What is precious is never to allow gradually the traffic to smother with noise and fog the flowering of the Spirit."

Imagination in human terms means a heightened sensitivity towards all life. One is only ethical, as Albert Schweitzer put it, "in the feeling of responsibility for all that lives." We as religious people often feel that we are sensitive. With imagination this sensitivity can be heightened in our relationships with our fellow human beings.

There is the story of the violinist who felt he could charm everybody, even wild animals. He goes to Africa and at the edge of the jungle starts to play. A series of wild animals one by one rush out to devour him, only to stop, mesmerized by his music. Then comes a tiger that pounces on the violinist and devours him. The elephant exclaims, "Why did you do that, he was playing such beautiful music?" The tiger lifts his paw to his ear and says, "What did you say?" Imagination can take us to the point where we become sensitive to the subtleties of situations that are not normally obvious. We may think we are sensitive, but because there are often mitigating circumstances, only with imagination can we grasp the reality.

Elliot Richardson, in his book *The Reflections of a Moderate Radical* and in a letter to me wrote: "Imagination is the only tool we have to grasp reality. The world is too small and our lives too short for the closed mind and the pinched heart. Imagination takes us beyond the usual to the extraordinary in our actions."

Freed from unnecessary guilt, we have the ability to use our minds, our imaginations and our good will to enhance justice, excellence and love. Freedom used wisely will portend a great future for the human race.

The Kenosha, Wisconsin *Evening News* of December 29, 1900, stated: "All things considered, this old world, wicked as it is, is a vastly better place to live in at the close of the nineteenth century than it was at the beginning, and it is a reasonable assumption that it will be a still more desirable place of residence at the close of the twentieth century than it was at the beginning, though none of us will be here to tell whether it is or not."

As we enter the twenty-first century, we should reflect on this assumption. If justice and good will go hand in hand with the advance of technology and science and the dissemination of knowledge, this century should be a more glorious one for more of the world's people.

I have great expectations for the future of this Church and our nation. Eleanor and I thank you for the privilege of serving you and sharing with you the past forty years. We look forward to the future with confidence and wish each of you joy and fulfillment in your lives.

Acknowledgements by Sermon Book Committee
Graham Sterling, Chair

The ways were plain to see and the worth of the journey undoubted, but this work could not have been published on schedule or offered for sale at an affordable price had not admirers of Rhys and Eleanor Williams contributed the front-end cost. The need was pressing and finite, so the Sermon Book Committee limited its appeal to just a few.

Now the scores of others, who would have contributed if invited, should focus on the equally important task of assuring that Rhys Williams' *Triumphant Living* becomes widely available and widely read. Possible steps toward this goal might include giving copies to family, friends and libraries, and publishing reviews in readers' favorite media.

Contributions will cover not only the cost of this first printing but subsequent printings as well. Rhys and Eleanor have donated all their rights to The First and Second Church in Boston. Total revenue from sales will go to the Church.

Timely completion of this First Edition of *Triumphant Living* and the opening of further opportunities were made possible by the valuable commitments of these friends of Rhys and Eleanor:

Oliver and Esther Ames	*Stephen and Rogina Jeffries*
Elizabeth Ames	*Susan Loring*
Godfrey and Janet Amphlett	*Horace and Ruth Nichols*
Hope Baker	*Ken and Marianne Novack*
George and Rita Cuker	*Pendennis and Francine Reed*
Robert Dancy	*George and Rebekah Richardson*
Daniel J. Finn	*David Sheets*
Andrew and Brenda Forbes	*Donald Sohn*
Howard and Darcy Fuguet	*Graham, Judith and Gordon Sterling*
Nigel and Madeline Harvey	*John and Nancy Sullivan*
Roger Husbands	*Katherine Winter*
James and Susan Jackson	

"Money, the life-blood of the nation, Corrupts and stagnates in the veins,
Unless a proper circulation, Its motion and its heat maintains."

Jonathan Swift: *The Run*, 1720